SPORTS SCANDALS

Sports Scandals

Peter Finley, Laura Finley,
and Jeffrey Fountain

Scandals in American History

GREENWOOD PRESS
Westport, Connecticut • London

Library of Congress Cataloging-in-Publication Data

Finley, Peter S.
    Sports scandals / Peter Finley, Laura Finley, and Jeffrey Fountain.
        p. cm. — (Scandals in American history, ISSN 1942–0102)
    Includes bibliographical references and index.
    ISBN-13: 978–0–313–34458–9 (alk. paper)
    1. Sports—Corrupt practices—United States. 2. Sports—Social
aspects—United States. I. Finley, Laura L. II. Fountain, Jeffrey. III. Title.
    GV718.2.U6F56 2008
    306.4'83—dc22   2008016095

British Library Cataloguing in Publication Data is available.

Library of Congress Catalog Card Number: 2008016095
ISBN: 978–0–313–34458–9
ISSN: 1942–0102

First published in 2008

Greenwood Press, 88 Post Road West, Westport, CT 06881
An imprint of Greenwood Publishing Group, Inc.
www.greenwood.com

Printed in the United States of America

♾™

The paper used in this book complies with the
Permanent Paper Standard issued by the National
Information Standards Organization (Z39.48–1984).

10   9   8   7   6   5   4   3   2   1

CONTENTS

SERIES FOREWORD

Scandal is a part of daily life in America. The evidence is everywhere, from the business world, with its Enrons, Ponzi schemes, and insider trades, to the political arena, where scandals are so pervasive that, for shorthand purposes, we simply add "-gate" to each new one (Watergate, Travelgate, Spitzergate, and so on). Cultural phenomena that are designed to entertain, inform, and distract us—television, film, popular music, sports, media—have also been touched by the fickle finger of scandal. Even religion, the one area of life that is intended to uplift and guide Americans, has not been immune to the taint of scandal.

Scandal, which can be defined as something that offends propriety or established moral codes and brings disgrace on anyone or any organization associated with it, is not a modern invention. It has been with us since the days of the Salem witch trials and Boss Tweed, and it resurfaces in many of today's breaking news events. To bring this subject into the open and to offer a wider historical view of such a major and often overlooked aspect of U.S. history—one that is of abiding interest to students—Greenwood developed this series of reference works. These volumes examine the causes and impacts of scandal within key areas of American life—politics, sports, media, business, popular music, television, film, religion, and more. Prepared by field experts and professionals, the volumes are written to inform and educate high school and undergraduate college students as well as to engage and entertain students and general readers alike. As reference tools, they place scandals within a wider social and cultural context. But as general histories, they are fun to read from cover to cover.

The volumes have been carefully written and edited to ensure that a diversity of viewpoints surrounding each scandal is included. Because many of the issues that touched off scandals have never been resolved, the books in this series can be used to spark classroom debate as well as to examine the ethical issues that come into play. Each volume is enhanced with a timeline, illustrations, and a bibliography so that students can read further and in more detail about subjects that pique their interest, as well as to augment the reading and learning experience.

PREFACE

I t could be argued that the history of the United States is rife with scandals. From the genocide committed by Christopher Columbus to Watergate to the current debate over CIA-perpetrated torture of prisoners, one can learn a lot about the values and structures prevailing in the country by better understanding its various scandals. Understanding what happened, who was involved, and the fallout from a scandal allows us to examine our cultural beliefs as well as critically look at our systems and institutions.

But why sports scandals? Surely those are not nearly so important. "It's just sport," some might say, "intended to amuse and entertain, and not worthy of this type of serious examination." We disagree. The sport industry is one of the biggest industries in the United States. At worst, it is the eleventh largest industry in the United States, and one estimate put it sixth. Second, sports receive a tremendous amount of media coverage. *USA Today,* the most widely read newspaper in the country, devotes one quarter of its coverage to sports. Third, there are few places where children are more likely to look for role models than the world of sports. Surely more high school students can tell you about their favorite sports stars than about a Supreme Court justice.

Indeed, sports scandals are instructive for all the same reasons as other scandals.

For instance, the current discussions about steroid abuse highlight the broader concerns about drugs in the last forty to fifty years. Although sexual harassment, sexual assault, and domestic violence have occurred throughout all of history, they were not problems that were discussed openly until the 1970s—thus the more recent coverage of cases involving athletes and coaches accused of rape, assault, or harassment. Learning about sports scandals also helps highlight social inequalities. For instance, the debate about whether shock jock Don Imus should have lost his job for calling the Rutgers women's basketball team "nappy-headed hos" is indicative of the competing attitudes about racially and sexually offensive commentary and the limits of free speech.

Sports scandals can be used to teach history as well, in that they are many times in sync with other historical events. Learning about Tommie Smith and

John Carlos raising their gloved fists at the 1968 Olympics can help people understand the civil rights struggle and the various responses to it. Likewise, Muhammad Ali's struggle to attain conscientious-objector status during the Vietnam War demonstrates some of the competing perspectives about that war and about the struggle for rights at home. More recently, former NBA basketball player Mahmoud Abdul-Rauf's decision not to stand for the playing of "The Star-Spangled Banner" paralleled the debate about what it truly means to be a patriot in this country and how much freedom, exactly, an athlete could have in expressing himself and his religious faith.

Like other scandals, sports scandals can prompt needed dialogue about and examination of institutions. Most often, they push sport teams and organizations to examine their own policies, as in the case of penalties for steroid use or recruiting violations. Sometimes scandals even usher in discussion of public policy and law, like the Duke lacrosse case did with the judicial system when three players were falsely accused of rape in 2006.

Sports scandals are certainly not unique to America. Although there are sports scandals in other countries, the focus here is on scandals involving American athletes, coaches, and teams, as well as leagues and events that are based here, such as the National Hockey League, Boston Marathon, and Little League World Series.

Certainly there is no dearth of scandals that could be examined. In fact, each chapter of this text could be expanded into a book, and many of the individual entries could as well. However, the objective of this text was to present the essential facts of many scandals, with attention to including the "rest of the story." We endeavored to present the impact of the scandals, including what happened to the people involved years after the story fell away from the front pages of the popular press.

Deciding which scandals to include was no simple task. We examined the literature on sports scandals in order to discern logical categories. Then, using that literature, we selected the entries that received considerable attention in sources including *USA Today, Sports Illustrated,* ESPN, and the Associated Press. We selected some of the most important scandals in several categories. A total of eighty-six entries is included. We then selected between five and sixteen scandals in each area, emphasizing the diversity of cases and varying responses to similar situations. While undoubtedly there were plenty of scandals in previous centuries, the vast majority of entries in this book occurred in the twentieth century. Part of that decision was tied to coverage, since media has certainly paid more attention to scandals in the world of sports in more recent times.

The book is divided into seven sections, examining sports scandals related to gambling, sex, drugs, cheating, violence, outrageous commentary, and odds and ends, for a total of eighty-six entries. It is our hope that readers not only learn about sports scandals, but enjoy the reading. We have tried to write in a user-friendly and engaging style and provide ample coverage of the scandal, its immediate fallout, and its legacy.

The authors all have a long history of involvement in sport, both personally as well as professionally. Jeffrey Fountain holds two degrees in sport administration and has helped run a large summer camp for several years. He is a professor of sport administration at Nova Southeastern University (NSU) in Florida. Peter Finley is also a professor of sport administration at NSU and the coauthor of two previous works on current issues in sport. In addition, he was a collegiate athlete on a national championship-winning cross country team, and a highly successful high school track coach. Laura Finley holds a Ph.D. in sociology and is director of the Center for Living and Teaching Peace in Florida. She has coauthored two books on current issues in sport, as well as numerous other publications. Like Peter, she was on a national championship-winning cross country team and was also a scholarship athlete on a Division I team.

Readers, including high school and college students as well as those in the general public, should find *Sports Scandals* a useful and intriguing examination of a very interesting topic. The references cited provide readers with an important tool for conducting additional research as well.

TIMELINE: SIGNIFICANT SCANDALS IN U.S. SPORTS

1866	Cyclist collapses during race in Europe after taking a combination of cocaine and heroin to enhance his speed and endurance.
1877 October 30	Louisville Grays expel players for selling games.
1919	Chicago White Sox fix the World Series.
1951 August October 13	Point-shaving scandal at City College of New York (CCNY). Ninety cadets resign from West Point, thirty-seven on the football team, for cheating. New York Giants steal signs to win pennant race.
1961	Thirty-seven basketball players from twenty-two colleges, including Columbia, St. John's, New York University, North Carolina State, and the University of Connecticut, are arrested for point shaving.
1967	International Olympic Committee (IOC) develops list of banned substances. Boxer Muhammad Ali's (Cassius Clay) title is revoked when he refuses to be inducted into the U.S. military.
1968 Summer	First doping tests at the Mexico City Olympics. U.S. sprinters Tommie Smith and John Carlos raise their fists in Black Power salute on the podium at the Mexico City Olympics.
1971	U.S. Supreme Court reverses Muhammad Ali's conviction of draft evasion.
1972 Summer	U.S. Olympic basketball team is denied gold medal in questionable call.
1975	International Olympic Committee bans anabolic steroids.

1977
December   Los Angeles Laker Kermit Washington punches Houston Rocket
                        Rudy Tomjanovich during game, referred to as "The Punch."

1978–1979   Point-shaving scandal at Boston College involving Mafioso
                        Henry Hill.

1980
April   Rose Ruiz rides subway to win Boston Marathon.

1983
July 23   Kansas City player George Brett tars his bat in game against the
                        Yankees.

1985   Tulane University drops men's basketball after point-shaving
                        scandal involving star John "Hot Rod" Williams.

1986   NCAA initiates drug testing program.
January   Beginning of collusion allegations in Major League Baseball.
February 28   Major League Baseball Commissioner Peter Ueberroth announ-
                        ces suspension of eleven players because of cocaine.
June 19   Boston Celtics draft pick Len Bias dies from cocaine overdose.

1987
February 25   Southern Methodist University is given NCAA death penalty
                        for recruiting violations.
April 7   Executive president of the Los Angeles Dodgers, Al Kampanis,
                        comments on *Nightline* that blacks are incapable of holding
                        management positions.

1988   Margo Adams files suit, claiming four-time American League
                        batting champion Wade Boggs breached a contract with her
                        when he failed to leave his wife.
January   Announcer Jimmy "the Greek" Snyder is fired from CBS for
                        making racist remarks.
Summer   Carl Lewis is awarded the 100-meter medal after Canadian Ben
                        Johnson tests positive for stanozolol.
Summer   Boxer Roy Jones Jr. is robbed of gold medal.

1989
March 1   A group of high school athletes sexually assault a mentally
                        retarded girl in Glen Ridge, New Jersey.
August 24   Pete Rose becomes fifteenth person banned from baseball due to
                        gambling.

1990
July 30   Major League Baseball commissioner Fay Vincent bans legend-
                        ary New York Yankees owner George Steinbrenner from
                        involvement with the team.

September 17	Reporter Lisa Olson faces sexual harassment in the locker room of the New England Patriots.

1991

September	Mississippi State football coach Jackie Sherrill has a bull castrated on the practice field to "motivate" his team.
November 7	Magic Johnson announces he is HIV positive.

1992

	Zamboanga City, Philippines, wins Little League World Series with ineligible players.
January 7	Figure-skater Nancy Kerrigan is attacked while preparing for the Olympic trials.
February 10	Mike Tyson is convicted of raping beauty contestant Desiree Washington.

1993

	Marge Schott, owner of the Cincinnati Reds, is suspended for making racist comments.
	NBA investigates Michael Jordan on allegations of gambling.
	Gambling scandal at Arizona State ends in seven men jailed.

1994

	Point-shaving scandals involving both men's basketball and football teams at Northwestern University in Chicago, Illinois.

1995

October	O. J. Simpson acquitted of murdering ex-wife Nicole Brown and her friend, Ronald Goldman.

1996

	Marge Schott again suspended for racist and insensitive remarks.
March	Denver Nugget Mahmoud Abdul-Rauf causes stir when he refuses to stand for national anthem.
July	Security guard Richard Jewell is wrongly accused of setting off bomb in Atlanta's Olympic Park.

1997

	Sportscaster Marv Albert is charged with misdemeanor assault and battery after attacking his date in a hotel room.
April	Professional golfer Fuzzy Zoeller makes racist comments regarding golfer Tiger Woods.
June	Heavyweight boxer Mike Tyson bites opponent Evander Holyfield's ear during match.
October	University of Michigan fires coach Steve Fischer due to scandal involving payments to Fab Five players.
December 1	Golden State Warrior Latrell Sprewell chokes coach P. J. Carlesimo during practice.

1998

March 25	Former football player Reggie White makes degrading and homophobic speech.

1999

January 30   Atlanta Falcon Eugene Robinson is arrested for soliciting a
                prostitute.
November 16   Former Carolina Panther Rae Carruth is accused of drive-by
                murder of his pregnant girlfriend.
December   Atlanta Braves pitcher John Rocker spews racist and homopho-
                bic insults.

2000

January   University of Vermont president Judith Ramaley imposes the
                death penalty on her own university's hockey team due to
                horrific hazing.
January 31   Baltimore Raven Ray Lewis is accused of murder in a post–
                Super Bowl melee.

2001   Three female students at the University of Colorado claim they
                were raped by players at a party.
December   George O'Leary resigns before ever coaching for Notre Dame
                when inaccuracies on his resume are made public.

2002   Salt Lake City bribes the International Olympic Committee to
                host the Winter Olympic Games.
February   Former NBA All-Star Jayson Williams shoots limousine driver
                and covers it up.
August   Federal agents investigate performance-enhancing substances being
                distributed from Bay Area Laboratory Co-Operative (BALCO).
October   Three former fraternity brothers attempt to fix the Breeder's
                Cup Pick Six.

2003   New York Giants tight end Jeremy Shockey announces he will
                not "stand" for having a gay teammate, while Detroit Lions
                president Matt Millen calls Kansas City wide receiver Johnnie
                Morton "a faggot."
                Real Olympic Park bomber, Eric Rudolph, is captured.
April   Iowa State coach Larry Eustachy is fired for partying with rivals'
                students after team loses.
May   Mike Price is fired before he even coaches a game at Alabama
                due to indiscretions with drinking and strippers.
June   Katelyn Faber accuses LA Laker star Kobe Bryant of rape.
June 12   Baylor basketball player Carlton Dotson shoots and kills team-
                mate Patrick Dennehy, leading to widespread cover-up at the
                school implicating the team's coach.
July   Former University of Michigan star Chris Webber pleads guilty
                to contempt charges for lying to a grand jury about taking
                money as a college player.

Summer	University of Washington coach Rick Neuheisel is fired for partaking in neighborhood betting pool.
September 8	Rush Limbaugh comments that black quarterback Donovan McNabb is over-rated, prompting public outcry and his resignation from ESPN.
October 13	Longtime Cubs fan Steve Bartman interferes with a foul ball, and the Cubs lose Game 6 of baseball's National League Championship.
2004	Former University of Colorado kicker Katie Hnida says she was molested and raped while on the team in 1999.
March	Vancouver Cannuck Todd Bertuzzi attacks Colorado Avalanche player Steve Moore during regular season game.
September	Rape case dismissed against Kobe Bryant.
November 19	Basketbrawl between Indiana Pacers and Detroit Pistons at the Palace of Auburn Hills, Michigan.
2006	University of Northern Colorado disgruntled punter Mitch Cozad is accused of stabbing the starting punter in his kicking leg. LaSalle University is found to have failed to report allegations of sexual assault involving players, in violation of Clery Act.
February	Operation Slapshot, an alleged hockey gambling ring involving a former player and a state trooper, makes the news.
March	Three Duke lacrosse players are accused of raping a stripper at a party.
July	Sprinter Justin Gatlin tests positive for steroids.
September	Miami Northwestern High School star Antwain Easterling has consensual sex with underage girl at school, prompting cover-up by school officials and threats to cancel season.
2007	
April	Shock jock Don Imus calls Rutgers female basketball players "nappy-headed hos."
April 25	Atlanta Falcon superstar quarterback Michael Vick is arrested for dog fighting.
Spring	All charges are dropped against Duke lacrosse players accused of rape and district attorney Mike Nifong is disbarred.
Summer	NBA referee Tim Donaghy is implicated in game fixing during prior two seasons.
August 9	Barry Bonds breaks homerun record under tremendous accusations that he used steroids.
September	Cyclist Floyd Landis is found to have doped his way to victory in the 2006 Tour de France.
October	Sprinter Marion Jones confesses to using steroids.

| | Isiah Thomas is found guilty of sexual harassment and ordered to pay $11.6 million to former New York Knicks executive Anuchua Browne Sanders. |
| December | George Mitchell reports widespread steroid abuse in Major League Baseball. |

2008

| January | Controversial, but highly successful, basketball coach Bobby Knight quits during the middle of the season for Texas Tech. |

Chapter 1

VIOLENCE: FIGHTS, BITES, MURDER, AND MAYHEM

In selecting the cases, this chapter casts a wide net. Included are many forms of violence in various degrees of severity, committed by athletes and retired athletes, both on and off the field. The selections are so varied because violence itself is never simple, nor is it easy to create a profile of who will be perpetrators or victims. All the cases, however, have had a tremendous impact on the sporting world, as is noted at the end of each entry.

Sadly, violence is a seemingly permanent fixture in U.S. culture, permeating virtually every institution. From world wars to the war on terror, the schoolyard to the backyard, many people use violence as a means of obtaining power and of responding to conflict. This is true in sports as well, although rather than a problem worthy of serious examination, it is often chalked up to being "part of the game." When excessive violence occurs in the course of a game or event, it is often treated as though it is trivial. Rarely has an athlete been prosecuted for in-sport violence, although this chapter highlights the cases of Marty McSorley and Todd Bertuzzi, which were exceptions. Although violence occurring in sport is generally directed at opponents, the cases of Latrell Sprewell (who attacked his coach) and Basketbrawl (which pitted players against fans), illustrate that not all violence is player to player.

In other cases, athletes perpetrate violent acts outside of the sport realm. Their actions impact not only their individual victim(s), but their teams, sports organizations, and the sport community as a whole. Many of the cases described in this chapter, from the double murders allegedly committed by O. J. Simpson to the murder of a Baylor University athlete, demonstrate the devastating impact of off-field violence and the cover-ups that sometimes follow.

THE PUNCH—RUDY TOMJANOVICH NEARLY KILLED

During the third quarter of an NBA game between the Los Angeles Lakers and the Houston Rockets in December 1977, a fight broke out that would be long remembered for a single, devastating punch. Los Angeles Laker Kermit

Washington, a six-foot-eight, 230-pound player, hit six-foot-eight, 220-pound Rudy Tomjanovich so hard that it literally crushed his face, nearly killing him. The altercation began with a minor scuffle between Lakers center Kareem Abdul-Jabbar and Rockets forward Kevin Kunnert. Sensing an impending brawl, Washington reacted when he saw movement out of the corner of his eye. He turned and punched, catching an unsuspecting Tomjanovich squarely on the face. "The Punch," as it would come to be known, was so vicious that Tomjanovich later said, "The next thing I remember was lying on the floor. There was a buzzing in my ears. I remember thinking that the scoreboard must have fallen on me."[1] Abdul-Jabbar compared the sound of the impact to a melon splitting on concrete.

It took three surgeries to repair Tomjanovich's face. Both eye sockets had been broken, along with his nose and jaw. Some teeth were knocked out. The surgeon who initially did the reconstruction compared it to putting a broken eggshell back together with Scotch tape. The last surgery involved an incision along the side of his nose to allow for the passage of tears. It was truly a miracle that he survived.

The NBA fined Washington and suspended him for twenty-six games. The Lakers traded him to the Boston Celtics and then he was moved to the San Diego Clippers, then to the Portland Trail Blazers, and later to the Golden State Warriors. Wherever Washington went, the reputation that The Punch had given him followed. He was a pariah in the league and deemed a thug by the fans. Washington never felt that the labels that were applied to him were accurate. Many would attest that he was, in fact, a kind and sensitive man who abhorred fighting. He has always claimed, and even took a lie detector test to support, that he simply saw a figure charging at him and reacted. In his heart, The Punch was an act of self defense.

Tomjanovich filed suit against Washington and California Sports, Inc. (owners of the Los Angeles Lakers), seeking millions of dollars in actual and punitive damages. Likewise, his team, the Rockets, filed suit seeking $1.4 million, claiming that the loss of the player caused the team to have a terrible season. The Rockets had been 49–33 the season before and slumped to 28–54 without the all-star player. Lawyers representing the Lakers claimed that Tomjanovich assumed the risk of being hit by playing pro basketball and that Washington acted in self-defense.[2] The Lakers lost the case and millions of dollars.

Although Washington's name will forever be linked to The Punch, he went on to have considerable achievements as a humanitarian activist after his playing days ended. He ran a program, called Project Contact, that took relief items including medical attention to areas in Africa that were suffering from the results of wars, famine, and disease. He made several annual trips to places such as Kenya, Burundi, Rwanda, and Uganda. At least 40,000 people benefited from the aid that his group delivered. *Boston Globe* columnist Bob Ryan, in an article about Washington's charitable work, called him, "a bookworm of a family man with a strong social conscience."[3] He also suggested that skin color likely had a lot to do with the demonization of Washington (he is black, Tomjanovich is white).

Tomjanovich played eleven years in the NBA, making the all-star team five times. The Houston Rockets retired his jersey. In 1992 he became the interim and then head coach of the Rockets. During his twelve seasons there, the team was a regular playoff contender and won NBA titles in 1994 and 1995. Tomjanovich was a part of the organization for thirty-four years as a player, scout, coach, and consultant. He left coaching following the 2002–3 season after being diagnosed with bladder cancer. Later, he briefly coached the Los Angeles Lakers and continued to work with USA Basketball as a director of scouting. In 2000, Tomjanovich led the Olympic team to basketball gold in the Sydney Games.

The Punch is significant for several reasons. First, it brought attention to the issue of violence in basketball, helping to demonstrate that it is not just the contact sports that can be dangerous. Second, the racial implications brought out by the case highlight a recurring issue in many sports—that is, the huge number of black players and the small number of black coaches.

NANCY KERRIGAN ATTACKED, STILL WINS OLYMPIC MEDAL

On January 7, 1992, figure skater Nancy Kerrigan was attacked after her practice at Cobo Arena in Detroit, Michigan, where she was preparing for the U.S. Olympic trials. Kerrigan had earned a bronze medal at the previous Olympics and was considered a contender to win in Lillehammer, Norway. The assailant ran by Kerrigan, clubbed her on the knee with a blunt object, and then disappeared into a crowd of people who were attending an auto show at Cobo Hall. The attack resulted in a very serious bruise on her right knee, calling into question whether she would be able to participate in the trials. She did withdraw from the competition, but, fortunately, the rules allowed U.S. Olympic officials to give her a spot on the team. The attack was the second assault on a high-profile female athlete in less than a year. Just eight months prior, in April 1991, tennis star Monica Seles was stabbed while she changed courts during a tournament in Hamburg, Germany. Her assailant, Guenter Parche, claimed he attacked Seles because of his devotion to her rival, Steffi Graf. Parche received a two-year suspended sentence.

One week after the attack on Kerrigan, two men were charged in Portland, Oregon, and another man surrendered in Phoenix, Arizona. Rival skater Tonya Harding's bodyguard, Shawn Eric Eckardt, was one of those indicted. He reportedly hired two men to attack Kerrigan. Derrick B. Smith drove the getaway car and Shane Stant hit Kerrigan with a collapsible metal baton. Eckardt claimed Harding and her husband, Jeff Gillooly, were involved in the planning and cover-up of the attack. U.S. Olympic officials hoped Harding, who qualified for the U.S. Olympic team, would withdraw from the Lillehammer games.

The United States Olympic Committee (USOC) also asked the International Olympic Committee (IOC) to consider declaring Harding ineligible for the games, a power that body holds. Records showed Harding had made two phone calls to the arenas in which Kerrigan was practicing, allegedly in an attempt to discern her practice schedule. Kerrigan said, "I can't understand any explanation of why something like this would occur. I don't think I could ever understand the answer, because I can't think that viciously."[4]

Harding had previously filed two restraining orders against Gillooly. Even though they were officially divorced, the two reconciled, and at the time of the attack, Harding considered Gillooly her husband. John McBride, a coach and owner of a skating rink in Portland, explained Harding was "a girl who was never taught or trained in how to deal with life.... My hat's off to the people who've dealt with her."[5] Gillooly was charged less than a week after the others. Harding proclaimed that she and Gillooly were innocent. However, she announced they were separating in order for her to concentrate on preparing for the Olympic Games.

On January 27, 1994, Harding admitted she learned about the attack shortly after it occurred, but had no role in planning it. The USOC announced it was deeply concerned about her admission and formed a five-member investigative committee in response. Harding expressed that she was sorry about what happened to Kerrigan. She said, "I am embarrassed and ashamed to think that anyone close to me could be involved. I was disappointed not to have the opportunity to compete against Nancy at the trials. I have a great deal of respect for Nancy."[6]

In the end, both Harding and Kerrigan competed in Lillehammer. Kerrigan won silver and Harding finished eighth, well out of medal contention. Gillooly pleaded guilty and was sentenced to two years in prison on racketeering charges. He was given the option of serving six months in Oregon's SUMMIT boot camp program. While there he had his name legally changed to Jeff Stone. Harding was sentenced to three years of probation and was stripped of the national title she won in Kerrigan's absence. Sean Eckardt also pleaded guilty to racketeering charges and was sentenced to eighteen months in prison. The two other conspirators, Shane Stant and Derrick Smith, also were sentenced to eighteen months for their involvement. The courts determined that Smith drove the getaway car and Stant was the actual assailant.

Harding continued to be involved in scandalous and questionable behavior over the years, often involving alcohol and fights with boyfriends. A video of her and Gillooly having sex appeared on the Internet, and stills from the tape were featured in *Penthouse* magazine. Harding claimed she was drunk at the time of the filming. She also appeared on a USA Pro Wrestling show in 1994. In 2002 Harding boxed against Paula Jones on the Fox network Celebrity Boxing show. In 2003 she made her official professional boxing debut, in which she lost in a four-round decision.

The case is still significant today. It demonstrated to many the cutthroat nature of a sport long known for its beauty and grace, and highlighted the fact that women, too, can commit or orchestrate violence in such a competitive environment. Additionally, it represented to many a classic example of "good versus evil," as Kerrigan was the beautiful princess to Harding's working-class brute. Further, although there are many scandals that have emerged from the Olympics, this was one of the most violent and certainly one of the worst to occur in a winter games.

O. J. SIMPSON IS CHARGED WITH DOUBLE MURDER

The nation was stunned as the story unfolded on national news: Beloved former football star and actor O. J. Simpson was accused of murdering former wife Nicole Brown Simpson and her companion, Ron Goldman, in a brutal attack at Brown Simpson's home in Brentwood, California. On June 12, 1994, neighbors out for an evening stroll encountered an agitated dog that led them to the bloody body of Nicole Brown Simpson. Officer Robert Riske was first on the scene and discovered the second body. Both victims had bled to death from multiple stab wounds. Nicole's throat was deeply slashed. Ronald's body bore multiple stab wounds and showed evidence he had struggled with the assailant. Shortly after, Los Angeles Police Department (LAPD) Central Robbery and Homicide Division detectives arrived and were ordered to inform Nicole's former husband, O. J. Simpson, that his ex-wife had been murdered but that their children were safe. Bloody shoe prints leading away from the bodies and toward a back alley, and a bloody glove and knit hat, were among the evidence found at the scene. Blood was found inside Simpson's Rockingham residence, including a bloody shoe impression in the carpet, and blood on his driveway, in the foyer of his house, and in his bathroom. Blood was also found in his white Ford Bronco. Elsewhere on the grounds, investigators found a single glove that matched the one found at the crime scene. Simpson himself had a deep cut on one of the fingers of his left hand. When investigators inquired about the cut during their interview with him fifteen hours after the murder, Simpson could not recall how he had gotten it.

The prosecution seemed to have a slam dunk case. They had a DNA match between Simpson's blood and the blood drops found on the scene, an analysis found the hairs inside the hat found at the murder scene were consistent with Simpson's hair, the matching gloves belonged to Simpson, and testimony from witnesses, including Brian "Kato" Kaelin, Simpson's limousine driver, and friend and retired policeman, Ron Shipp, verified he had no alibi for the time of the murders. Further, Shipp testified that Simpson spoke of dreams he had of killing Nicole and his concern that the dreams would affect a lie detector test. The prosecution argued that Simpson had not only the means and opportunity to commit the crime, but the motive to do so as well. They brought up previous allegations of his abusive behavior towards Nicole, introducing the

O. J. Simpson smiles after being found not guilty of the
murder of his ex-wife, Nicole Brown Simpson, and her
friend Ronald Goldman. Courtesy of AP Photo/POOL,
Myung Chun.

world to recordings of 911 calls that Nicole had made and photographs of her
with bruises all over her face.

The defense strategy focused on besmirching the Los Angeles Police Department, arguing the case against Simpson was a conspiracy concocted by racist
officers. They repeatedly brought up the possibility that evidence was either
planted, contaminated, or both. Because the investigation and analyses were so
botched, jurors were instructed that they could not trust the results of the
DNA, hair, and other tests. In what is often called the Trial of the Century,
Simpson was acquitted in October 1995. A February 1997 civil trial, however,
found him liable for the wrongful deaths of Nicole Brown Simpson and Ronald
Goldman. Simpson was ordered to pay $33.5 million in compensatory damages
to the victims' survivors. The trial received tremendous media attention, with
CNN alone providing more than 600 hours of coverage. An estimated 150 mil-
lion Americans were watching live at the moment the verdict was announced.

Orenthal James Simpson first captured the hearts of Americans as a running back at the University of Southern California (USC), where he won the

Heisman Trophy in 1968. He went on to play for the Buffalo Bills and attained all-pro status. In 1985 Simpson was inducted into the NFL Hall of Fame. During and after his professional career, Simpson was well known for his work as a pitchman for various companies, most notably Hertz rental cars. He began acting towards the end of his NFL career, appearing in several films including the *Naked Gun* comedies.

According to author Gregg Barak, Simpson has avoided making any payments to date, as he often, but not always, denies responsibility for the deaths. In fact, until recently, Simpson seemed to be living a life of luxury in South Florida, where he plays golf regularly and is a part of the nightlife in South Beach. State law protects his Kendall, Florida, home from seizure, and the families are unable to touch his NFL pension and the income from his personal production company, which is allegedly $300,000 per year. Simpson made a different statement in a 1998 *Esquire* magazine cover story, in which he said for the first time, "Let's say I committed this crime ... even if I did this, it would have been because I loved her very much, right?"[7] More recently, the scandal continued as Simpson announced he was writing a book titled, *If I Did It*. The book was to be published by HarperCollins and chronicles the "hypothetical" account of the slaying of Nicole Brown Simpson and Ron Goldman. In February 2007 the partial transcript of an interview Simpson did with publisher Judith Regan became public. In it, Simpson made several comments that certainly indicated his guilt. Regan was later fired by HarperCollins amid public outcry about the publisher attempting to profit from the double murders. In the summer of 2007, the families of the deceased won the rights to the book. The Browns are to receive the first 10 percent of the gross proceeds and the Goldmans the rest.

In 2007, however, Simpson's charmed life appeared to fall apart once more. He was accused of having directed several men in the armed robbery of sports memorabilia from a Las Vegas hotel room. Most of the memorabilia was related to Simpson's athletic career. Simpson allegedly orchestrated the break-in to get what he claimed was "his stuff." He was freed in September 2007 on $125,000 bail pending trial, but he was returned to jail in January 2008 on allegations that he violated the conditions of his bond.

As noted, many have proclaimed the O.J. Simpson trial the Trial of the Century. Not only was Simpson accused of a brutal double murder, but the case had all kinds of other drama. It brought to the public, who viewed the trial in record numbers, more juicy and lurid details than a fiction novel, including a beloved celebrity, live chase, an abusive relationship, racism, and police corruption.

MIKE TYSON BITES EVANDER HOLYFIELD

Voted the number one sports story of 1997 by the Associated Press, heavy-weight champion Mike Tyson lost his boxing license in Nevada when he bit off a portion of Evander Holyfield's right ear during the third round of their World Boxing Association Heavyweight Championship rematch on June 28 at the MGM Grand in Las Vegas. Tyson was disqualified from the bout, slapped with a $5.24 million fine, and had the $30-million purse for the fight withheld. Tyson claimed he bit his opponent in response to Holyfield's repeated head butts. When the referee, Mills Lane, and the ring doctor did not immediately stop the fight after a first bite of Holyfield's ear, Tyson bit Holyfield a second time. The second, and more vicious bite, removed a piece of the top of the ear. Mitch Libonati, who worked for the MGM Grand as an official boxing-glove cutter, was supposed to cut the gloves off Holyfield at the conclusion of the fight. Instead, Libonati had the unfortunate experience of recovering Holyfield's missing flesh. He explained, "It looked like a piece of sausage, cut off at the edge. It was about half the size of my pinky finger."[8] The ring doctor determined that Holyfield could continue to fight, but Lane signaled the fight was over. Of the post-fight activity in the ring, columnist Stephen Brunt wrote, "Like a little dog confronted by a big dog, only finding courage being held in its master's arms, Tyson was full of moxie once the ring filled with a cast of thousands. He made a show of trying to get at Holyfield."[9] Tyson allegedly took a swing at an officer during the post-fight melee, although Tyson denied this occurred.

Not only did the incident prompt national outrage, but it was also fuel for a competition amongst journalists, who sought to creatively describe what happened. Across the globe, journalists came up with the most amusing ways to describe Tyson's latest blunder. Duncan Johnstone of the Wellington, New Zealand, *Sunday Star Times,* commented, "It doesn't get much worse than biting off pieces of your opponent's ear. Mike Tyson reached a new low with his Hannibal Lecter impersonation on the ear of Evander Holyfield in their heavyweight boxing clash."[10] A headline in the *Austin American Statesman* read, "Views on a champ, a chomp, a chump."[11] The columnist wrote, "Most of us have never bitten anybody, at least not since we learned to walk. The great heavyweights Muhammad Ali, Joe Louis, Jack Johnson never bit like this. Of course, they never had to. They had other weapons, such as punches. Now we know for sure: Tyson bites. On what was Tyson working behind his camp's closed doors? His overhand right? Or his overbite? Was he jabbing and crossing and hooking or was he flossing and brushing and rising? C'mon, champ! Chomp!"[12] Mark Purdy of the *San Jose Mercury News* commented, "The Sounds and the Fury? Try the incisor and bicuspid. And a disgrace."[13] Michael Madden of the *Boston Globe* opined, "Like a 3-year-old in a temper tantrum, Mike Tyson bites. Like a 3-year-old, Mike Tyson is told not to bite, but he goes out and bites again. Laugh at him. He deserves nothing else."[14] Mark Whicker's headline in the *Orange County Register* read, "Call him ear-responsible: Tyson delivers punchline to the joke that is boxing." Whicker went on to say, "The next stop, beyond outrage, is laughter. You wonder how Mike Tyson could go from Fighter of the Year to Biter of the Ear."[15]

Tyson grew up on the streets. He was brought to a training camp in Catskill, New York, by Gus D'Amato, known for taking in troubled street kids with an interest in boxing. Teddy Atlas, who himself had been a street fighter, was Tyson's first trainer. Atlas claimed all the other kids changed while at Catskill, but Tyson "always had people who helped him avoid consequences."[16] Atlas explained that Tyson always tried to end things too quickly. When the outcome was not quick, or when he could not overpower or intimidate, he would submit. He commented, "You saw that against Buster Douglas. Once Douglas wouldn't back down, Tyson submitted. He didn't try to win that fight. Tyson was what I call a 'game quitter' that night. I said when he got out of prison [for his rape conviction], 'The first time Tyson faces a pro, he'll get beat.' Evander Holyfield isn't the greatest talent, but he is a pro. Holyfield has spent his life facing things. He prepared for what he was going to face in Tyson."[17] According to Atlas, Tyson submitted to Holyfield in their first fight on November 10, 1996. Several days before the fight, the Tyson camp announced he planned to withdraw from the fight unless the Nevada Boxing Commission pulled Mitch Halpern as referee. Atlas argued this was Tyson creating an excuse in advance—if he did not win the fight, he could tell everyone it was the ref's fault.

As further punishment for the biting incident, Tyson was required to undergo therapy to help him manage his anger. An interview five months after the fight made it clear that Tyson was still a deeply troubled man. Tyson explained that he didn't know what happened during the fight, he "just snapped." He told interviewer Alex Wallau, "I truly think everyone hates me. I truly believe that. Because no one gets punished more than I do. But I understand. I'm a big boy and I believe big boys have big ordeals."[18] Many had a hard time viewing Tyson as downtrodden, especially given that the interview took place in his sixty-one-room mansion on seventeen acres in Connecticut. He also said this about biting Holyfield: "I shouldn't have done that, because for that one moment I just forgot he was a human being."[19] Tyson described himself as unstable. "I'm pretty erratic and spontaneous. I'm the most extremist [*sic*] fighter who ever lived. I know I have to change, but I don't know if I can do it. It's scary to change. This is just the way I am."[20]

LATRELL SPREWELL CHOKES HIS COACH

On December 1, 1997, the National Basketball Association was rocked by an alarming act of violence when a player attacked and threatened to kill a coach. Like every professional sports league, the NBA had dealt with fights between players, both at games and practice. But the sports world was abuzz when Golden State Warriors guard Latrell Sprewell, who had been a three-time All-Star, choked first-year head coach P. J. Carlesimo at practice.

Sources said that Carlesimo was giving instruction to Sprewell and walking across the court toward him. Sprewell responded, "I don't want to hear it today."[21] Carlesimo continued his rant. Sprewell said, "Don't come up on me, don't come up on me."[22] Carlesimo kept coming. The argument became increasingly heated and Sprewell finally threatened to kill the coach. Carlesimo responded, "I'm right here."[23] The Golden State Warrior guard then attacked the coach, choking him for between ten and fifteen seconds and dragging him to the ground before teammates intervened. Sprewell was ordered to leave practice. He came back and, as players tried to calm him, threw a punch that glanced off Carlesimo's head.

The Warriors initially announced that it would suspend Sprewell for at least ten games, which would have cost the player nearly $1 million. Team management then set about trying to trade Sprewell. Their efforts, perhaps surprisingly, received considerable interest from up to ten other teams. After conversations with the NBA league office, however, the organization soon changed its position and announced that the team was terminating the final three years of Sprewell's four-year, $32-million contract. "This is the correct, moral, and ethical thing to do," team general manager Garry St. Jean said at the time.[24] The NBA then suspended Sprewell for one year (eighty-two games), which effectively prevented him from becoming a free agent and immediately signing with another team. Sprewell's suspension would ultimately cost him $6.4 million. He also lost endorsement deals that included a contract with Converse. Through arbitration, the suspension was reduced to the remainder of the season (sixty-eight games), but Sprewell did not play again until being traded to the New York Knicks in January 1999, slightly over one year after the incident.

There was initially considerable public backlash against Sprewell. Over time, though, journalists began to search for answers as to why a player would jeopardize his career in such a shocking manner. For many, the answer lay with the coaching style on which Carlesimo relied to motivate athletes. He had a reputation for being tough and willing to get in the face of his players. One journalist called him a "hand grenade with a whistle" who relied on foul language and a "brusque style."[25] Sprewell's agent, in defense of his client, made the point, "One of the issues that has not been examined here is how far can a coach go with his conduct? Are there any limits, or do all players have to deal with abuse and mistreatment?"[26] Sprewell was not the only player who took exception to the treatment that Carlesimo dished out. A former player under Carlesimo, Rod Strickland, said, "There were times when I felt like choking him. He's got a pretty annoying personality. I know Spree's going to get all the beef for this one. It's not just one player here, one player there. P. J. is the common denominator."[27]

For his part, Sprewell certainly had to shoulder much of the blame; particularly given that this was not his first incident of this type. Two years prior he had an altercation at practice with a teammate, Jerome Kersey, which led to a fight. Sprewell left practice that day and returned with a two-by-four board.

He was being restrained by teammates when he said that he would return with a gun. Team officials were concerned enough that he was serious that they kept Kersey in the locker room for three hours before deeming it safe to let him leave.

Sprewell seemed a changed man when he arrived in New York. He had several successful seasons and won over the fans with his substantial work ethic. He represented the Knicks in the 2001 All-Star game. He was traded to Minnesota in 2003 and had one productive season there. At the beginning of his second season in Minnesota, however, the team offered him a contract extension that Sprewell considered a lowball offer. Offended by the three-year, $21-million contract offer, he said, "I have a family to feed." He went on to say, "Why would I want to help them win a title? They're not doing anything for me."[28] He was working under a contract that paid him over $14 million per year at the time, so the offer did represent a significant pay reduction. The NBA fans, however, were not impressed with his comments and he went on to have one of the worst seasons of his career. He has not played since. Perhaps the most significant thing about the case was the public debate about whether it is athletes or coaches that are most out of control. While many faulted Sprewell for behaving poorly, others noted that coaches often treat athletes as if they are chattel. Like other cases in this chapter, the fact that a black athlete stood accused of wrongdoing against a white person brought up racial issues as well that still remain in the world of sports. Some wonder if black athletes can ever get fair treatment in a system that is still run largely by whites.

RAE CARRUTH ORGANIZES MURDER OF HIS GIRLFRIEND

Former Carolina Panthers player Rae Carruth was charged with first-degree murder for the drive-by shooting of his pregnant girlfriend, Cherica Adams, on November 16, 1999. Adams gave birth to a son through an emergency Caesarean section, but then died one month after the shooting. The baby lives with Adams's mother and has cerebral palsy as well as developmental problems. Three other men were charged in the shooting as well. Prosecutors dropped the charge against Wendy Cole, who was accused of harboring a fugitive. Cole allegedly helped Carruth flee North Carolina after his murder charge. Carruth was captured in the trunk of Cole's car in a motel parking lot in Tennessee. No reason was cited for dropping the charge.

The prosecution contended Carruth planned to kill Adams because he did not want to pay child support and that he used his vehicle to block Adams's car so his hired gunman could shoot her.[29] His defense attorneys claimed that codefendant Van Brett Watkins acted alone as the triggerman, and that he was angry with Adams and Carruth over a drug deal. Jurors heard a 911 call Adams made shortly after being shot in which she implicated Carruth. They read notes she scribbled from the hospital in her final waking moments. They also heard testimony from an emergency medical technician and a Charlotte police officer, both of whom said Adams told them Carruth was present at the shooting. The most damaging evidence the jury heard was from codefendant Michael Kennedy, who testified without a plea deal and against the advice of his lawyers that Carruth asked him to be the driver for the shooting and paid him $100 to buy the gun used to kill Adams. The admitted shooter, Watkins, testified with graphic detail about pointing the gun at Adams and pulling the trigger five times. He claimed he was paid by Carruth to shoot her. Carruth's ex-girlfriend, Candace Smith, testified that Carruth confessed to her that he had been involved with the shooting, and former NBA player Charles Shackleford corroborated that statement.

Carruth was acquitted of first degree murder, for which he faced potential execution, but was convicted of conspiracy to murder. He is serving a minimum prison sentence of eighteen years, eleven months. Van Brett Watkins pleaded guilty to second-degree murder. He was sentenced to a minimum of forty years, five months in prison, although he received forgiveness from Adams's family during the sentencing hearing. Saundra Adams, Cherica Adams's mother, commented, "He looked at all of us squarely in the eye. He was much more of a man than some of the others, namely Mr. Carruth."[30] Michael Kennedy, the driver, was sentenced to at least eleven years, eight months for driving the car from which Watkins fired. The fourth defendant, Stanley Drew Abraham, faced similar second-degree murder and conspiracy charges. He pleaded guilty to lesser accessory charges and was sentenced to ninety days in jail and five years probation.

In a televised interview from prison, Carruth told reporters that he and Adams were no more than sex partners. He said, "I didn't even know her last name until we went to Lamaze class."[31] When asked why he fled North Carolina after Adams died, Carruth said he thought everyone was against him. "Who was going to speak up for me? You have the guys that did it lying. Cherica was there and she's gone. The media has already said, 'This is what happened.' What did I have left?"[32] Some called Carruth's verdict and sentence a compromise, and argued he should have faced more time in prison or even execution. The jury foreman, Clark Pennell, stood by the verdict, saying, "I don't think there is anyone on the jury who could look you right in the eye and say they felt we made the wrong decision."[33] In March 2005 Carruth was denied a request for a new trial. Judge Charles C. Lamm Jr. rejected the defense motion, which claimed that a 911 call made by Adams should not have been introduced because it violated his constitutional right to confront his accuser.

Carruth's crime is significant in the world of sport because it demonstrates not only the callousness of some athletes, but it also highlights the overrepresentation of athletes in crimes against women. Carruth's attitude about women became very clear during the trial and in interviews, and unfortunately echoes that of many (although certainly not all) athletes who see women as objects for their satisfaction, not human beings.

MARTY McSORLEY COMMITS ASSAULT ON THE ICE

Boston Bruins defenseman Marty McSorley, known in the National Hockey League more for his fighting than for his finesse and goal scoring, was suspended and tried criminally for savagely attacking the Vancouver Canuck Donald Brashear with 2.7 seconds remaining in a game in February 2000. McSorley had been in the league seventeen years at the time and had been suspended at least five times. The Canucks had a 5–2 lead when McSorley skated up, out of Brashear's view, and smashed his stick with both hands against Brashear's head. His head hit the ice and his helmet flew off. His body twitched and blood streamed from his nose. Brashear sustained a concussion from the attack and had a grand mal seizure.[34] Earlier in the game, Brashear and McSorley had fought, with Brashear landing several hard blows and dragging McSorley to the ice.

Brashear was held overnight in a Vancouver hospital. The next day, he told reporters he did not recall the hit, but had viewed it on tape. He commented, "It looked worse than it was. It looked like I was dying. I wasn't dying, but it's a concussion. There are no bones broken. That was the main concern. Still, I have bad headaches and my face is swollen."[35] McSorley apologized, saying, "I apologize to Donald Brashear and all the fans who had to watch that. I embarrassed my hockey team ... I got way too carried away. It was a real dumb play. I'm still in shock at what I did. I have to come to terms with what I did. There's no excuse. It was so stupid, I can't believe I did it."[36]

Some players denounced McSorley for the attack. Canucks left wing Brad May said, "We couldn't believe what we saw and we didn't know what to do. It was crazy out there. I have no respect for that guy ever again. Anybody who has ever had respect for him should lose it."[37] Others stood up for McSorley. Vancouver captain Mark Messier, a former teammate of McSorley's on the Edmonton Oilers' Stanley Cup teams, said, "Marty has always been an honest player. He has always been a tough player and he's always played the game hard and played the game tough."[38] Keith Primeau of the Philadelphia Flyers noted that he believes the players do have a code of conduct and generally police themselves.

McSorley was suspended for one calendar year. Bruins general manager Mike O'Connell said he had no interest in re-signing McSorley after the incident. McSorley was free to sign with any other team immediately, but could not play until February 21, 2001. Whether criminal law should pursue the case was a matter of considerable debate. Canucks general manager Brian Burke said he didn't believe the police should be involved. Even representatives from other professional sports weighed in on the topic. Chicago Cubs first baseman Mark

Grace commented, "Every time a guy uses the crown of his helmet in the NFL, now the police will be involved? You get a red card in soccer and the police will be involved? Not that what McSorley did is excusable, because it's not. But the games are better off when they're policed by us."[39] Some experts concurred, maintaining the law should only be involved when the league proves to be unwilling or incapable of handling the situation. Others supported criminal prosecution. Dan Doyle, executive director of the Institute for International Sport at the University of Rhode Island, explained why the McSorley case warranted external investigation. "The difference in [the McSorley] incident is that the other guy didn't have a chance to get out of the way. And I think there is a difference when a person is, in effect, defenseless."[40] McSorley was convicted of assault with a weapon in a Canadian court. He faced possible jail time, but was sentenced to eighteen months probation.

Prior to McSorley's attack on Brashear, the longest suspension the NHL had ever imposed for an on-ice hit was in 1993. Washington Capital Dale Hunter received a twenty-one-game suspension for a blind-side check on New York Islander Pierre Turgeon after a playoff goal. Police had previously been involved in on-ice conflicts. In 1970 Wayne Maki of the St. Louis Blues and Ted Green of the Boston Bruins were charged with assault for an incident in a 1969 preseason game. Both were acquitted. In 1988 Minnesota Wild's Dino Cicarelli was fined $1,000 and spent one night in jail after hitting Luke Richardson several times in the head with his stick. Studies of baseball and basketball have shown that punitive action serves to deter further incidents of fighting in professional sports. Clearly, the significance of the case is that McSorley received the lengthiest suspension for on-ice violence to date, a signal to athletes that perhaps there are some actions that are not acceptable as part of their sport.

RAY LEWIS ACCUSED IN MURDER TRIAL

On January 31, 2000, Baltimore Ravens linebacker Ray Lewis and his entourage were involved in a bloody melee at a post–Super Bowl party in Atlanta. As his crew left a nightclub in the wee hours of the morning, they had an altercation that erupted into a street fight. By the time it ended, two men, Jacinth Baker and Richard Lollar, were dead from stab wounds. In the ensuing chaos, Lewis and his friends jumped into an awaiting limousine and fled.

Lewis was charged with two counts of murder and four other felony counts. Also charged were two members of his entourage, Reginald Oakley and Joseph Sweeting. As the criminal case progressed, it became apparent that a guilty verdict against Lewis was highly unlikely, as there was scant, if any, evidence to suggest that he had stabbed anyone. In an effort to ensure a conviction, prosecutors agreed to a plea deal with Lewis that required him to testify against the other two defendants. At the time of the plea agreement, Irwin R. Kramer, a

Baltimore defense attorney who was following the case, noted that the "prosecution is starting to run out of gas, and it doesn't seem like they had much in the tank in the first place."[41]

Lewis pleaded to a misdemeanor obstruction of justice charge and was sentenced to a year of probation. His testimony against Sweeting included the claim that he brandished a knife in the limousine and said, "Every time they hit me, I hit them," as he made punching motions.[42] Regardless of Lewis's testimony, both defendants were acquitted of all charges and nobody else was ever tried or convicted for the murders.

Evidence presented in the case prior to the plea agreement suggested Lewis possibly had a role in a cover-up. His limousine driver admitted on the stand that Lewis had told the others to keep quiet about what happened. Evelyn Sparks, who was in the limousine, testified that she saw another passenger dump a white laundry bag into a garbage bin at a fast food restaurant. Prosecutors were convinced it contained Lewis's bloodstained white suit, which was never recovered. Lewis's lawyer, Ed Garland, maintained that Lewis's only crime was to tell his companions to keep their mouths shut and that he gave an incomplete statement to police.

Lewis returned to the Baltimore Ravens, where he was playing under a four-year contract worth $26 million, reflecting his status as a top defensive player in the league. He was fined $250,000 by NFL commissioner Paul Tagliabue for conduct "detrimental to the league." In a letter to Lewis, from which the NFL released excerpts, Tagliabue wrote, "When an NFL player engages in and admits to misconduct of the type to which Mr. Lewis has pled here, the biggest losers are thousands of other NFL players, present, past, and future."[43] He was taken to task by sports writers for failing to recognize in the letter that the real losers were the victims and their families, which included the young daughter of Lollar.

Lewis led the Ravens to the Super Bowl title in the season following the double murder. He spent the annual Super Bowl media day fending off questions from reporters about his role in the murders and cover-up. For Lewis, all that mattered and all he would talk about was football. He maintained that what he had told prosecutors was true, that he did not know actually who did the stabbing. He acknowledged that he thought about the incident sometimes. "But that's on my time," he said, as he turned the conversation back to the game.[44]

A little more than a year after the stabbings and in the wake of Lewis's Super Bowl victory, two civil suits were filed against Lewis and his codefendants. One was filed in the name of India Smith, the daughter of Lollar by his girlfriend Kellye Smith. It sought $11 million in punitive and compensatory damages. The defense attorneys who represented Lewis in the criminal case called the civil case "totally without merit." The other case was brought by the grandmother of Baker and sought $10 million. Both cases were settled for an undisclosed amount, although newspapers reported a $1 million agreement in the case filed on behalf of India Smith. Lewis's attorney would not verify that amount, but he did say, "The parties have reached an amicable resolution,"[45] after three mediation sessions, which allowed Lewis to avoid a pending trial.

In November 2002 Lewis was used in the marketing campaign for an NFL-licensed video game. In an advertisement he was shown walking across a field and sneering into a camera, and saying, "Your momma can't save you now." Sports columnists questioned the appropriateness of the comment and the use of Lewis to sell a video game to children.[46]

Interestingly, many professional football players, while they expressed disdain for violent crime, used this case and others in this chapter to argue that athletes are subject to unfair media scrutiny. Professional athletes have complained that they are held to higher standards than the average person, and that when they do anything even moderately wrong, it becomes the subject of immense discussion on television, radio, and in newspapers and magazines. That this argument emerged after an athlete was accused of murder is telling. The debate about how much of an athlete's off-field life should be relevant to his career continues, with no end in sight.

JAYSON WILLIAMS SHOOTS HIS LIMO DRIVER

As former NBA All-Star Jayson Williams gave a tour of his home to friends and members of the Harlem Globetrotters in February 2002, he accidentally shot and killed his limousine driver, Costas "Gus" Christofi, as he handled a shotgun. Williams then convinced nearly a half dozen people to help him cover-up the shooting, claiming to police that Christofi committed suicide.

Williams was charged with a variety of crimes for the shooting and subsequent cover-up. According to testimony, Williams took the loaded shotgun from a cabinet in his master bedroom, uttered an expletive at Christofi, presumptively in jest, and then snapped the weapon shut. It discharged, striking Christofi in the chest. He died within minutes. Witnesses said Williams dropped to his knees and wailed, "Oh my God. Oh my God. My life is over."[47] At trial, the defense argued that the gun malfunctioned and the shooting was accidental. An expert testified for the defense that the shotgun's firing mechanism was worn and fouled with wood chips, rust and oil, allowing it to discharge when closed. The prosecution called experts to dispute that the gun malfunctioned, and claimed that the handling of the gun was reckless to the point of being criminal. Noting that Williams had been drinking and handling a loaded gun in a room full of people, prosecutor Steven C. Lember told the jury, "When you play with deadly weapons, 'accident' is no defense."[48] Witnesses admitted that before police arrived, Williams wiped the gun down and put it in Christofi's hands before he stripped naked and swam in his indoor pool. A friend was directed to get rid of his clothes. Williams's brother, Victor Williams, called 911 and told the operator that Christofi had committed suicide, but voices could be heard in the background saying, "Tell [the operator] that he reached for the gun," and "Wipe the gun off."[49]

In April 2004, Williams was convicted on four charges of tampering with evidence and trying to cover up the death of Christofi. Two of Williams's friends pleaded guilty to evidence tampering and testified in the case. Four Globetrotters players testified with immunity. Williams faces a maximum penalty of thirteen years in prison on those convictions, but a sentence of five years is more likely. He was acquitted on three of four shooting-related counts, including the most serious charge he faced, aggravated manslaughter. The jury, however, deadlocked 8–4 on a charge of reckless manslaughter and the prosecution opted to pursue a new trial. Williams remains free on bail and sentencing on the convictions was postponed until the resolution of the reckless manslaughter case.

A series of appeals prolonged the case, which had been scheduled for March 2005. The sides wrangled over whether the facts regarding the cover-up could be entered as evidence in the new trial, and whether a new trial was tantamount to double jeopardy. The appeals panel rejected the double jeopardy claim, but agreed that, since Williams had already been convicted of the cover-up, the evidence pertaining to that crime would be limited in the new trial. The case is slated for trial in the summer of 2008.

In the time between trials, Williams attempted a comeback of sorts, playing for the minor-league Idaho Stampede in the Continental Basketball Association in 2005. "I respect the legal process and understand the road before me, yet I desire to use the gifts and skills God has given me as a basketball player," he said at the time.[50] Williams, a former St. John's University star and 1990 NBA first-round draft pick, had signed an $85-million, six-year contract with the New Jersey Nets in 1999 before retiring in 2000 after a series of injuries that included a broken leg from a collision with a teammate. He had been employed as an NBA analyst for NBC, but was suspended after the shooting. The Williams case also brought up issues of the line between on and off field, and whether athletes have any obligation to be role models. It also demonstrates that although compared to the general public they face relatively light sanctions for their indiscretions, athletes do suffer tremendous financial losses when they screw up.

BAYLOR BASKETBALL—THE MURDER OF PATRICK DENNEHY

In NCAA history there might never have been a more shameless, tragic scandal than the Baylor basketball scandal of 2003. The program, under Coach Dave Bliss, was rife with NCAA violations that came to light after one player murdered another, and then the coach attempted to mastermind a cover-up of under-the-table payments to players that included besmirching the deceased as a drug dealer.

The scandal began when Carlton Dotson shot and killed teammate Patrick Dennehy on June 12, 2003, while they were firing pistols at a gravel pit. Dennehy was reported as missing one week later, after his family could not contact him and became worried. Dotson was arrested in Maryland, his home state, after calling authorities and saying that he needed help because he had "voices in his head." According to authorities, he confessed to killing Dennehy, but told an FBI agent that it was self-defense. He claimed that Dennehy had tried to kill him at the gravel pit but his gun jammed, allowing Dotson to shoot first. Dotson, speaking to reporters, denied that he had confessed. Dennehy's Chevrolet SUV was found June 25, without license plates, in Virginia Beach, Virginia. Within days of Dotson's arrest, but six weeks after he was reported missing, Dennehy's badly decomposed body was found near the gravel pits outside of Waco, Texas. He had been shot twice in the head.

Between July 30 and August 1, assistant coach Abar Rouse taped conversations that he had with Coach Bliss, some of which included players. Bliss had been making payments to Dennehy to cover his tuition and other expenses, in a clear and calculated violation of NCAA rules. He feared that the violations would be uncovered through the investigation into the murder. On the tapes, Bliss could be heard concocting a story to paint Dennehy as a drug dealer who paid his own tuition. Rouse turned the tapes over to Baylor and NCAA investigators. The *Fort-Worth Star Telegram* obtained copies. On one tape, Bliss said, "I think the thing we want to do ... and you think about this ... if there's a way we can create the perception that Pat [Patrick Dennehy] may have been a dealer. Even if we had to kind of make some things look a little better than they are, that can save us."[51] In an attempt to coerce a player to go along with the plan, he said, "if Dotson hadn't killed Dennehy, we wouldn't be in this jam. So we don't deserve to be in this jam. The reason we're in this jam is because of a dead guy and a guy that murdered him, and that isn't fair for you and me and Abar to be in this jam.... We're the victims."[52] Bliss was forced to resign August 8 after admitting that two players were given improper payments. He admitted to the cover-up attempt after the tapes were in the hands of media outlets. NCAA schools are barred from hiring Bliss without showing "just cause" and getting NCAA clearance until 2015.

Dennehy's stepfather, Brian Brabazon, reacted angrily to the tapes, saying of Bliss, "What a callous, cold-hearted person he is. He's lied all the way through. He never told the truth about any of this until he was caught each time."[53] Dennehy's girlfriend was particularly upset when she read that Bliss had said, on tape, "Dennehy is never going to refute what we say.... Now he's dead, so he isn't going to argue with me at all."[54]

Dotson was initially ruled incompetent to stand trial and was sent to a state mental hospital. He claimed to be hallucinating and believed people were trying to kill him because he was Jesus. Experts at the facility believed he was faking. Just as the murder trial was set to commence, Dotson surprisingly pleaded guilty without a sentencing agreement. He was subsequently sentenced to thirty-five years in prison. In 2006 Dotson attempted to appeal. He was denied the request because he had waived the right to appeal by pleading guilty.

The NCAA considered shutting down Baylor's basketball program, but reconsidered in light of Baylor's self-imposed sanctions that included the forced resignation of Coach Bliss, a loss of scholarships, and a ban on postseason play. Still, the sanctions were stiff; the program was placed on five years of probation and was banned from playing nonconference games for one season. Regarding a complete shutdown, the NCAA Division I chairman for the committee on infractions, Gene Marsh, said, "We walked up to the edge and then stepped back."[55] He continued, "We considered this to be a death penalty case. But we looked at the cooperation from the school and the honest and blunt approach they took about what their programs were. You have to give some credit along the way to a school that cooperates."[56] The NCAA noted that the violations were egregious and showed a clear lack of institutional control. They included handing out more scholarships than allowed by giving players over $30,000 in prohibited benefits, making impermissible donations to amateur teams with prep standouts, and covering up failed drug tests by players. Baylor University basketball came as close as any program has come to receiving the NCAA "death penalty" since Southern Methodist football actually did and lost the 1987 and part of the 1988 seasons.

To avoid a possible lawsuit, Baylor reached a settlement with Dennehy's mother, Valorie Brabazon in May 2004. Neither side provided details, but Brabazon, through her attorney, released a statement reading that her family wanted "to thank Baylor, its administrators, and staff for responding with sensitivity and caring concern for their needs, since the time of Patrick's untimely death in the summer of 2003."[57] Dennehy's father, Patrick Dennehy Sr., had filed a wrongful death suit against the school. It was dismissed because, according to the judge, the death was not foreseeable.

Valparaiso head coach Scott Drew, at only thirty-two years old and with one season as a head coach, agreed to take on the challenge of leading Baylor basketball into the future. He had assisted his father, Homer Drew, at "Valpo" for nine years before taking over the team and leading it to a 20–11 season and a National Invitation Tournament appearance. Drew met the monumental challenge at Baylor head-on, and by the 2006–7 season the team was showing signs of becoming competitive. Operating with a full complement of scholarships for the first time since the scandal, the team finished 15–16, the most wins for the program in six years.

The scandal in this case ran deep, permeating the entire basketball program. Coach Bliss's actions, and the NCAA's response, hopefully served as an important reminder that no individual or organization is above the law. Time will tell if the message was received.

TODD BERTUZZI DISGRACES HOCKEY

All-Star right-winger Todd Bertuzzi of the Vancouver Canucks lost more than $500,000 in salary when he was suspended from the National Hockey League for seventeen months, missing twenty games, for assaulting Colorado Avalanche player Steve Moore during a regular season game in March 2004. In addition, Bertuzzi was sentenced to a year of probation and eighty hours of community service when he pleaded guilty to assault in a Canadian court. As a condition of his probation, Bertuzzi could never play against Moore again. In addition to the sanctions against Bertuzzi, the Canucks were fined $250,000.

With the Avalanche holding an 8–2 lead, Bertuzzi grabbed Moore from behind, punched him in the side of the head, and landed on top of him as Moore fell to the ice. Moore was motionless on the ice, lying in a puddle of blood, before he was carted off on a stretcher. Moore sustained a concussion and broken bones in his neck. It was doubtful he would ever play hockey again. Allegedly, the attack was retaliation for Moore's hit earlier in the game that sidelined Vancouver captain Markus Naslund for three games and left him with a concussion. Two days after the attack, Bertuzzi made a tearful public apology, claiming that he had no intention of hurting Moore and that he felt awful about what happened. Some critics said he never attempted to apologize directly to Moore, but Bertuzzi claimed he tried to do so more than ten times.

The case generated a great deal of media attention. Many people felt Bertuzzi's punishment was not harsh enough. Some called for a complete ban on fighting in hockey. Players generally defended the importance of fighting to the sport. Florida Panthers enforcer Darcy Hordichuck said, "People don't have a clue about the role fighting plays. If you took police officers out of society, what's going to happen? It's not like I run around and try to take people's heads off out there. Guys run around and think they're tough. If you take a cop out of the equation, everybody is going to run around and there's no control."[58] Given that hockey was waning in its fan base and coverage at the time, some people involved with the NHL were upset that the media selected to emphasize only the worst of the league. "All [the media have] done is crucify my player," said Vancouver general manager Brian Burke.[59]

In August 2005, Bertuzzi returned to hockey, appearing first at Canada's Olympic orientation camp where he would play for Team Canada. He was also cleared to play in the NHL again, where he was due to make more than $5.2 million from the Canucks. He announced, "Today is a new beginning for me and my family. There's no way I can change what happened in the past, but I'm going to do what I can to make sure my career and my life aren't defined by what happened on March 8, but rather by what I did before and, most importantly, what I do after."[60] Many welcomed Bertuzzi back. Wayne Gretzky, Team Canada's executive director, pronounced, "Todd feels worse about what happened than anybody. He has been punished and served his time."[61] Moore was surprised Bertuzzi was reinstated to the NHL. He said, "It's difficult to see that he's able to play again when I still have a long way to go, and not just in hockey, but with my health."[62] At that time, the Colorado Avalanche would not commit to re-signing Moore if he was cleared by doctors to play again, although they had offered to allow him to return to Denver and work with the team's medical staff.

Moore filed a lawsuit naming Bertuzzi, former Canucks forward Brad May, Canucks coach Marc Crawford, former Canucks general manager Brian Burke, and Orca Bay Sports and Entertainment, owner of the Canucks. His first case was dismissed by a Denver court, which suggested the case should be filed in a Canadian court. He filed in Canada in February 2006. By November 2007, Bertuzzi's lawyer offered $350,000 to settle the case. Moore rejected that offer, which he considered an insult. He is seeking $15 million. Although important in many ways, perhaps the greatest impact of this case was to show the disparity in views about the proper treatment of on-field violence. While many athletes and sports fans defended the sentence and welcomed Bertuzzi back to the game, others emphasized the fact that, were it to have occurred off the field, Bertuzzi's assault would likely have garnered him a more significant punishment. Additionally, most ex-cons, as Bertuzzi now is, struggle to find any type of employment, and surely are not offered the great opportunity Bertuzzi was.

BASKETBRAWL

Basketbrawl, as it has come to be known, was the third most important sports story of 2004, according to newspaper and broadcast members of the Associated Press. It began when Detroit Piston Ben Wallace was fouled by Indiana Pacer Ron Artest, hard, with 45.9 seconds left in a November 19, 2004, game. Wallace responded by shoving Artest, and other players began pushing and shoving one another. Artest ended up lying on the scorer's table. Then a fan threw a cup of icy soda, hitting Artest, who flew into the stands in a rage. Teammate Stephen Jackson followed him in the attack on fans. Players and fans alike got involved in the ensuing melee, which resulted in suspensions for many players and lifetime bans from the Palace of Auburn Hills for some fans.

Five Pacers—Artest, Jackson, Anthony Johnson, David Harrison, and Jermaine O'Neal—were tried criminally and pleaded no contest to misdemeanor assault and battery charges. Artest, O'Neal, and Jackson all received one year of probation, sixty hours of community service, and $250 fines. Before sentencing, judge Julie Nichols reminded the players that, like it or not, they are role models. All but Harrison were suspended by the NBA. Four Pistons were also sanctioned by the league. Initially, O'Neal was suspended for twenty-five games, but an arbitrator reduced his suspension to fifteen games in late December 2004. Combined, the nine players lost nearly $10 million in salary. Artest received the most severe sanction from the league—a one-year suspension, without pay. Artest went on to play for the Sacramento Kings. Stephen Jackson was suspended without pay for thirty games.

Both Artest and Jackson had criminal histories, including violent offenses. Artest pleaded no contest to a misdemeanor domestic violence charge, and Jackson pleaded guilty to a felony criminal recklessness charge. As part of his community service, Artest spoke to youth about black empowerment, but was far from apologetic about the incident. "Someone started trouble and I ended it. I would always encourage you to protect yourself but in certain situations if you can avoid them, avoid them."[63] Artest also told kids about his past as a drug dealer and how he started to get into trouble when he was thirteen.

Bryant Jackson, a fan who got involved in the brawl when he threw a metal chair, was initially sentenced to two years of probation. In February 2007, he was sentenced to six months in jail when a judge determined he had violated his probation by not paying $6,000 in restitution or attending anger-management classes. John Green, the man who threw the cup, was sentenced to thirty days in jail on an assault and battery charge. Green was also banned for life from the Palace for Pistons games, and the Pistons executive vice president John Ciszewski said he would be arrested for trespass if he ever shows up at the stadium. Green was also required to complete Alcoholic Anonymous and anger-management classes. He acknowledged his guilt and claimed it was the dumbest thing he had ever done. Misdemeanor assault and battery charges were dropped against William Paulson when videotapes revealed he was defending a friend against an attack by Artest. A lawsuit by Charles Haddad, who alleged he suffered permanent migraines, memory loss, trouble sleeping, inability to socialize, and an aversion to bright lights after being punched by Indianapolis forward Jermaine O'Neal, was dismissed in October 2006. The defense showed that Haddad had flown to Las Vegas the day after the brawl and regularly traveled there, suggesting his claims were false. The U.S. District Court jury determined O'Neal had punched Haddad, but he was justified in doing so because he was protecting his teammates.

Indiana lost a lot of games after the brawl, as it was required to substitute players to cover the loss of three of its five best scorers. Although there were vows made to do whatever possible to ensure nothing like Basketbrawl happened again, critics claimed little changed. While the NBA did add another uniformed police officer near the bench and curbed the sale of alcohol, the most significant rule change the league made between seasons was to add a new dress code for the players. Sportswriter Dave Zirin explained that Basketbrawl highlighted a bigger problem. "Those fans in Auburn Hills, $50 tickets in hand, believe it is not only their right but their duty to throw punches at opposing players if the opportunity presents itself."[64]

More than two years later, Artest was booed as he was introduced at the Palace in a game between the Pistons and the Kings. Pistons fans heckled Artest about a CD he had made, his Mohawk haircut, and the black supportive sleeves he wore under his shorts. The brawl dominated headlines for weeks and later inspired an episode of NBC's hit show, *Law and Order.*

NORTHERN COLORADO BACKUP PUNTER STABS THE STARTER IN THE LEG

In an assault that drew immediate comparisons to the attack on Nancy Kerrigan at the 1994 Olympic Ice Skating Trials, the backup punter at the University of Northern Colorado stabbed the starting punter in his kicking leg in an attempt to gain the starting position during the 2006 season.

Mitch Cozad had failed to make the team in two attempts at the University of Wyoming prior to transferring to Northern Colorado to pursue his dream of being a collegiate punter. He made the team, but did not earn the starting position. Prosecutors claimed that his act was one of desperation to do off the field what he could not do on it. So, under the cloak of darkness he attacked his kicking rival, Rafael Mendoza Jr., in the parking lot of Mendoza's apartment complex.

As Cozad ran off, Mendoza told a passerby that he had been stabbed and asked the person to follow the fleeing Dodge Charger. The car was later seen at a liquor store, where an employee called police after seeing two men in sweatshirts peel tape off the Wyoming license plate, which read 8-KIKR.

The plate led police to Cozad's mother in Wheatland, Wyoming, and then quickly to Cozad. In a feeble attempt to cover his tracks, he told police that the car had been stolen the night of the stabbing. Police searched his dorm room and found two black sweatshirts. Then, as police interviewed a girlfriend who Cozad claimed as an alibi, he further damaged his case by sending her text messages that appeared to encourage her to lie on his behalf. After initially claiming he was with her all night, she then recanted and said that he was not. Even more damning, she told police that earlier in the evening he had asked her, "What would you think would hurt the most, being hit with a car, being beaten with a baseball bat, or getting stabbed?"[65]

Cozad was charged with attempted first-degree murder and second-degree assault. On August 9, 2007, a jury found the twenty-two year old guilty on the assault charge, but acquitted him on the more serious charge. In October 2007, Cozad was sentenced to seven years in prison. Kevin Aussprung, who reportedly had driven Cozad's car after the attack, was treated as a witness in the case against Cozad and was never charged for any part he may have played in the attack. In opening and closing arguments, Cozad's lawyer had pointed at Aussprung as the guilty party. Weld County district attorney Ken Buck said, "If I saw proof he was more involved [we] would have charged him. But I never saw proof."[66]

Interestingly, this case did not draw the same amount of attention as did other less severe examples cited in the chapter. Buck summed up the case, however, by saying, "The message is that in America, we take sports too damn seriously. It's never appropriate to hurt someone … over something as stupid as gaining the starting position in football."[67]

MICHAEL VICK BUSTED FOR BAD NEWZ KENNELS

On April 25, 2007, police executed a warrant at a home in Surrey, Virginia, that belonged to Atlanta Falcons superstar quarterback Michael Vick. The previous day, his cousin had been arrested on drug charges and listed the home as his address. What authorities found led to the downfall of a man who had become the face of the NFL, known for dazzling highlights and the ability to single-handedly redefine the quarterback position. Police found sixty-six dogs and a training complex that was used to prepare them to fight for their lives in brutal and vicious dog fights. As the local investigation appeared to be dragging, federal officials executed their own search warrants in July, digging up the land and yielding dog remains. Vick's fall from grace was almost immediate, and many considered it "the sharpest fall of the biggest active star in NFL history."[68]

Within weeks of finding the dogs' remains, Vick and three other men were indicted on federal charges for dog fighting and related activities that occurred

Flanked by U.S. marshals, Michael Vick is escorted into the federal courthouse in Richmond, Virginia, where he faced charges for dogfighting in relation to his Bad Newz Kennels operation. Courtesy of AP Photo/Haraz N. Ghanbari.

over a six-year period through an operation called Bad Newz Kennels. Vick had begun to bankroll the scheme almost immediately after being drafted into the NFL. Included were charges for breeding dogs for fighting, hosting fights, and killing dogs that performed poorly. As public sentiment turned against Vick and sponsors begin to drop his contracts, Vick pleaded not guilty in a federal court in Richmond. He proclaimed his innocence, saying, "Today I pleaded innocent to allegations made against me ... I look forward to clearing my good name."[69] His lawyer promised "a hard-fought trial," indicating that they were pursuing their own investigation on Vick's behalf. Vick went on to blame his family and friends for taking advantage of his generosity in using the house, which he claimed he rarely visited.

Any plans Vick had to mount a credible defense were sunk when codefendant Tony Taylor pleaded guilty only days after being indicted and agreed to cooperate with the prosecution. Just over two weeks later, Vick's other two codefendants, Purnell Peace and Quanis Phillips, also pleaded guilty to a single charge of conspiracy, saying they traveled with Vick to dog fights and described "executing approximately eight dogs that did not perform well in testing sessions."[70] They admitted the dogs had been hanged and drowned, and that Vick had taken part in the killings. The eighteen-page indictment said that Vick was consulted before one dog was wet down and electrocuted. In addition, they asserted that Vick had bankrolled the entire operation.

Three days after he became the lone remaining defendant, and in an abrupt about-face from his declaration of innocence, Vick, through his lawyer, announced that he had reached an agreement to plead guilty to the federal charges, and that he wished to apologize to everyone who had been hurt by this matter. His problems, however, were compounded a month later when a grand jury in Surrey County, Virginia, indicted Vick and his codefendants on an additional state charge of dog fighting. The grand jury declined to indict on eight counts of killing dogs, which could have put Vick and his crew in prison for forty years. It was clear that a legal battle was impending regarding whether the state charges were a violation of the Fifth Amendment's ban on double jeopardy.

Only one day after the indictment on the state charge was handed down, it was announced that Vick had failed a court-ordered drug test he had taken only seventeen days after he pleaded guilty to the federal charges. As a result of his positive test for marijuana, Vick was confined to his residence at night, ordered to wear an electronic monitoring device, and directed to have mental health counseling while he awaited his December sentencing. While some of his Falcons teammates, including wide receiver Joe Horn, swore they would remain close to Vick regardless of whether he ever played another down in the NFL, others began to distance themselves. Safety Lawyer Milloy commented that he was ready to move on and concentrate on football instead of things that were beyond his control.

As Vick awaited sentencing, two banks filed federal lawsuits against him for failure to repay loans. One suit was filed by a South Bend bank that claimed Vick refused to pay for cars used for a car rental business, costing the bank over $2 million. The suit sought unspecified damages. The other, filed by a Canadian bank, sought over $2.3 million that it claimed Vick planned to use for real estate investments.

Vick had signed a ten-year, $130 million contract with the Falcons in 2004, at the time among the largest in the league. The guaranteed portion totaled $44 million. The Atlanta Falcons announced that it would pursue repayment for a portion of that. In addition to being indefinitely suspended from the NFL, Vick also lost lucrative sponsorship contracts with Rawlings, Nike, Reebok, and Upper Deck. Vick was sentenced on December 10, 2007, to twenty-three months in prison. Whether he would ever again set foot on an NFL field remained to be seen. Peace and Phillips had been sentenced to eighteen and twenty-one months, respectively. Taylor, who provided much of the information used to build the case against Vick, was sentenced last, and to only two months in prison.

The Vick case brought up all kinds of issues. One of these was outrage from domestic violence advocates. Although they deplored the crime, some advocates used Vick's sentence as a vehicle to express outrage at the fact that abusers many times receive lesser punishments for harming their partners than Vick did for harming animals.

Chapter 2

DRUGS: COCAINE, STEROIDS, AND AN ASTERISK

In late 2007, as this book went to press, former U.S. senator George Mitchell reported the results of a lengthy investigation into steroid use in Major League Baseball. The results were alarming, yet at the same time, not altogether surprising. Mitchell found widespread use of performance-enhancing substances involving athletes from the benchwarmers to the biggest stars. The reason few were completely surprised by the results of the investigation was that most sports fans realize that use of performance-enhancing substances has become a staple of modern athletics. All that has changed recently is perhaps the number of users and the types of drug. Today, drugs are being specifically manufactured by chemists to beat the tests that are administered to athletes by leagues that are falling behind in attempts to maintain a level playing field and a clean game.

Sports organizations have grappled with how to handle this pervasive problem, vacillating between denying there is a problem to enacting tough measures with long suspensions for players who fail a test. Moving forward, the leagues will grapple with determining what to do with records that were clearly set in a time when sports were rife with drug use. What is clear is that the win-at-all-costs mentality endemic to sports in the United States has created a culture whereby many athletes feel they have no choice but to use drugs in order to remain competitive. Not exclusive to team sports, drug-related scandals have permeated individual-based sports to an alarming degree as well.

In addition to performance-enhancing substances, some sports scandals involve athletes who have destroyed themselves through their use of other illicit drugs. With it, they have had a negative impact on their families, friends, teammates, and the entire sports world.

MAJOR LEAGUE BASEBALL COCAINE SCANDAL, 1985

In 1985 Major League Baseball was engulfed in a major drug scandal when an investigation by federal prosecutors in Pittsburgh revealed players were buying cocaine from local dealers. In May 1985 up to twelve players reportedly testified to a federal grand jury. Commissioner Peter Ueberroth remarked, "I think it's going to be bad," when asked about the grand jury inquiry.[1] The next month, the federal grand jury indicted seven men for drug trafficking. Fortunately for Major League Baseball, no players were indicted or even named as unindicted coconspirators. However, the investigation revealed that a considerable number of players were using cocaine. Evidence pointed to cocaine being sold to players in almost every Major League ballpark in the National League, and that transactions were so commonplace that "in some cases the athletes were able to pin down sales by recalling who the opposing pitcher was on a given date."[2] The prosecutors reported that the drug transactions between the players and dealers were always for small amounts of cocaine, however the frequency of drug deals for some players was alarmingly high. Prosecutors indicated one player paid for over $100,000 worth of drugs in one year.

In September 1985 the trial of Curtis Strong, a Philadelphia caterer, began. He was charged with sixteen counts of cocaine distribution. Lonnie Smith was the first player of several to testify in the case after receiving immunity from the prosecution. During his testimony, he named other players when asked about drug use in Major League Baseball. Joaquin Andujar, Gary Mathews, Dickie Noles, Dick Davis, and Keith Hernandez were all named as players using cocaine with Smith during his playing days with the Phillies and Cardinals. Smith also mentioned the names of players taking amphetamines, including Bake McBride, Nino Espinosa, and Mike Schmidt. When Keith Hernandez testified, he admitted using cocaine since the 1980 season and referred to that time period as one of "romance between baseball players and the drug."[3] Under cross-examination, Hernandez named Bake McBride, Nino Espinosa, Larry Bowa, Greg Luzinski, Randy Lerch, and Pete Rose as teammates that "supposedly" used amphetamines, or "greenies," as the players called them. Keith Hernandez's and Dodgers infielder Enos Cabell's testimony named Dave Parker, Jeff Leonard, Lary Sorenson, Al Holland, J. R. Richard, Dale Berra, Rod Scurry, John Milner, and Bernie Carbo as MLB players using cocaine during the early 1980s.

Pittsburgh Pirates Dale Berra, son of the legendary Yogi Berra, and Dave Parker also testified during Strong's trial. Their testimony painted the Pirates organization in a particularly ugly light. They testified that team leaders Bill Madlock and Willie Stargell were the "people to see for amphetamines in the Pirates clubhouse."[4] If all the major leaguers were not granted immunity, they could have faced charges for drug possession and use, smuggling, illegal transportation, and distribution of cocaine.

At the conclusion of the two-week trial, Strong was found guilty on eleven felony counts of selling cocaine. Major League Baseball found itself with a black eye after seven players testified about not only their current and past drug use, but also about the drug use of their teammates. Even the great

Willie Mays was accused of having "red juice" (a mixture of fruit juice and amphetamines) in his locker by retired Pirate John Milner.[5] While Madlock, Stargell, and Mays all denied the allegations, the cloud of suspicion hung over all of baseball, and fans were forced to wonder which players were into illegal drugs and which were playing while strung out.

On February 28, 1986, Major League Baseball commissioner Peter Ueberroth announced eleven players were suspended because of cocaine. Seven of the players were suspended for one year but were able to buy their way out of the suspension by paying 10 percent of their base pay to local drug rehabilitation facilities. Ueberroth believed they had prolonged drug use and facilitated distribution among players.[6] Four players were suspended for sixty days, with the option to give 5 percent of their base pay to a rehabilitation facility to have the suspension waived. These four players had used, but not distributed drugs. All eleven players also had to perform community service and submit to drug testing for the rest of their careers. The seven players receiving the harshest penalty were the players involved in the Pittsburgh drug trials: Joaquin Andujar, Dale Berra, Enos Cabell, Keith Hernandez, Jeff Leonard, Dave Parker, and Lonnie Smith.

This case was significant for many reasons, but in particular for its timing. In the 1980s, crack cocaine was decimating cities across the country. The fact that professional athletes were using cocaine highlighted the fact that use of the drug was widespread.

THE TRAGIC DEATH OF LEN BIAS

As a star of the University of Maryland's basketball team in 1986, six-foot-eight forward Len Bias wowed coaches and fans alike with his powerful, yet graceful moves, his acrobatics, and his confidence on the court. Bias was Maryland's all-time leading scorer and a two-time Atlantic Coast Conference Player of the Year. The excitement about Bias continued as he was the Boston Celtics' number-one draft pick, and the second overall selection for the 1986–1987 season. Excitement turned to shock when twenty-two-year-old Bias was found dead from a cocaine overdose on June 19, 1986. His death prompted a dramatic overhaul of the Maryland athletic program, as the athletic director and two head coaches resigned. Its impact went beyond the world of basketball, however. It was the impetus for national debate about drugs and spurred a massive antidrug campaign by Congress.

On June 19 at approximately 6:30 A.M., Bias collapsed in his dorm room after a "cocaine party" with his friend Brian Tribble and teammates Terry Long and David Gregg. According to Long and Gregg, there were "scoops" of cocaine available. Bias had bragged, "I'm a horse, I can take it." He suffered three seizures before paramedics arrived.[7] He was pronounced dead at approximately 8:50 A.M. A search the following day revealed nine grams of cocaine in

Bias's car. The following week, Maryland state medical examiner John Smialek reported that there was no evidence Bias had ever used cocaine, only to announce less than two weeks later that Bias often used the drug.

Maryland coach Charles "Lefty" Driesell resigned in the wake of the scandal, amid allegations he tolerated drug use and academic deficiencies among his players.[8] Driesell was widely denounced for calling cocaine performance enhancing, saying at a conference on drugs that "if you know how to use cocaine and use it properly, it can make you play better." He said his comment was based on research he had done thirty years prior for his master's degree, but that it was misinterpreted, and he meant that cocaine acts as a stimulant and thus increases heart rate and the production of adrenaline.[9] He said, "It was interpreted entirely wrong. Good gracious, I've made a living coaching. I would never allow my athletes to use or suggest that they use steroids or cocaine or anything to enhance their performance." Driesell, who was known for making "alarming public statements," went on to be assistant athletic director for fundraising.[10] Athletic director Dick Dull left Maryland a few weeks after Driesell. Football coach Bobby Ross also resigned, even though he had nothing to do with the basketball team and its problems. He cited a lack of support for his efforts to improve the school's athletic facilities and was resentful that his reputation was sullied by guilt by association with the athletic department as a whole.

Terry Long and David Gregg, who were with Bias when he died in his dorm room, were kicked off the team before the start of the 1986–87 season. These losses crippled the team, which had its worst season ever and did not win a single Atlantic Coast Conference game. Brian Tribble, a friend of Bias, was acquitted in June 1987 of charges of providing Bias the cocaine. During the trial, testimony showed that many people had knowledge of Bias's cocaine habit and had warned him to cool it. Driesell, who testified for the prosecution, professed he did not know about Bias's drug problem and commented, "Obviously, I was shocked he was fooling with drugs because I had talked to him about it, his lawyer had talked to him and his parents had talked to him. We knew he was going to be worth a couple of million dollars and we were all trying to make sure he didn't go near it [drugs]."[11] He claimed he saw no evidence of drug use during Bias's senior year.[12] Charges of cocaine possession and obstruction of justice against Long and Gregg were dismissed in exchange for their testimony against Tribble.

In February 1987 a Prince George's County grand jury issued a scathing report about the University of Maryland athletic programs. The report said, "The university's decision to have a major athletic program which was based to a large extent on the talents of students who had less than a reasonable chance of graduating ... was not only appalling, but abominable."[13] The grand jury recommended the university shorten the men's basketball season, increase the use of drug testing, hire more police, and make greater use of student informants.

Interestingly, Maryland's vice chancellor, Dr. A. H. "Bud" Edwards, announced that, one year later, the school saw a major increase in student enrollment. Private donors gave approximately $4 million more than they had the year prior to Bias's death, and the number of donors expanded by 3,000 people. Edwards commented that the school had changed dramatically in that year. "We think we have a whole new University of Maryland. We're feeling quite good about it. It's behind us. We don't spend 10 seconds a day thinking or talking about it here. It's a year old, that stuff."[14] Bias's mother, Lonise, was not so prepared to put the tragedy behind her. She became a national spokesperson against drug abuse.

National Basketball Association executives vowed to make greater use of detectives to investigate the private lives of players suspected of drug abuse. NBA executive vice president Russell Granik commented, "Drugs is a dirty business, and I think you've got to fight dirty to rid yourself of this horrendous problem. If it appears that you're infringing on one's individual rights, as the players will argue and yell, I think the greater good dictates a strong position to help eradicate this cancer."[15] The players union expressed concern that such tactics would be used nefariously by teams trying to find a way out of contracts. Another suggestion to protect the league was to expand drug testing. Drug testing, now widely employed by the government, in corporations, the military, schools, and athletic programs, was in its infancy at the time. The NBA only tested athletes when it had reasonable cause to believe there was drug use.

Driesell went on to coach at James Madison and Georgia State before retiring in 2003, in the middle of his forty-first season. He was named to the National Collegiate Basketball Hall of Fame in 2007.

Like the 1985 Major League Baseball cocaine scandal, Bias's case highlighted the widespread use of cocaine and its dangers, and helped to usher in reforms that went beyond the world of sports. Unfortunately, many of them, like drug testing, were hurried in without full consideration of their effectiveness and other concerns.

BAY AREA LABORATORY CO-OPERATIVE (BALCO)

In August 2002, Federal agents were tipped off that there was an illegal steroid distribution ring working out of the Bay Area Laboratory Co-Operative (BALCO) in Burlingame, California. The following June, elite track and field coach Trevor Graham, who was aware of the use of undetectable designer steroids in his sport, retrieved a used syringe from a trash can and gave it to the U.S. Anti-Doping Agency (USADA). It was used to detect and create a test for the designer steroid that would later be identified as Tetrahydrogestrinone (THG). Graham named Victor Conte, the owner of BALCO, as the source of the drug. Within months authorities searched BALCO and found steroids, human growth hormone, and testosterone. They also searched the home of Greg Anderson, fitness trainer for baseball superstar Barry Bonds. They found performance enhancing drugs and $60,000 in cash, as well as documents that detailed drug use by several professional athletes. As the story unfolded, public interest centered on the undetectable drugs, called the cream and the clear, and on which athletes may have used them.

In October 2003 the USADA retested samples collected at the national track and field championships from the prior June. Several athletes tested positive for THG, revealing that the BALCO drugs were, indeed, being used by top-level athletes and had escaped detection through the initial round of testing.

From the outset, *San Francisco Chronicle* reporter Mark Fainaru-Wada was on top of the story. He was soon joined by coworker Lance Williams. By 2004 they had secured copies of grand jury testimony that they used to quote baseball player Jason Giambi and sprinter Tim Montgomery as admitting they had used the steroids. They reported that Barry Bonds and baseball player Gary Sheffield testified that, while they used substances that matched descriptions of the cream and the clear, they did not knowingly take steroids.

In October 2005, three of the conspirators in the BALCO scandal entered into a plea deal. Conte was sentenced to four months in prison and four months of house arrest for conspiracy to distribute the undetectable steroids and for money laundering. Greg Anderson was sentenced to three months in prison and an equal time of home confinement for conspiring to distribute steroids to professional baseball players and for money laundering. BALCO vice president James Valente was put on probation for steroid distribution. Judge Susan Illston expressed frustration that the sentences could not be more severe and questioned the judgment of the prosecutors for pursuing a case that, in the end, resulted in such minor punishments. Judge Illston later sentenced track and field coach Remi Korchemny, who had a minor involvement with BALCO, to a year of probation for giving an athlete the sleep disorder drug modafinil. He was also ordered to avoid contact with the other BALCO defendants.

The fifth man convicted was the creator of the designer steroid. Patrick Arnold, a chemist from Illinois and an executive with a nutritional supplements company, had successfully synthesized the steroids to be undetectable via the testing used at the time. Arnold had gained fame in 1998 as the marketer of the steroid-like substance "andro," which was used by Mark McGwire when he broke the single-season home run record. Arnold supplied "the clear" to Conte, who distributed it to twenty-seven athletes including Olympic track star Marion Jones. For his part in the scandal, Arnold served three months in prison.

In March 2006, Fainaru-Wada and Williams released their book about Barry Bonds and the BALCO scandal, *Game of Shadows*. In it, they claimed that Bonds became jealous of the attention heaped upon Mark McGwire and Sammy Sosa during their epic home run race in 1998. He then sought an edge to improve his own game. The book also explained how Jason Giambi approached Bonds's trainer, Greg Anderson, about improving his game, and how that led him to use the cream and the clear. The book led to diminished fan support for Bonds as he pursued the career home run record. A considerable amount of the information for the book was drawn from grand jury testimony that was illegally leaked to the authors. They refused to divulge the name of their source, and U.S. district judge Jeffrey White ordered them imprisoned for up to eighteen months unless they testified. As their case was on appeal, the source of the leak came forward. Surprisingly, it was a lawyer who had represented Conte and Valente and he had been personally complaining about the leak, even seeking a mistrial on the basis that the leak prevented a fair trial for his clients. The lawyer, Troy Ellerman, was sentenced to two-and-a-half years in prison in a plea deal in which he admitted to four charges, including disclosing the transcripts in violation of a judge's order. Even with time reduced for good behavior, Ellerman will serve far longer than any of the BALCO conspirators. The charges against Fainaru-Wada and Williams were dropped.

Of the leaked BALCO grand jury testimony, it was Barry Bonds's testimony that drew the most attention. While he admitted to using a cream and a clear liquid substance provided by Greg Anderson, he maintained that he believed it was an arthritis cream and flaxseed oil. Fainaru-Wada and Williams claimed in *Game of Shadows* that the flaxseed oil story was concocted by Conte, among other cover stories. Conte reportedly also advised his clients to tell authorities that the "C" on their doping charts stood for Vitamin C and not "the cream." His position was that all the athletes could beat the case if they refused to admit anything, particularly that they ever knew they were taking a steroid. It is possible that the BALCO convictions have not ended. Barry Bonds was indicted in November 2007 on four counts of perjury and one count of obstruction of justice. Greg Anderson, who had previously refused to testify regarding Bonds's involvement, could be called to testify. He had already spent over a year in prison for contempt. He was released at the time Bonds was being indicted. It appears that he will face added prison time if he does not testify, should the case go to trial.

BALCO altered the cumulative sports conscious, sending a clear message about the extent to which athletes will go to excel, and the uphill battle that drug testers face in trying to catch them. Dr. Don Catlin, whose UCLA lab used the soiled syringe to discover the previously undetectable steroid THG, said the scandal was as big as they come, adding, "It has totally changed the landscape of drugs in sports."[16]

There were numerous impacts of the steroid scandal that were aimed at slowing the spread of performance-enhancing drug use. Major League Baseball enacted new and tougher drug-testing policies and penalties. Then, fearing that Congress would intervene because the policies were criticized by antidoping organizations as laughably weak, MLB created even newer policies with more testing and more severe sanctions for failed tests. Congress acted to increase the potential prison time for steroid dealers. State high school athletic associations across the country launched programs to educate students about the dangers of steroid use.

The BALCO scandal did little to slow Conte in his highly successful business ventures as a supplements guru. At his sentencing he had claimed he would "share what I have learned about the rampant use of drugs at the elite level of sport and more specifically, to explain exactly how elite athletes routinely beat the existing anti-doping programs."[17] To date he has not followed through on that pledge. He continued to believe that beating drug tests was easy to do and that cheating was widespread. Regarding the Sydney Olympics in 2000, Conte said he guessed that half of the 11,000 athletes used illegal performance-enhancing drugs.

After serving his brief sentence, Conte returned to work, renaming his business Scientific Nutrition for Advanced Conditioning (SNAC). He sells a product called ZMA to professional athletes including Barry Bonds, as well as to bodybuilders, combat sports fighters, and Oakland Raiders and Texas Rangers personnel. The zinc and magnesium supplement is touted as a natural muscle builder. Within a year of his release from a federal work camp, Conte was driving a $170,000 silver Bentley and claiming he had a million-dollar annual income.

FLOYD LANDIS STRIPPED OF TOUR DE FRANCE TITLE

In 2007 American cyclist Floyd Landis became the first man in the 105-year history of the Tour de France to win the race and then lose the title for a doping offense. The 2006 champion, who won with an incredible and unlikely solo effort on the epic seventeenth stage, tested positive for an abnormal testosterone-to-epitestosterone level, and subsequently was found to have synthetic testosterone in his system. After the USADA found him guilty, Landis sought an arbitration hearing. The case with the USADA was a soap opera, rife with accusations of shoddy lab work and witness intimidation. In the end, two of three arbitrators held up the results that showed Landis's comeback victory was drug assisted, although all three arbitrators agreed that the lab work that produced the positive tests was suspect and not done to World Anti-Doping Agency rules. Only a successful appeal to the Court of Arbitration for Sport (CAS) can save his crown. Barring an unlikely reversal, Landis will forfeit his title and face a two-year ban from the sport.

Landis had shocked the cycling world when he regained his form overnight during the 2006 Tour, after collapsing miserably on the sixteenth stage over mountainous terrain. Although he managed to finish, he went from race leader to eleventh place, over eight minutes back. Every contender and team director wrote him off as finished in the race for the individual title. Thus the shock to all when Landis stormed back better than ever the next day, attacking the field 125 kilometers from the finish, holding his advantage to a solo victory and riding right back into contention. He went on to an improbable victory in what was considered one of the strangest Tours ever. The story took a decided turn for the worse when Landis's team, Phonak, announced that he had failed a drug test. Many experts, who doubted that his Stage 17 exploit was possible without some help, were not surprised by the announcement.

Landis proclaimed his innocence and offered a variety of explanations, most of which seemed far-fetched, at best. In addition to claiming he had naturally high testosterone, which apparently had never caused a problem with testing in the past, he also blamed the testosterone spike on his drinking habits. He claimed to have binged on Jack Daniels the night before his epic ride into history. When asked directly if he had ever doped, he gave the less-than-convincing response, "I'm going to say 'no' to that."

Landis committed over $2 million to clearing his name. Much of the money was donated by fans that paid for the opportunity to ride their bikes and have a meal with Landis. He fought an uphill battle in the arbitration against the USADA, which was 34–0 in such cases, prompting Landis to call the system a "kangaroo court."[18] Much of the testimony dealt with the quality of the testing and whether specific protocols were followed by the lab, with each side calling experts to buoy its position.

The testimony became explosive when former Tour de France champion Greg LeMond, the first American winner of the event, took the witness stand. He claimed that in a conversation with Landis he had suggested that living with a secret was a difficult and awful thing to do, sharing that he had been sexually abused by a relative as a young boy. He claimed that Landis responded to his admonition to confess by saying, "What good would it do? If I did, it would destroy a lot of my friends and hurt a lot of people."[19] Landis shared the story of LeMond's sexual abuse with friends and posted an open letter to LeMond on an Internet site in which he threatened to "out" LeMond if he "ever opens his mouth again and the name Floyd comes out."[20] A friend of Landis, Will Geoghegan, even called LeMond the night before his scheduled testimony and threatened to expose his abuse at the arbitration hearing. LeMond, infuriated, filed a police report and told the story during his testimony. Landis fired Geoghegan, who had acted as his business manager, but the damage to Landis's reputation and his case was clear and profound.

In September 2007, nearly four months after the hearing, the arbitrators released their eighty-four-page decision. Two of three arbitrators were convinced Landis had doped his way to victory. "Today's ruling is a victory for all clean athletes and everyone who values fair and honest competition," said

USADA CEO Travis Tygart.[21] Landis said, "I am innocent and we proved I am innocent."[22] At the time of writing he had appealed the result to the Court of Arbitration for Sport.

In an open letter to fans that appeared on his Web site, Landis claimed, "If any good has come of this, we have shown that the anti-doping system is corrupt, inefficient and unfair." He continued, "I still have hope that the system can, and will be, changed so that no other athlete has to suffer through this process only to be denied a clean chance at justice."[23]

For many, the case was just more evidence that all professional sports are infested with performance-enhancing substances. Some believe cycling is no more than a three-ring circus of doped-up freaks, and some fans have denounced the sport until they see evidence that its athletes are competing clean. They might have a long wait ahead of them.

BARRY BONDS, HOME RUN KING (WITH AN ASTERISK)

In the history of sports reporting, it is likely that the word *asterisk* never appeared in the sports pages more than on the morning of Wednesday, August 9, 2007. The night before, at 8:51 Pacific Time, Barry Bonds of the San

Barry Bonds found life on the road more challenging as he approached the all-time home run record and fans made their feelings clear. Courtesy of AP Photo/Steven Senne.

Francisco Giants hammered a pitch 435 feet into a throng of crazed fans. He rounded the bases in his signature home run trot for the 756th time in his twenty-three-year career. He had eclipsed the home run record of 755, held for thirty-three years by baseball legend Hank Aaron. The sellout crowd of 43,154 rose to its feet. Most cheered. Many booed. The heat cranked up on the debate of the asterisk.

To his chagrin, Bonds had, over the preceding years, become the poster boy for baseball's steroid era, a time when the sport lacked adequate drug testing, and suspicion ran rampant that the sport's biggest sluggers were the product of blatant steroid abuse. Perhaps no moment, aside from Bonds breaking the single-season home run record, more directly forced baseball fans to decide how much they trusted the players and yearned for a clean game. Columnist Dan Connolly of the *Baltimore Sun* wrote that the moment "polarized a country that isn't sure whether to celebrate a new hallowed sports number or mourn the passing of the torch from a respected baseball legend to one mired in controversy."[24]

Columnists and fans around the country called for the new record to be denoted with an asterisk, indicating that it was set under circumstances that, at best, could be called dubious. Even baseball commissioner Bud Selig struggled with the new record. He attended the game in which Bonds tied the record, but literally jammed his hands into his pockets rather than applaud the effort. As Bonds broke the record, Selig was reportedly, and perhaps ironically, meeting with former senator George Mitchell, who was heading baseball's investigation into performance enhancing drug use in the sport. When asked why he didn't acknowledge the hitter's accomplishments along with those of other players, like Tony Gwinn and Cal Ripken Jr., Selig responded, "They've never done anything to embarrass the game."[25]

Bonds had been a great player throughout his career. However, his physical transformation at an age when most players are past their peak was stunning. He had been a lanky player, highly skilled, but not necessarily a powerhouse. He walked into the Giants' clubhouse in 2000 as a transformed man, rippling with new muscles. How he acquired his new body was documented by *San Francisco Chronicle* reporters Mark Fainaru-Wada and Lance Williams in their book *Game of Shadows*. They made the case that Bonds had used steroids for several years, beginning in 1998, including the secret drugs called the cream and the clear from BALCO. Their two-year investigation cited court documents, including leaked grand jury testimony from the BALCO case, and interviews with over 200 sources. The authors claimed that Bonds used human growth hormone and steroids, including one used to fatten cattle. Bonds never sued the authors for their claim. Particularly curious was that his trainer, Greg Anderson, who secured the drugs from BALCO, languished in prison for over a year as opposed to testify about whether Bonds used steroids. In fact, Anderson was jailed three separate times on contempt charges but remained tight lipped. Even Bonds's longtime mistress claimed she saw him inject steroids. In 2004, the *San Francisco Chronicle* published leaked grand jury testimony from the BALCO case. In it, slugger Jason Giambi admitted to using steroids that he obtained from Anderson. Bonds said that he thought the substances that prosecutors defined as the cream and the clear were flaxseed oil and arthritic balm.

As Bonds transformed before the very eyes of baseball fans everywhere, his stats improved as well. He had hit 292 home runs in his first ten years in the league, and then, as most players would normally decline with age, he bulked up and blasted 464 home runs in the next eleven-plus seasons, including the single-season record of 73 in 2001.

Given the evidence against Bonds, it was a wonder that many fans still supported him in the home run chase. An ESPN/ABC News poll found that 52 percent of fans hoped he would not break the record and 73 percent thought he had used steroids. Race played a factor in opinions, as whites overwhelmingly hoped he would not break the record and most black respondents hoped he would.

As the asterisk debate raged, newspapers ran attention-grabbing headlines. The *New York Post* ran "756" with the numbers formed with syringes. The *Philadelphia Daily News* ran a 756 with an asterisk. The *Daily News* front page screamed "King of Shame," and the *Boston Herald*'s back page headline was "King Con."[26] *Pittsburgh Post-Gazette* columnist Gene Collier offered up some new nicknames for the new home run king, including the Great Scambino and the Colossus of the Cream and the Clear.[27]

Hank Aaron, for his part, was a class act throughout. He kept a low profile as Bonds approached his record, but vowed not to be there to share the moment. It was a surprise to many that he recorded a congratulatory speech that was played at the ballpark moments after Bonds rounded the bases. Whether the congratulation was heartfelt was debatable. One columnist wrote that the speech "had all the sincerity of a hostage video."[28] Bonds also received congratulations from President George W. Bush, which hardly was congruent with his State of the Union address in which he called for eradication of steroids from professional sports.

Legendary sports commentator Bob Costas said, "There's no denying Bonds' greatness as a player. There is certainly a reasonable basis to doubt the authenticity of his late-career achievements."[29] Bonds said, "This record is not tainted at all, at all, period."[30]

The historic home run ball sold at auction for a staggering $752,467 to fashion designer Mark Ecko. He created a Web site that allowed fans to vote on the fate of the ball. Visitors to the site selected from donating the ball to the Baseball Hall of Fame in Cooperstown, New York, as it was, donating it after branding it with an asterisk, or putting it on a rocket and blasting it into space. After launching the site, Ecko cast the first vote. "I voted for the asterisk," he said.[31] Over 10 million votes were cast. The results suggested that the public held significant doubts about the accomplishment, as two-thirds of voters wanted the ball either branded or sent into space. The winning choice was to brand the ball with an asterisk and send it to Cooperstown, with 47 percent of the votes. Representatives of the Hall of Fame acknowledged that they would accept the branded ball.

At the time of writing, Barry Bonds had been indicted for lying to a grand jury regarding his steroid use and obstructing justice in the process. He had entered a plea of not guilty. If convicted, he faces a sentence of up to two-and-a-half years in prison. The outcome will have importance beyond Bonds, as it may represent a new era in holding athletes accountable for their personal decisions. Although there is hope the case will be a harbinger of major systemic change, many say this is unlikely.

Chapter 3

GAMBLING, GAME–FIXING, AND SHAVING POINTS

Millions of Americans gamble. From the weekly purchase of lottery tickets, to the yearly bus trip to Biloxi, to the annual Super Bowl and NCAA basketball tournament office pools, many types of gambling are generally considered innocuous. Most gamblers keep their activity under control, devoting only a set amount of money they are comfortable losing. Others, however, cannot control their gambling, and the end result can be devastating.

Gambling takes on a whole different tone when it involves athletes or coaches betting on sports, because many times they are betting against their own teams. More than just impacting personal integrity or finances, when players or coaches gamble it puts the integrity of the entire team and league on the line. Gambling scandals involving athletes and coaches take a number of forms, running the gamut from point shaving (winning a game but allowing the opposition to keep the score close) to flat-out losing on purpose. Although referees have always been accused of making unfair calls by bitter fans, recently accusations of widespread gambling by referees have emerged as well (and in at least one case have been proven). Some of the nation's most celebrated athletes, including Michael Jordan and Pete Rose, have been embroiled in gambling scandals.

1877 LOUISVILLE GRAYS—GAME FIXING

Throughout the history of competitive sports in America, gamblers have sought to influence the outcome of games for their own profit. Ensuring an honest and uncorrupted game has been one of the biggest challenges facing sport. From the beginning of the development of modern baseball in the 1840s and 1850s, crooked players made it nearly impossible to portray the sport as clean and honest entertainment. Once the National League came into existence in 1876, the effort by the league to "restore integrity to the game" was apparent. The first scandal for professional baseball, as we know it today, happened in 1877 and involved the Louisville Grays.

The upstart league began play in 1877 with six teams. From the outset the league faced challenges to its longevity, including the Cincinnati team disbanding after starting 3–16 and the Hartford team failing to draw home crowds. Cincinnati later reorganized and played out a schedule of exhibition games, while Hartford moved its home games to Brooklyn. By mid-August, the Louisville Grays stood alone in first place and seemed to be pulling away from the rest of the fledgling league. Boston trailed by three-and-a-half games with about one-third of the sixty-game schedule remaining.

The Grays departed for a road trip in mid August, which would be fraught with suspicious losses and leave the team trailing Boston, ending its hopes of winning the pennant. The Grays won none of their seven official games and only one of three in an exhibition series with lowly Cincinnati, by that time winners of only nine of forty-six games. Over the span of games, the team committed over five errors per game, although the Louisville *Courier-Journal* reported that number was close to the average for the league. Still, something seemed amiss with the team.

The on-field performance of the team during the road trip was not the only issue raising eyebrows. As the losing streak was ongoing, the vice president of the Grays, Charles E. Chase, received an anonymous telegram from Hoboken, New Jersey, which, at the time, was known as a gambling haven for baseball betting pools. The telegram informed Chase that the Grays were underdogs in their next game against Hartford, and that "it was clear something was radically wrong with the players on the Grays" and the telegram warned him to "watch your men."[1] The Grays lost the game to Hartford. Chase soon received another telegram that was more precise about the second game against Hartford, saying it would be a "crooked affair" and the "Grays will lose." The Grays did in fact lose the second game against Hartford, the final official game of the road trip. The loss was the result of errors at critical times in the ball game.

A sportswriter named John Halderman, who suspected something was wrong with the Grays, wrote articles that implied the directors of the team knew something. He pressured the players individually until outfielder George Hall unknowingly gave him enough information that he could accuse Grays' pitcher Jim Devlin and outfielder George Hall of crooked play. Halderman, who was also the nephew of the club president, forced the team directors to investigate, threatening that he would "take the matter into his own hands."[2] During an interview, Hall was made to believe that Devlin had confessed. Hall came clean about taking money to throw games, and he also pointed a finger at Devlin and reserve player Al Nichols. Once Devlin learned that Hall had confessed, he also admitted to the scheme and placed the blame on Nichols. According to Devlin and Hall, it was Nichols who knew a gambler named James McCloud, who paid the three players to throw a few games. The players, however, maintained that none of the games they lost on the 0–7 road trip were thrown. Because the three players had communicated with McCloud through telegraph, the team directors requested that all the players on the Grays give permission to examine their Western Union records. All the players complied with the request except for the shortstop, Bill Craver. His noncompliance forced the directors to banish him from the team even though there was no evidence he threw games.

The review of telegraphed messages proved that Devlin, Nichols, and Hall were involved in the game-fixing scheme. On October 30, 1877, the Louisville Grays officially expelled the three players for selling games and dismissed Craver for suspicion of misconduct. The league ratified the expulsions during its annual meeting in December.

In the end, the scandal actually brought down two franchises. The St. Louis Browns had to withdraw from the 1878 season because it had signed both Devlin and Hall for the following season. Once the league banned the players, the hopes of the financially troubled team were crushed, and it folded. The Louisville Grays were unable to attract enough talented players to the scandal-ridden team, and the owners also had to withdraw from the 1878 season. Devlin and Craver both sought reinstatement and were denied. Each, ironically, became a police officer. Hall also tried to get back into the game and was denied doing so as the fledgling league took a firm stand in handling its first-ever case of crooked players. Clearly, the significance of this case is that it was the first (although unfortunately not the last) to clearly identify the major problem of athletes throwing games. It highlighted the difficulty in clearly discerning where cheating has occurred, and it decimated two teams in the process.

WORLD SERIES FOR SALE! THE 1919 CHICAGO BLACK SOX

In 1917 the Chicago White Sox put together an impressive season and easily dominated the competition, winning one hundred games and clinching the pennant race by nine games. The team concluded that season by winning its second championship (the first was in 1906), defeating the New York Giants 4–2 in the best-of-seven series. Unfortunately, the following year was plagued with problems both on and off the field. Battling injuries, the team won only fifty-seven games. The off-the-field problems were related to World War I, and the drop in attendance and revenue as the result of playing a shortened season.

The 1919 season started amid uncertainty, and owners reduced salaries. Despite the fears of the owners, fans flocked to baseball games looking for happier times after the war. Baseball saw the overall attendance more than double from 3 million in 1918 to over 6.5 million in 1919.

The White Sox bounced back from their poor 1918 season and went 88–52, taking the American League Pennant race by three-and-a-half games over the

Cleveland Indians. The Chicago White Sox faced the Cincinnati Reds in the World Series, which had been extended to a best-of-nine-games series so the owners could capitalize on the increased popularity of the sport that year. The 1919 World Series would go down in history as one of the biggest sports scandals of all time. Some of the accounts have been questioned throughout the years, with regard to specific details of the scandal, as the people involved gave different versions of the story years after the fact. The definitive truth may never be known as to who was involved and to what extent. Nonetheless, by the time it was over, eight players were banned for life from Major League Baseball. The scandal has remained a part of popular culture due to films like *Eight Men Out* and *Field of Dreams*.

Most accounts portray the owner of the Chicago White Sox, Charles Comiskey, as a "tightwad and a tyrant," and his tightfistedness as one of the main reasons why players were underpaid and thus more willing to fix the World Series.[3] One example of Comiskey's cheap and abusive tactics of his players revolved around pitcher Eddie Cicotte being benched so he couldn't win his thirtieth game and receive a $10,000 bonus in 1917 (for dramatic effect, this was changed to 1919 in the movie *Eight Men Out*). While this is a commonly cited story told to illustrate the motives of the players, evidence to the contrary exists regarding Comiskey's tightfistedness and the story of Cicotte's bonus.

The players involved, each of whom would be banned for life, were pitcher Eddie Cicotte, centerfielder Oscar "Happy" Felsch, first baseman Arnold "Chick" Gandil, leftfielder Joe "Shoeless Joe" Jackson, infielder Fred McMullin, shortstop Charles "Swede" Risberg, third baseman George "Buck" Weaver, and pitcher Claude "Lefty" Williams.

Although versions vary, the most popular telling of the 1919 World Series scandal centers around first baseman Arnold "Chick" Gandil, generally considered the instigator of the fix and the ringleader of the now infamous Black Sox. Accounts described two separate plans to fix the World Series. The first involved professional gambler Joseph "Sport" Sullivan's meeting with Gandil, at which Gandil demanded $80,000 up front to get other players to help throw the Series. Gandil then approached star pitcher Eddie Cicotte, who joined the fix for $10,000 up front. Once Cicotte was on board, Gandil set forth to recruit more players, and, on September 21, 1919, a meeting took place in Gandil's hotel room that involved all eight players associated with the scandal. The second plan to fix the World Series involved gamblers Bill Burns and Bill Maharg, who approached Cicotte with their proposal to pay the players to lose.

Both plans lead back to well-known gambler Arnold Rothstein. Each plan was presented to him because he had the means to bankroll the payments to the players. Rothstein backed the plan by Sullivan and gave him $40,000 up front for the players. He turned down the plan by Burns and Maharg. Rothstein reportedly placed over $270,000 in bets on the Reds once the scheme was in motion. Of the $40,000 Sullivan was supposed to give to the players, he only gave them $10,000, which lead to frustration and anger among the players. However, the players had another place to turn because Abe Attell, an associate of Rothstein, had told Burns and Maharg that Rothstein would back their plan. Attell raised his own money to fix the Series, and the day before the first game, he offered to pay the players $20,000 after each loss.

Cicotte was the starting pitcher for the White Sox in the Series opener against the Cincinnati Reds. He opened the game by hitting the leadoff batter, which was supposedly a sign indicating that the fix was on. His pitching did not improve and he was pulled by the fourth inning, down 6–1. The Reds easily won the game 9–1. Williams started Game 2 for the White Sox, and during the fourth inning, although he was known for his control, he walked three batters and then gave up a triple to Larry Kopf. The Reds won the game 4–2. After Game 2, Burns delivered $10,000 to Gandil and inquired about Game 3, which Gandil confirmed the team would also intentionally lose. However, because they had only received a small portion of the money promised, the players changed their minds and won the home game 3–0. Gandil drove in two of the three White Sox runs. Before Game 4, Gandil demanded $20,000 from Sullivan, threatening to call off the fix. Sullivan produced the $20,000 and the Chicago crowd saw the Sox lose again, 2–0, with Cicotte committing two errors and cutting off a throw home from Shoeless Joe Jackson. Cincinnati had a commanding 3–1 lead in the Series. It is reported that Gandil gave Risberg, Felsch, Williams, and Jackson each $5,000 after Game 4 and that Weaver did not receive any money. Game 5 was scoreless until the sixth inning, when both Risberg and Felsch committed errors, allowing the Reds to score four runs. Gandil, Risberg, Felsch, Williams, and Jackson were a combined 0–15 at the plate in the game, while Weaver went 2–4. After the 5–0 loss in Game 5, and the Reds ahead 4–1 in the Series, the players became upset because their $20,000 for losing the game was not paid. The players did not throw Games 6 and 7 and the White Sox won both. Rothstein was unhappy and he told Sullivan to make sure the Reds won Game 8. Sullivan contacted a Chicago "thug," who paid a visit to Williams, who was slated to be the Game 8 starting pitcher. Williams was told, "Don't make it past the first," and his family was threatened if he failed to throw the game.[4] In Game 8, Williams did not last fifteen pitches, giving up four hits and four runs in the first inning before being pulled. The Reds went on to win the game 10–5 and the Series 5–3.

Rumors of a possible fix continued through early 1920. Comiskey publicly supported his players and offered $20,000 to anyone with information that proved him wrong. Hugh Fullerton, a Chicago sportswriter, wrote a powerful article demanding that the owners deal with the gambling problem, and it was published during the baseball winter meetings. However, the 1919 fix was not exposed until a grand jury was convened to look at another possible fix involving a Cubs–Phillies game on August 31, 1920.[5] New York Giants pitcher Rube Benton testified in that case that he had seen a telegram the previous September, sent to a teammate, claiming the White Sox would lose the 1919 Series. He further testified that he learned later that Gandil, Felsch, Williams, and Cicotte were in on the fix. Benton even admitted that he bet on the Series, using the information. He won the bets and was never disciplined by the league.

A few days later, Maharg provided a reporter with details of the scandal for an article. Cicotte was called to testify and he admitted the Series was fixed. Shoeless Joe Jackson admitted he was promised $20,000 and actually received $5,000, but he claimed he did not do anything to throw the games. As Jackson left the courthouse, the famous "Say it ain't so, Joe!" line was supposedly uttered by a young boy. A number of sportswriters and historians have claimed that those words were never actually spoken—that it is merely a myth that has grown out of the scandal and has gone relatively unquestioned. Even Jackson adamantly denied that the encounter ever took place.

The eight players went on trial in September 1920, ending any chance Chicago had of repeating a World Series berth in 1920. That season also saw the owners appoint Federal Judge Kenesaw Mountain Landis as Major League Baseball's commissioner. The sworn confessions of Cicotte, Jackson, and Williams strangely disappeared before the trial and the prosecution was not allowed to inform the jury that they ever existed. After only two hours of deliberation, the players were acquitted. Despite the victory inside the courthouse, the newly appointed commissioner banned the eight players for life. To this day, and despite many attempts for reinstatement, especially for Buck Weaver and Shoeless Joe Jackson, none of the eight Black Sox was ever reinstated.

GAMBLING AND THE EARLY YEARS OF THE NFL

Gambling scandals have touched every major sport in America including professional football during its early years. In 1946 the Chicago Bears were set to play the New York Giants in the championship game, and the point spread favored the Bears to win by ten points. Then heavy betting reduced the spread to seven-and-a-half points, as word spread about a possible fix. Prior to kickoff, the spread ballooned to thirteen points, as word leaked out that two Giants players would be held out of the game as an investigation began. The police investigation concluded with an interrogation of New York Giants starting quarterback Frank Filchock and fullback Merle Hapes.[6] Alvin Paris, a novelty store owner who was under police surveillance, had offered $2,500 to Filchock and Hapes to fix the game. The police learned about the scheme because they had Paris's phone tapped. Both Filchock and Hapes turned down the bribe to fix the championship game; however, they did not inform anyone in the front office or with the league about the offer. Once the investigation became public, the two players faced the wrath of the commissioner. NFL commissioner Bert Bell suspended Filchock and Hapes indefinitely, as the rules of the league required. This forced the issue regarding giving the commissioner more power, and in 1947 the owners gave him the power to suspend "anyone connected to the league for life if they were involved in crooked operations."[7]

Filchock and Hapes were considered guilty of actions detrimental to the NFL for failing to report the bribe offered by Paris. While this was not a major scandal, it heightened the awareness of possible outside influences by the gambling community. The road was paved for the more publicized gambling problem that occurred in 1963. In 1962 Commissioner Pete Rozelle was investigating "unusual activity" of several football teams including the Green Bay Packers and the Detroit Lions. Packer halfback Paul Hornung, a Heisman Trophy winner and first-round draft pick, was under investigation, along with Detroit Lions defensive lineman Alex Karras. On April 17, 1963, Commissioner Rozelle announced that "there was clear evidence some NFL players knowingly carried on undesirable associations, which, in some instances, led to their betting on their team,"[8] and that both Hornung and Karras were suspended indefinitely for wagering on NFL games. Five other Detroit players were fined $2,000 each for wagering on the 1962 championship game. The punishment proved to be less than severe, however. Only eleven months after suspending Hornung and Karras, Rozelle reinstated both of them. Rozelle was named "Sportsman of the Year" by *Sports Illustrated*, the first time an executive was given the honor.

WIDESPREAD "GAME FIXING"—1951 COLLEGE BASKETBALL

In spring 1950 City College of New York (CCNY) had the best college basketball team in the country. During this time in college basketball history the city of New York was host to some of the best teams in the country, including Fordham, Long Island University, Manhattan College, New York University, and St. Johns. CCNY topped them all. With its starting lineup of hometown players, CCNY was just as popular as the New York Yankees and the Brooklyn Dodgers, and helped get 18,000 people into Madison Square Garden to watch doubleheader basketball games. CCNY became the only college basketball team ever to win both the NCAA championship and the National Invitation Tournament (NIT) in the same year, at a time when the NIT was considered the more prestigious tournament. Unfortunately, a year later the team would be at the forefront of one of the largest point-shaving scandals in history, forever tarnishing the 1949–50 team's spot in history.

On January 18, 1951, sports editor Max Kase of the *New York Journal-American* reported the first of many stories about point shaving in college basketball during the late 1940s and early 1950s, thanks to a tip from district attorney Frank Hogan. Hogan arrested two former basketball players from Manhattan College and three bookmakers. They were all charged with bribery and conspiracy. The arrested former players were Manhattan College's Henry Poppe, the school's career-scoring leader, and Jack Byrnes. In the 1949–50 season, each player had received over $5,000 to shave points in basketball games against Siena, Santa Clara, Bradley, St. Francis College, Brooklyn College, and New York University.

The scandal began on January 11, 1951, when Poppe approached Junius Kellogg, the first black player in Manhattan College history, offering him $1,000 to shave points. Kellogg informed his coach of the offer. The coach, in turn, informed the president of the college. Subsequently, the police were informed. The police had Kellogg accept the offer to fix the January 16 game against DePaul. Poppe informed Kellogg courtside before the game that the team could win the game, but not by more than ten points. After the game, Poppe was arrested and implicated Byrnes in the scheme. Byrnes was arrested a few hours later.

District Attorney Hogan continued his pursuit of point shavers. One month after the Manhattan College scandal, the other shoe dropped on CCNY.[9] On February 18, three CCNY players were arrested; they admitted throwing three games during the 1950–51 season, for which each player received a few thousand dollars. Within days of the arrests of these CCNY players, sixteenth-ranked Long Island University (LIU) saw three players arrested and admit to receiving $18,500 to fix seven games. Among them was Sherman White, who had been named Player of the Year by *Sporting News* only one day prior, and was merely seventy-seven points shy of the all-time collegiate scoring record.

Newspapers then carried stories of other accounts of players involved in point shaving, including more CCNY players. At first, most basketball fans in the country concluded that the point shaving was confined to the New York area and the sleazy underworld of the big city. That belief was shattered when players from the University of Toledo and the University of Kentucky were implicated as well. "They couldn't reach my boys with a ten-foot pole," Kentucky's legendary coach Adolph Rupp said. Unfortunately, he was wrong, and Kentucky's basketball program was suspended for the 1952–53 season.[10] In total, thirty-two basketball players from seven schools (CCNY, LIU, Bradley, NYU, Kentucky, Manhattan, and Toledo) were named in the point-shaving scandal of 1951. Most players received suspended sentences, with a few serving several months in jail. Eight players were either acquitted or had the charges dropped. The harshest punishments were reserved for the gamblers who enticed the players. Nine men classified as fixers or gamblers behind the point-shaving schemes were also arrested. Salvatore Sollazzo received the longest sentence—eight to sixteen years in state prison.

GAME FIXING CONTINUED—1961 COLLEGE BASKETBALL

If fixing basketball games could be considered an art form, Jacob (Jack) Molinas would be Pablo Picasso. Instead, it is a crime and his work to master the craft would land him in prison. Both an outstanding player and a career gambler, Molinas was as intrigued with the challenges of shaving points and not getting caught as he was with breaking down the opposition's defense and scoring at will. And while many point shavers want to win the game, albeit by a closer-than-expected margin, Molinas would lose a game outright as long as he felt the financial score was sufficient.

In 1949 Molinas was playing in Madison Square Garden in the state high school basketball finals and was the dominant player on the court. Unfortunately for his teammates, he had taken several hundred dollars to lose the game. He had even personally wagered against his own team. Of course, by that time gambling was old hat for Molinas, who had started laying wagers when he was only twelve, and was associating with mobsters by the time he ran the hardwoods at the high school level.

Molinas's partner in crime was Joe Hacken, a basketball fanatic who had multiple convictions for bookmaking. Together, they would fix games over several years and involving hundreds of players. Hacken claimed to have fixed his first game at the tender age of eighteen. Hacken and Molinas were "doing business" when Molinas was playing for Columbia University; they would continue together until arrested in 1961.

In 1953 Molinas finished his college basketball career, earning All-American honors, and was selected fourth overall in the NBA Draft by the Fort Wayne Pistons. During his rookie year with the Pistons, he was selected to the All-Star team and seemed destined for greatness. As it always would, his penchant for gambling got the best of him, as he was suspected of wagering on his own team; he was banned for life from the NBA on January 10, 1954.[11] Molinas insisted he only bet on Pistons games, and always for his team to win, but at least one game raised suspicion. Against the Boston Celtics, in a game in which Molinas was benched early, he immediately committed two flagrant fouls when he returned to the court with only a minute left in the game.

Even though Molinas was out of basketball, he continued to fix games and sell them to organized crime groups and individuals. For example, he would charge $25,000 to "buy a game" and then use some of that money to bribe players and, on occasion, referees. Molinas took his schemes to another level, dramatically increasing his risk, when he started making judgment calls and predicting which games he could sell to mobsters without actually paying any players. He also started selling games to more than one person to maximize his profit from each fix. Possibly the best "fixers" in basketball history, Molinas and Hacken had an estimated 476 players from twenty-seven schools under their control, and fixed at least forty-three games between 1957 and 1961.

Molinas made $10,000 in his single season with the Pistons, which paled in comparison to the $50,000 a week he made with Hacken at the peak of their point-shaving scheme. The point shaving was brought to light in 1961 with the arrest of thirty-seven players from twenty-two colleges including Columbia, St. John's, New York University, North Carolina State, and the University of Connecticut. Most of the players confessed when questioned by police. In 1962 Molinas was implicated as the ring leader, and his connections with top mob guys were revealed, including Mafia chief Tommie "Ryan" Eboli and Capo Vincent "The Chin" Gigante of the Genovese crime family.

Molinas was found guilty of bribing players to fix games on the testimony of players from the University of Utah, Bowling Green State University, the University of Alabama, and the College of the Pacific. He was sentenced to ten to fifteen years in prison, most of which he served at Attica. He was released after serving only five years, and became the inspiration for the film *The Longest Yard*, starring Burt Reynolds. Upon his release, Molinas moved to Hollywood to traffic pornography and furs. He was murdered in 1975 at the age of forty-three by a gunshot wound to the head while standing in his backyard. His killing may have been linked to the murder of a business partner, Bernard Gustoff, who was beaten to death less than a year prior. Molinas had collected on a $500,000 insurance policy, and the *Los Angeles Times* reported within days that there were possible links.

Perhaps the most famous player hurt by an association with Molinas was Connie "The Hawk" Hawkins, who many consider the 1960s equivalent of Julius Erving. Hawkins was broke and on Christmas holiday when he borrowed $250 from Molinas in 1961 while he was a freshman at the University of Iowa. Hawkins's brother Fred repaid the loan before the scandal of 1961 broke. Even though Molinas and Hacken repeatedly stated that Hawkins was never part of any game fixing, in spite of their efforts to recruit him, his association with Molinas caused an early end to his college career. He never played in a single varsity game for Iowa.

In 1964 Hawkins was eligible for the NBA draft. Although he was not banned by the league, no team would take him. Nor would they take him in the 1965 or 1966 drafts. After the 1966 draft, the NBA Board of Governors and Commissioner Walter Kennedy banned him from the league. Hawkins played with the Harlem Globetrotters, and in the inaugural season of the American Basketball Association. In 1969, after a *Life* magazine article detailed his likely innocence, and with an antitrust lawsuit against the NBA working its way through the courts, the door was finally opened for Hawkins to play in the NBA. The two sides settled the suit and he received $1.295 million. Hawkins went on to have an outstanding NBA career and was elected to the Basketball Hall of Fame in 1992.

BOSTON COLLEGE POINT SHAVING, 1978–1979

In 1980, during the ongoing federal investigation into the 1978 theft of $5.8 million from the Lufthansa cargo terminal at JFK International Airport in New York, convicted felon turned government informant Henry Hill (popularized in the 1990 movie *Goodfellas*) revealed a point shaving scheme he masterminded involving the 1978–79 Boston College basketball team. Hill coauthored a *Sports Illustrated* article in February 1981 that outlined the scheme involving three Boston College basketball players: Rick Kuhn, Jim Sweeney, and top-scorer Ernie Cobb. Once the investigation concluded, and with the help of unindicted coconspirator Henry Hill, five men were charged, tried, and convicted of racketeering, bribery, and crossing state lines to commit a crime for their roles in point shaving of six Boston College games. The only Boston College player charged during the first trial was Rick Kuhn, along with Paul Mazzei, a convicted drug trafficker, Anthony and Rocco Perla, brothers who knew Kuhn and introduced him to Mazzei, and Jimmy "The Gent" Burke, who was made famous by Robert De Niro's portrayal of him as Jimmy Conway in *Goodfellas*. Burke was the FBI's prime suspect as the mastermind behind the Lufthansa robbery; that crime remains unsolved.

Of the six Boston College games cited in the indictment, the gambling syndicate only won money on three. In each, the group bet against Boston College. On two occasions, against Providence College and Holy Cross, the crew lost its money as Boston College won by too many points and then lost by too few. One game was a "push," when St. John's, a nine-point favorite, won by exactly nine points. The crew made money on the other three games, against Harvard, UCLA, and Fordham. Henry Hill claimed gambling profits of $75,000 to $100,000 from the point shaving scheme.

Jim Sweeney became a government witness and testified about his role in the scheme. Sweeney admitted accepting $500 from Kuhn, but denied doing anything on the basketball court to help shave points. Ernie Cobb was trying out for the New Jersey Nets in 1980 when the FBI interviewed him. Cobb was tried separately in 1984 and found not guilty despite admitting to receiving $2,000 from the gambling syndicate. He testified he believed the money was for information about the team's chances of winning and not for point shaving.

Rick Kuhn received up to $2,500 for each fixed game. He was sentenced to ten years in prison for his role. Anthony and Rocco Perla were sentenced to ten and four years in prison, respectively. Jimmy "The Gent" Burke was handed the longest sentence of all defendants—twenty years and a $30,000 fine. Despite the Organized Crime Strike Force's effort to incarcerate Jimmy Burke for his suspected role in the Lufthansa heist, or any of the numerous murders he was suspected of carrying out as an associate of the Lucchese crime family, in the end it was his role in the Boston College point-shaving scheme of 1978–79 that landed him in prison, where he died of lung cancer in 1996. What makes this scandal noteworthy, aside from the point shaving itself, was the involvement of major crime syndicates. No small operation, this scandal drew attention to the complexity of gambling schemes and the depths to which some would go to fix a game.

TULANE UNIVERSITY DROPS MEN'S HOOPS

College basketball was rocked by a point-shaving scandal again in the spring of 1985, when eight people were indicted. Included were three Tulane basketball players. Among them was the team's star player and NBA hopeful, John "Hot Rod" Williams. Adding to Tulane's problems was the fact that the investigation revealed cash payments to players. In exchange for agreeing to play at Tulane, Williams admitted receiving $10,000 in a shoebox, plus an additional $100 a week from his coach.[12] Coach Ned Fowler and his two assistants resigned once the payments to the player became public; the coaching staff was not aware of the point shaving, however.[13] So shamed was the university by the scandal that the board and trustees agreed with Tulane President Eamon Kelly's decision to drop men's basketball in April 1985, after seventy-two years of sponsoring the sport.

The scheme began with a meeting between senior forward Clyde Eads and Tulane business major Gary Kranz, in which they agreed to trade basketball gear for cocaine. To help acquire more athletic equipment, through theft, Eads brought senior forward Jon Johnson into the deal. According to grand jury testimony, within weeks point shaving became a topic of discussion among the group. The point shaving started when Kranz wanted to fix the February 2 game against Southern Mississippi. The investigation concluded that the scheme involved two additional games: the Virginia Tech game on February 16, and the Memphis State game on February 20. There was talk of including a fourth game, against Louisville, but the players refused, as they always wanted to win that game. They did, breaking an eighteen-game losing streak.

The investigation was launched after the February 20 game when rumors started to fly and Tulane benefactor Ned Kohnke, disturbed by things he was hearing about the basketball program, went to district attorney Harry Connick. Kohnke, who often worked out with Eads, convinced the player to admit his involvement. Eads and Johnson were given immunity for their testimony, and they named three other Tulane basketball players: "Hot Rod" Williams, David Dominique, and Bobby Thompson, along with Kranz and his fraternity brothers Mark Olensky and David Rothenberg. Two suspected bookmakers, Roland Ruiz and Craig Bourgeois, were also arrested.

According to the D.A.'s office, Olensky and Rothenberg gathered $34,000 to wager on the Memphis State game, with $18,000 spread between ten different Las Vegas casinos, another $10,000 with Birmingham bookies, and the remaining $6,000 with a Tulane bookmaker. As the indictments were handed down, senior guard Bobby Thompson, Olensky, and Rothenberg all pleaded guilty to avoid prison time. Their sentences were suspended, and they were placed on probation and ordered to pay fines directly to local charities. Dominique pleaded to lesser charges.

"Hot Rod" Williams went to trial, as he denied any part in the point-shaving scheme. The first attempt to convict Williams was declared a mistrial in August 1985. Williams, a projected first-round NBA draft choice before the scandal, was selected in the second round of the 1985 draft by the Cleveland Cavaliers, despite warnings from the league about the risk presented by his legal status. The owners of the Cavaliers paid Williams's legal expenses. However, the team had to withdraw the contract they had offered Williams after the mistrial because the NBA did not allow teams to sign players with point-shaving charges still pending. Williams sat out a year while awaiting a second trial and passed the time by playing for the Rhode Island Gulls of the U.S. Basketball League for $15,000. NBA first-round picks were making about $350,000 a year.

In June 1986 a six-member jury acquitted Williams on all five charges by a unanimous vote. The jury was not swayed by the testimony of six others involved in the scheme, who they thought testified only to lighten their own sentences. Further, they considered there to be a complete lack of solid evidence. Williams made the NBA All-Rookie team in 1986 and went on to play thirteen years in the NBA with three different teams.

Tulane University reinstated men's basketball in 1989. Under coach Perry Clark, the team struggled through a 4–24 season, but began a run of success the following season that saw the team enjoy national rankings and post-season play with regularity over several seasons. The Tulane scandal is instructive in that it demonstrates that in sports there is usually a second chance. Whether that is a good or bad thing is still open to debate, but regardless, both team and player eventually emerged from the scandal and went on to success.

PETE ROSE BANNED FROM BASEBALL

In 1963 Major League Baseball was introduced to a player who would prove to be among the most controversial in the history of the game. It was Pete Rose's rookie year for the Cincinnati Reds, and his impact would be immediate. During spring training he was nicknamed "Charlie Hustle" by Whitey Ford and Mickey Mantle because he would sprint to first base after receiving a walk. Throughout his career, Rose played the game at a high level of intensity, and the nickname stuck. Hall of Fame player Joe Morgan once said, "He played every game like it was the seventh game of the World Series."[14] Rose was loved by Cincinnati fans because he played with unparalleled vigor. In the 1970 All-Star Game, in an attempt to score the winning run, he literally ran over catcher Ray Fosse, surprising and angering many fans who perceived the All-Star game to be an exhibition. Fosse was severely injured and was never quite the same player again. Rose, questioned after the game about the play, said, "Nobody told me they changed it to girls' softball between third and home."[15] Rose earned his reputation as a hard-nosed player and is legendary for his prowess at the plate. Unfortunately for baseball, he is perhaps better known for his gambling habits and lifetime suspension from the game.

During his long baseball career, Rose set nineteen MLB records, including most games played (3,562), most singles (3,215), and one of the most coveted records in baseball, the career hits lead (4,256 hits). Rose started and finished his baseball career in Cincinnati with stops in Philadelphia and Montreal. As he approached the end of his playing career, he transitioned into a player/manager role for the Reds from 1984 through the 1986 season. In 1987 he

The Pete Rose gambling scandal made the cover of *Time* in July 1989. Just over a month later MLB commissioner Bart Giamatti banned him from baseball for life. Time & Life Pictures/Getty Images.

was taken off the forty-man roster, but continued to manage the team. From 1984 to 1989 Rose managed 786 games and had a winning percentage of .525.

In February 1989, during spring training, MLB commissioner Peter Ueberroth summoned Pete Rose to New York for a meeting. A month later the commissioner announced that MLB "has for several months been conducting a full inquiry into serious allegations" about Pete Rose, but the commissioner did not specify what the "serious allegations" were. Ueberroth went public with the inquiry because he knew of a forthcoming *Sports Illustrated* article about the investigation.[16] As rumors of a serious gambling problem started to surface, Rose said, "I'd be willing to bet you, if I were a betting man, that I have never bet on baseball."[17] The March 27, 1989, *Sports Illustrated* story about Rose's gambling named several key people in the scandal, including alleging that Ron Peters was Rose's "principal bookmaker," and that his friends, Paul Janszen and Tommy Gioiosa, helped place bets for him. John Dowd, a Washington lawyer, was in charge of the Pete Rose gambling investigation. He constructed a 225-page report that was delivered to the new MLB commissioner, A. Bartlett Giamatti, on May 9, 1989.

In late June, under orders from the Ohio Supreme Court, the confidential Dowd report was released to the public. The report alleged Rose wagered on baseball games and, most importantly, on his own team. Rose faced a lifetime ban under Rule 21(d) of Major League Baseball, which read, "Any player, umpire or club or league official or employee, who shall bet any sum whatsoever upon any baseball game in connection with which the bettor has a duty to perform, shall be declared permanently ineligible."[18] The report named three bookmakers and five intermediaries that Rose used to place bets between 1985 and 1987. Rose was reportedly wagering at least $10,000 a day on sports, including fifty-two Cincinnati Reds games in 1987—always betting for the Reds to win. On August 24, 1989, Pete Rose became the fifteenth person banned for life from baseball and the first since 1943. A settlement was reached with Commissioner Giamatti that allowed Rose not to admit to the gambling allegations, but banished him for life from the game he loved. Only days after banishing Rose from baseball, Giamatti had a heart attack and died at the age of fifty-one.

Rose's troubles did not end with his expulsion from baseball; in 1990 he pleaded guilty to filing false income tax returns and was sentenced to five months in federal prison, 1,000 hours of community service, and a fine of $50,000. In February 1991, with Rose approaching eligibility to be included on the ballot for the Baseball Hall of Fame, the Hall's board of directors voted to leave his name off the ballot. The Hall maintained that the only way Rose could be included on a future ballot would be if he was reinstated by the commissioner before December 2005, which was his last year of Hall of Fame eligibility.

Rose continued to deny that he wagered on baseball until he had a private meeting with Commissioner Bud Selig in November 2002. Rose went on to publish an autobiography titled *My Prison without Bars*. As the book was set for release, Rose went on ABC's *Primetime* and admitted he had bet on baseball. Bud Selig did not reinstate Rose before the deadline passed on Baseball Hall of Fame eligibility. Debate over whether Rose deserves to be in the Hall of Fame rages on. To this day, Rose is banned from the sport he loves and dominated for so many years, and his name is still not enshrined in the Hall of Fame. When the topic of sport scandals is mentioned, Rose's name inevitably comes up.

THE MICHAEL JORDAN GAMBLING CONSPIRACY

The National Basketball Association twice investigated Michael Jordan, generally considered the best player in league history, for his high-stakes gambling habits. The second probe concluded in fall 1993 as Jordan made a surprising retirement from the game, prompting questions about whether the two events were related. NBA commissioner David Stern said they were not. Jordan, thirty at the time, claimed the retirement came as he lost motivation to play, having led the Chicago Bulls to three consecutive NBA titles and the 1992 Olympic team to gold in Barcelona. He had also lost his father, James Jordan, in a tragic murder only months after claiming the third NBA title. Jordan was offended by questions as to whether there could be links between his gambling and the murder. Two teenagers were caught when they used James Jordan's cell phone. They were convicted of the murder and sentenced to life in prison.

The league had not taken action against Jordan after initially investigating his gambling losses during golf and card games with James "Slim" Bouler, a convicted cocaine dealer. Jordan testified in Bouler's drug and money-laundering trial in 1991 that he had lost $57,000 to Bouler. He was not questioned about checks, totaling $108,000, made out to bail bondsman Eddie Dow, but the money was to cover gambling losses according to Dow's attorney.

The second investigation was prompted when San Diego businessman Richard Esquinas coauthored the book *Michael and Me: Our Gambling Addiction ... My Cry for Help*, in which he claimed Jordan had lost $1.25 million to him over ten days on the golf course. Jordan confirmed that they negotiated a $300,000 settlement to cover the losses. Esquinas agreed to settle for less than he was owed because he feared for his safety and believed he would never be paid the full amount. He claimed that in a phone conversation, Jordan said to him, "Rich, I'd just might as well shoot you as to give you a check for $1.2 million."[19] Jordan released a statement saying, "I have played golf with Richard Esquinas with wagers made between us. Because I did not keep records, I cannot verify how much I won or lost. I can assure you that the level of our wagers was substantially less than the preposterous amounts that have been reported."[20]

Jordan's gambling also was scrutinized by the league and the media because he was seen gambling in an Atlantic City casino the night before the Eastern Conference finals second game against the New York Knicks in 1993. Reports placed Jordan in the casino as late as 2 A.M., although he denied he was there that late. David Stern said in a press conference that the issue was closed, but at the same time deputy commissioner Russell T. Granik said the league was yet to interview Esquinas and that the league's security personnel would pursue loose ends.

Esquinas cooperated with the investigation and said later that the league was particularly interested in a visit he had to Jordan's home on March 29, 1992. While watching college basketball on television, Jordan had a phone conversation. Esquinas claimed that Jordan discussed a betting line over the phone, saying to the other party, "So you say the line is seven points?"[21] Apparently the league never asked Jordan about the phone call because the league never even interviewed him before concluding the investigation and announcing there had been no wrongdoing. The investigation was closed almost immediately after Jordan announced his retirement. The lawyer for Richard Esquinas questioned the veracity of the investigation given that Jordan was never interviewed about the point-spread conversation.

While away from basketball, Jordan pursued a baseball career. By all accounts, he was not a good player, even at the minor league level. Through his lone season he batted a meager .202 and hit only three home runs. He played for the Birmingham Barons, a farm team of the Chicago White Sox. The White Sox were owned by Bulls owner Jerry Reinsdorf, who inexplicably continued to honor Jordan's $3.9 million basketball contract while he played minor league baseball.

In March 1995 Jordan announced he would return to the NBA with a two-word press release that read, "I'm back."[22] He played seventeen games to close the season, and the Bulls were eliminated in the conference semifinals. He returned the following season and led the Bulls to a second run of three titles in 1996, 1997, and 1998.

Questions have lingered among basketball fans as to whether Jordan's gambling played a part in his hiatus from the NBA. Although solid evidence has never surfaced that he bet on basketball or was secretly suspended from the league, some fans cite two of Jordan's own comments as disconcerting. First, when he retired amid the gambling investigation in 1993, he commented that he might return to the NBA, saying, "If David Stern let's me back in the league, I may come back." This begged the question, why wouldn't the commissioner, who had cleared him of wrongdoing, welcome back the league's marquee player? The question was never put to Jordan, but sports columnists fueled the theory that he was asked to take a year off and address his gambling issues.[23] Jordan added to the intrigue by saying, "It doesn't mean I'm not going to play basketball somewhere else ..." as he stressed that he was leaving "the NBA."[24] Second, when Jordan retired after the 1999 championship, he thanked Stern for giving him the "opportunity" to play basketball. Again, nobody asked how, exactly, Stern had given him an opportunity. NBA officials have consistently denied the allegation that there is a connection. NBA vice president Brian McIntyre said, "There is no smoking gun. Anyone who links the two subjects is dead wrong."[25]

Jordan was interviewed for CBS's *60 Minutes* in October 2005. He admitted, "Yeah, I've gotten myself into [gambling] situations where I would not walk away and I've pushed the envelope." He continued, "It's very embarrassing … one of the things you totally regret. So you look at yourself in the mirror and say, 'I was stupid.'"[26] Jordan returned after his second retirement to play two more seasons with the Washington Wizards, from 2001 to 2003. He is currently a part owner of the Charlotte Bobcats.

The most significant thing about this scandal is who it involves. Jordan was more than an icon in basketball. He was considered a celebrity and generally held up as one of, if not the number one, best player ever. Not only was he tremendously skilled on the court, but he was viewed as a generally decent human being who lived a relatively "normal," albeit affluent, life. The scandal brought doubt about all of these things and has sullied his reputation to some degree.

NORTHWESTERN UNIVERSITY FOOTBALL POINT SHAVING

It was the third quarter of a Northwestern and Iowa football game in 1994. Northwestern was on the one-yard line and almost certain to score. Running back Dennis Lundy took the handoff cleanly, drove toward the end zone and, inexplicably, fumbled away the ball. Iowa, a six-point favorite, would win the game 49–13 and easily cover the point spread.

In the locker room after the game, an assistant coach overheard player Rodney Ray accuse Lundy of intentionally fumbling the ball. The assistant reported the incident to head coach Gary Barnett. Northwestern hired an investigator, who determined that Lundy and basketball player Dion Lee had been betting on college sports. Both were suspended by the school and information was turned over to the United States Attorney's office. Ultimately, Northwestern would be commended for cooperating with the federal investigation. The university, however, would also take a severe public relations hit as it came to light how deep the gambling problems ran on campus and among the athletes.

Lundy's original story was that he had a sprained wrist from the previous play and that he was "hit on the arm real good, and the ball just came out."[27] The videotape did not demonstrate this to be true. He would later recant this story and told a federal judge that he fumbled on purpose to help ensure he would collect on a $400 bet he had placed against his own team. Lundy would ultimately be sentenced to a month in prison and subsequent probation for lying to a federal grand jury investigating campus gambling.

Northwestern became the first school to suffer the ignominy of having both its men's basketball and football programs tied to illegal gambling at the same time. The football scandal came to light only a week after two basketball players, Dion Lee and Dewey Williams, were sentenced to a month in federal prison for point shaving during the 1995 season. *USA Today* columnist Joanne Gerstner wrote, at the time, "Northwestern projects itself as one of the nation's elite universities, on par with top-shelf institutions such as Stanford and the Ivy League schools. But the twin scandals serve as a reminder that scandal and disgrace aren't confined to so-called renegades."[28]

The football scandal differed from previous point-shaving incidents for three reasons, according to *New York Times* columnist Bill Dedman. First, point shaving generally occurs in basketball, where fewer players control a greater amount of the action. Second, point shaving generally involves a favored team still winning, but by fewer points than expected (they win the game but lose against the spread). In the case of Northwestern football, the goal was to lose the game by more points than expected. Third, the players put up their own money, whereas in most cases it is the outside influence of seasoned gamblers that leads to the scandal.

Dion Lee had masterminded the plan to gamble on basketball games with the help of former Notre Dame football player Kevin Pendergast. Both men saw the arrangement as a way to escape mounting gambling debts. Lee would keep the score low and ensure that the team lost the games while allowing the opposing teams to cover the spread. Pendergast arranged the bets against Northwestern and promised Lee a cut of the winnings from games against Wisconsin, Penn State, and Michigan. Pendergast was responsible for between $40,000 and $70,000 in bets. He paid Lee a mere $4,000. Williams was recruited into the scheme for $700, as another player to help keep Northwestern's scores down. Pendergast lost all of his money in the final game of the scheme when Northwestern failed to lose by over twenty-five points to Michigan. He was sentenced to two months in prison, and he and Lee were ordered to spend five years speaking on college campuses about the dangers of gambling.

The Northwestern gambling scandal even touched players who had never bet on a game or been engaged in efforts to fix the outcome of games. Former Northwestern cornerback Dwight Brown was the last of a group of athletes to be sentenced. He was sentenced to thirty days in jail for lying twice to a grand jury investigating gambling on Big Ten campuses. The federal investigation caught eleven former football and basketball players. All pleaded guilty: five to perjury, four to point shaving, and two to illegal gambling.

Through the 1990s gambling affected college sports at universities across the country. Gambling rings involving athletes were found at the University of Maine, University of Rhode Island, and Bryant College. Football and basketball players at the University of Maryland and Holy Cross were suspended for betting on college sports. Boston College football players were suspended for gambling, including betting against their own team.

A 1999 study conducted at the University of Michigan sought to fathom the depths of gambling among male college athletes. Results indicated that almost half had bet on college sports, with about five percent having bet on their own games, admitting to shaving points, or providing inside information to gamblers. Equally troubling was that a second Michigan survey of game officials revealed that 20 percent had bet on the NCAA basketball tournament, and two admitted that their knowledge of the point spread affected how they called a game.

BOSTON COLLEGE FOOTBALL SCANDAL

On November 6, 1996, Boston College again had its athletic program thrust into the national spotlight for the all the wrong reasons. The school had suspended thirteen football players for gambling on professional and college sports in violation of NCAA rules. Eleven of the thirteen players were suspended from the football team for wagering from $25 to $1,000 on other games, including the World Series and college and professional sports. Two of the thirteen players were caught wagering on a Boston College football game, and both bet against Boston College to cover the spread against Syracuse. The total amount wagered on the Syracuse game was $450. The players lost their wagers when Boston College won the game 45–17, easily covering the thirteen-point spread.

In a *Boston Herald* article on November 14, 1996, two of the suspended football players spoke out (on condition of anonymity) very bitterly about the situation. One player said, "I know I did the wrong thing.... But a lot of others did wrong, too, and we're taking the fall for everyone who ever laid a bet."[29] In the interview, one of the players claimed that at a team meeting only weeks before, twenty-five to thirty football players acknowledged some type of gambling. The investigation also uncovered student bookies, and one reportedly provided a list of over 500 clients on the campus.

When asked to comment on coaches' responsibility towards preventing gambling by athletes, Boston College basketball coach Jim O'Brien responded, "On the list of priorities, agents have been No. 1, followed by drugs and the general topic of physical abuse of women. Gambling has been way down on the list."[30] Surrounded by rumors of his imminent termination at the conclusion of the season, head football coach Dan Henning resigned on November 25, 1996, only weeks after the gambling scandal unfolded.

ARIZONA STATE UNIVERSITY BASKETBALL POINT SHAVING

The Arizona State University (ASU) scandal began with a $100 wager on the outcome of a professional football game. It would end with seven men behind bars and shame brought to the campus of Arizona State University. At the center of the scandal was college basketball player Stevin "Hedake" Smith, who had agreed to shave points in ASU basketball games to help escape mounting debt from gambling. He then enlisted the help of teammate Isaac Burton.

It was during the 1993 basketball season that Smith would place a bet with a classmate to back up his comments about a professional football game. Smith lost. "And within weeks was betting on anything I could," he said.[31] He would eventually owe a reported $10,000. It was then that he was approached with an offer that he believed was too good to refuse. Smith agreed to fix ASU basketball games for $20,000 per game.

The scheme was relatively simple in design: Smith and Burton would ensure that the opposing teams would stay close enough in the games to cover the point spread. ASU could still win the game, but they had to make sure the opponent was closer than the spread that Las Vegas odds makers created to motivate gambling on the game. Smith and Burton accomplished this by failing to score when they had the ball or by playing less-than-stellar defense. Smith would admit that even in a game in which he scored a career-high thirty-nine points, against Oregon State, his defense was intentionally lacking. He said that he just "stepped back a half step and he had the room he needed" to score.[32] While Arizona State won that game by six points, Oregon State covered the spread, and the gamblers, who had bet on OSU, won their bets.

The plan was hatched by Benny Silman, a popular bookie on the ASU campus and to whom Smith owed the $10,000. Silman suggested a payment plan that would allow Smith to even make a handsome personal profit. The plan also involved Joseph Gagliano Jr., a Phoenix investment adviser, Vincent Basso, a schoolmate of Gagliano's, and Chicago bookmakers Joseph Mangiamele and his father Dominic Mangiamele. All five would be charged with money laundering and illegal sports betting.

The gamblers won their bets on the first four games they fixed, all in the 2003–4 season. ASU beat both Oregon and Oregon State, but failed to cover the point spreads. Against Southern California, ASU was a seven point favorite, but actually lost the game by twelve points. It was during the fifth game, against Washington, that things fell apart. Arizona State started the game very poorly, with players missing fourteen consecutive shots. However, after halftime, they played much better and won the game by eighteen points, easily covering the spread and breaking the bank for the gamblers who had bet against them.

The gamblers had amassed their winnings from the first four games and, through intermediaries, had placed many wagers on the Washington game, likely totaling $1 million spread across many casinos and online betting sites. Each bet was made in a sum of less than $10,000, which allowed the transaction to avoid reporting requirements by the federal government. Prior to the game, Las Vegas casinos suspended betting because the wagers far surpassed the volume of money generally bet on this type of game and because an over-whelming amount of it was bet against Arizona State.

David Price, an associate commissioner for the Pac-10 Conference, received a call early in the day of the ASU—Washington game, alerting him to the fact that wagers made on the game were "fishy."[33] The caller, a bookie, told him that many young, novice gamblers were making uncharacteristically large wagers on what would generally be considered a meaningless game. And they were all betting that ASU would not cover the spread. Price contacted the Nevada Gaming Control Board, which affirmed that it was suspicious of the activity and planned to interview the players. Media reports later suggested that the players were tipped at halftime that authorities were onto the fix, so they reversed course and played well in the second half.

Investigations by both the Pac-10 Conference and the Nevada Gaming Control Board found no wrongdoing, and the scandal temporarily died out. In spring 1997, however, the investigation was resurrected when information was provided to the FBI, possibly from friends of Silman who had been arrested on unrelated charges and hoped to secure plea deals.

By June 1999, the five gamblers and two players were convicted and sentenced to prison or probation. Silman and Gagliano were sentenced to forty-six and fifteen months in prison, respectively. Joseph Mangiamele was sentenced to three months in jail, which reflected his "high level of cooperation in the case."[34] Dominic Mangiamele was sentenced to three months of home detention because his involvement was limited. Basso was sentenced to a year in prison.

Smith, who pleaded guilty to conspiracy to commit sports bribery, was sentenced to one year in prison. His true punishment was greater than that, though. According to his attorney, the scandal killed any hopes he had for an NBA career, and he ultimately filed for bankruptcy. At his sentencing, Smith said, "I realize what I did was wrong. I wish I could redo it."[35]

Isaac Burton seemed the most contrite for his involvement. "I made a mistake. A dumb, well-publicized mistake. I wish they hung articles about me in every college locker room, so kids could learn from my mistake," he said. Burton had been playing in Australia when the FBI came to visit in 1997. Like Smith, he pleaded guilty and was sentenced to two months in jail. He had taken $4,300 for his part in the scheme. "I thought I was rich," he said. "I didn't know that $4,300 is nothing. I didn't think."[36] One thing this case highlights is that gambling-related scandals are not always lucrative. They always, however, bring unwanted negative attention to a team, and many times to an entire sport.

RIGGING THE BREEDERS' CUP—THE PICK-SIX WAGERING SCHEME

Three former fraternity brothers nearly pulled off the greatest scam in horseracing history when they applied computer expertise to fix the Breeders'

Cup Pick Six in October 2002. Their plot was undone by bad luck or greed, as they claimed the lone winning ticket by picking the correct winner of six consecutive races. The win drew attention because some of the races were won by long shots, reducing the likelihood that anyone would have picked correctly. When the Breeders' Cup Classic was won by Volponi, which had started at long odds of 43–1, the prize pool swelled to over $3 million and seasoned handicappers believed that picking all six races was impossible. When the conspirators tried to claim the prize, they found that an investigation was already underway.

They were described as computer geeks who had found careers in information technology after graduating from Drexel University, where they were members of the fraternity Tau Kappa Epsilon in the 1990s. They kept in touch over the years, and then, at age 29, stumbled on a way to exploit the computer system that takes bets. Programmer Chris Harn worked for Autotote, which processes bets, when he discovered that he could manipulate betting tickets after the early races were completed in a multirace wager. He enlisted the help of friends Glen DaSilva and Derrick Davis. Harn placed bets through a telephone betting account created in Davis's name. After the first four races, Harn created a ticket with all four winners and then bet on every horse in the remaining two races. The bet cost the group $1,152, but it was sure to win. Autotote launched an internal investigation and fired Harn, labeling him a "rogue software engineer."[37]

Harn pleaded guilty to fraud and money laundering and received the lightest sentence of the trio, at one year and one day. "I realize I've hurt a great number of people. Forgiveness is earned, not granted, and I hope to pay my debt to society not with words but with my future actions," Harn said.[38] If he had not agreed to help authorities, Harn faced up to seven years in prison. Many were troubled that the mastermind was given a lighter sentence than his accomplices. Davis and DaSilva were sentenced to thirty-seven months for wire fraud and twenty-four months for fraud and money laundering, respectively.

Racing fans were outraged that the scam seemed to be treated as a victimless crime when, in fact, the seventy-eight rightful winners who had picked five race winners would have been denied their winnings, about $44,000 each, if the trio had not been detected. DaSilva's attorney suggested the prosecutors were wise to offer a short sentence for a plea, given that there was no paper trail or hard evidence. "They never would have made the case," he said for a *Vanity Fair* article.[39] Prosecutors maintained that they would have made the case, but that the plea brought immediate closure.

Harn and his crew had used their system in previous months, winning smaller amounts on races in Illinois and New York through the off-track-betting phone account. Although some of the rightful winners were found and paid, it is unclear whether all of the money could ever be properly allocated. Ultimately, they were done in by their big win being simply too big. On a day when too many eyes were on horse racing, judge Charles Brieant commented, "A little less arrogance and they would have done it on a day other than the Breeders' Cup."[40]

When two men partnered to legally win over $2.6 million in a Pick Six in 2003, they were not surprised when racing fans were skeptical. After careful examination of the ticket, the money was awarded and excited winner Graham Stone commented about the scrutiny, "That was fine ... I've never even been to Drexel."[41] This scandal demonstrates that no sport is immune from unscrupulous behavior. Further, it shows that even the most technologically advanced cheats cannot always evade scrutiny.

NEUHEISEL FIRED, WINS HUGE SETTLEMENT

Successful football coach Rick Neuheisel was fired from the University of Washington in summer 2003 after lying to NCAA investigators about his participation in an auction-style NCAA basketball pool the previous two years. The firing, however, was no open-and-shut case as it became apparent that both the university and the NCAA made serious missteps in the process, which allowed the coach to launch a civil lawsuit seeking millions of dollars. He accused the university of wrongfully terminating his contract and the NCAA, among other things, of encouraging the firing.

Neuheisel admitted betting more than $11,000, winning $18,523, in neighborhood pools for the 2002 and 2003 NCAA basketball tournaments. These bets were a violation of NCAA rules. However, Washington compliance officer Dana Richardson had sent an e-mail to coaches in 1999, and again in 2003, that authorized participating in pools with friends. In the memo she wrote, "The bottom line of these rules is that if you have friends outside of ICA [the intercollegiate athletic department] that have pools on any of the basketball tournaments, you can participate."[42] Richardson's position was erroneous and reflected that she had not properly reviewed all information available to her from the NCAA before issuing the memo. NCAA rules prohibit gambling on college sports by all athletic department staff.

When it appeared that firing Neuheisel for gambling was going to present the university with a problem, given the presence of the Richardson memo, the primary reason for his dismissal changed to focus on the lies told to the NCAA investigators, as well as his "untruthfulness" with then-athletic director Barbara Hedges about an interview he had with the San Francisco 49ers,[43] which had caused the university some embarrassment. While the NCAA did find that Neuheisel had violated NCAA gambling rules, it did not sanction him, citing the internal memo that authorized the behavior. Particularly concerning was that Hedges, according to Neuheisel's lawyer, Bob Sulkin, tried to cover up the existence of the e-mail altogether. "She knew the e-mail [memo] is death to the university," he said.[44]

As the cause for firing shifted away from gambling and towards the coach's dishonesty, the university faced a contractual problem. Under the terms of the contract, his lies would be considered minor transgressions and not likely meriting his firing. As Sulkin pointed out in court, "The contract doesn't say you can add up all the acts."[45] Sulkin defined the cause for firing in this way, "There has never been an issue about dishonesty. Dishonesty is nothing but a subterfuge. What they did was, to try to get a lesser penalty for themselves, was fire Rick Neuheisel.... The NCAA was out to get Rick Neuheisel."[46]

Neuheisel's case against the NCAA had a number of components, including defamation from NCAA officials, including NCAA president Myles Brand. The coach felt that comments from NCAA officials acted to pressure Washington to fire him, in part because the university believed doing so would soften the NCAA sanctions that were likely forthcoming. The investigation that initially focused on his gambling habits had spiraled into minor recruiting violations and revealed that several athletic department employees, including compliance director Dana Richardson, competed in NCAA basketball pools. The university would ultimately be placed on probation for two years, but the penalty could have been worse.

As the case progressed, Neuheisel's lawyers demonstrated that the NCAA interviewed the coach in violation of its own recently passed bylaws that stated investigators must notify interviewees of the purpose of the interview in advance. The NCAA had not done so and, in essence, had blindsided the coach. The bylaw had been passed into effect only six weeks prior to the June 2003 interview.[47] Neuheisel initially lied about whether he had been in the gambling pools. He recanted his story the same day and admitted participation.

Twenty-one months after the legal battle began, Neuheisel walked out of court with a $4.5 million settlement in his favor. He received $2.5 million from the NCAA, $500,000 from the university, and secured an agreement that the university would not seek repayment of a $1.5 million loan. "I feel fully vindicated," Neuheisel said. "Obviously, they're going to have their stories, too, but I feel like this is the best scenario."[48] The settlement brought to a close five weeks of testimony. The case was set to go into closing arguments and the jurors, reportedly, were leaning in Neuheisel's favor.

Neuheisel had worked as a volunteer coach at the high school level for two years following his dismissal from Washington. He accepted a position in the professional ranks, with the Baltimore Ravens, in 2005. Over four seasons with the Washington Huskies he had a 33–16 record that included a Rose Bowl victory and a third-place national ranking in 2001.

University of Washington athletic director Barbara Hedges announced her retirement within months of Neuheisel's firing. She had been at the helm at UW for nearly thirteen years. Compliance director Dana Richardson received a letter of reprimand and is no longer a university employee. However, the

Pac-10 Conference determined her mistake was an honest one. In fact, UW law professor Robert Aronson supported Richardson's interpretation of the NCAA rules, which many coaches and compliance officers believe are complicated and sometimes convoluted. He said, "You know, I could make a pretty good argument, in fact I think Dana's made a pretty good argument for why there is something in here [NCAA gambling rules] that is allowed."[49] The situation with Neuheisel supported what critics of the NCAA had long contended—that is that rather than focus on some very significant problems in college sports (like many of those documented in this text), the organization many times polices minutia.

OPERATION SLAPSHOT SCARES NATIONAL HOCKEY LEAGUE

In the first season back on the ice for the National Hockey League following the 2004–5 lockout, the last thing hockey needed was a gambling scandal. Fortunately, what seemed to threaten the sport's revival turned out to be far less damaging than many anticipated when it first made news in February 2006. The name of the investigation alone, Operation Slapshot, implied that the sport of hockey was heavily involved when New Jersey authorities announced that a former player (coaching at the time) and a state trooper had been charged with running a gambling ring that handled millions of dollars. The former player, Rick Tocchet, played in the NHL from 1984 to 2002 and was the assistant to Wayne Gretzky on the Phoenix Coyotes' bench at the time.

As concerning as Tocchet's involvement in the gambling ring was, more problematic for hockey was that Janet Jones, Gretzky's wife, was named as a high roller who placed bets on sporting events with the bookies. She married Gretzky in 1988 and they have five children together. They were known to frequent Las Vegas casinos. The National Hockey League had no more iconic figure than Wayne "The Great One" Gretzky. Immediately there was fear that hockey could face a similar situation as Major League Baseball had with Pete Rose betting on his sport. Jones immediately claimed she had never placed a bet for her husband, and he denied involvement in the ring and defended his wife against accusations that she had done anything wrong.

As the case moved forward, there were no ties made to hockey betting and the sport dodged a potentially fatal blow. The gambling had, in fact, been on college and professional football and basketball games. The amounts wagered were staggering; in one forty-day period, the gamblers handled more than $1.7 million in wagers. Of the three men charged, the authorities appeared most interested in state trooper James Harney, who took bets while sitting in his patrol car watching traffic. Harney pleaded guilty to conspiracy, promoting gambling, and official misconduct and was sentenced to five years in prison. James Ulmer, who acted to pass wagers from bettors to Tocchet and Harney, pleaded guilty but cooperated with prosecutors in exchange for a light sentence of two years of probation. Janet Jones and other bettors were never charged because placing bets, even with bookmakers, is not illegal in New Jersey.

Fifteen months after the case began, it ended with Tocchet's guilty plea to promoting gambling and conspiracy to promote gambling. He was sentenced to two years of probation. Tocchet had faced up to five years in state prison, but there is a presumption against incarceration for first-time offenders who plead guilty to third- or fourth-degree crimes.

In July 2007, Tocchet was playing in the World Series of Poker while awaiting his sentencing on August 17. He survived the first day of play, but did not return to the tournament for the second day, essentially vacating his chips amid speculation that he decided being in a high-stakes gambling event could hurt him in both his sentencing hearing and his attempts to get back into hockey. Janet Jones also played in the event, which had a $10,000 entry fee. She was eliminated in the early going. Tocchet was reinstated by NHL commissioner Gary Bettman in February 2008 and resumed working with Wayne Gretzky and the Phoenix Coyotes as an assistant coach.

NBA OFFICIAL TIED TO GAMBLING ON GAMES HE WORKED

The National Basketball Association faced the most dreaded form of scandal for a sports league when, in summer 2007, thirteen-year-veteran referee Tim Donaghy was accused of fixing games for the purpose of gambling throughout the two prior seasons. Officials who had worked with Donaghy had thought he had a bright future. Mike Mathis, who officiated NBA games for twenty-six years, said, "I would have told you he had a hell of a future. He had moxie, arrogance, a little over the edge. But he had the cojones to make calls at the end of games and to make them on superstars the same as on anybody else."[50] His future took a precipitous downturn when he began providing inside information to gamblers regarding which officials would work which games (which was not public information), and about the relationships certain officials had with specific players. The gambling operation came to light after the FBI stumbled across it while investigating the Gambino crime family.

As soon as the story broke that Donaghy was involved in gambling, local sports writers began revisiting games he had worked, looking for odd outcomes. They quickly found them. Donaghy had worked a game in which the underdog New York Knicks upset the Miami Heat after being awarded thirty-nine free throws. The Heat had shot only eight. Donaghy also worked Game 3 of the Spurs-Suns playoff series, which was roundly criticized as being horribly officiated. The Suns' Amare Stoudemire played only twenty-one minutes, relegated to the bench with foul after foul, while the Spurs' Tim Duncan ran wild for thirty-three points and nineteen rebounds.

The now infamous NBA official Tim Donaghy oversees a Washington Wizards–New Jersey Nets game in April 2007. He would soon become the source of one of the league's worst gambling scandals. Courtesy of AP Photo/ Haraz N. Ghanbari.

Donaghy pleaded guilty in August 2007 to conspiring to commit wire fraud and conspiring to transmit wagering information across state lines. While he did not plead guilty to fixing games, some of the tips he gave involved games he worked. It is assumed that he was also making bets and calls in his own interest, but that was not part of the plea agreement. His sentencing, originally scheduled for November 2007, was rescheduled for January 2008. Donaghy's legal problems may have not all been addressed by the plea deal. Maricopa County (Arizona) attorney Andrew Thomas submitted requests to the NBA and FBI to determine if the Suns were cheated by a fixed game in the loss to the Spurs.[51] He could file charges if evidence supports his belief.

NBA commissioner David Stern believed the event to be isolated and called Donaghy a "rogue, isolated criminal," even though there had hardly been sufficient time or an investigation to make that determination.[52] This begged the question; if the league did not know about Donaghy until informed about his activity by the FBI, how could the league know that no other referees were involved? Some journalists called for Stern to resign should he be wrong, and other referees be implicated later. Journalists also wondered how Stern could call the event "unforeseeable"[53] when he also had claimed that the league took every precaution to avoid just such an incident.

It appeared the damage to the NBA would be kept to a minimum (in part due to the Michael Vick dog-fighting scandal dominating headlines at the time). Then, as part of his cooperation requirement, Donaghy informed law enforcement officials that twenty other referees had violated NBA rules against gambling. With the exception of gambling on horse races that occur outside the NBA season, the referees were not allowed to gamble. "You are not permitted to bet if you're a referee," Stern said. "The legal betting will cost you your job. The illegal betting, depending on the context, may cost you your freedom."[54] A law enforcement source said that Donaghy's disclosure seemed to come in an attempt to offer any information that could lighten his sentence.

The NBA launched a review of league rules and practices relative to gambling and its officiating program. Lawrence B. Pedowitz, a former chief of the criminal division in the U.S. Attorney's Office for the Southern District of New York, was asked to lead it. At the time, the NBA had no indication from the FBI that any other officials had actually wagered on or affected the outcome of NBA games, according to NBA spokesman Tim Frank. Pedowitz determined that Donaghy was the lone official involved in gambling on games. However, as Donaghy suggested, about half the officials admitted to violating the league's gambling rules. In a surprise move, Stern did not fire them as he had said he would do. Rather, he suggested the rules were antiquated and announced that the league would refine them, allowing for some casino gambling by referees during specific parts of the year. The league also will make public the names of the officials assigned to games, reducing the potential impact of this as inside information. Stern added, "We're developing a wide array of statistical screens that we will use ... to detect signs that something might be amiss."[55]

The impact of the Donaghy scandal could be felt throughout sports, but in basketball in particular there was anticipation that fans would openly question calls, accuse officials of being "on the take,"[56] and perhaps even call a referee "Donaghy" when they don't like or agree with a call.

Chapter 4

SEX: ASSAULT, HARASSMENT, COVER–UPS, AND ACCUSATIONS

stimates are that one in four women in the United States will at some point in her life be the victim of domestic violence. Likewise, one-quarter of all college-aged women suffer an attempted rape. These are horrifying statistics. It is well-documented that athletes are overrepresented as accused rapists and abusers, although conviction figures do not show such an overrepresentation. Some maintain that male athletes are targeted by women who claim to have been assaulted so they can attain money or fame. Others say the low conviction rates are another sign that athletes are privileged. Rather than demonstrating innocence, the argument is that athletes are not convicted because of the general hero-worship of athletes in the United States.

Some of the cases included in this chapter do not involve rape or domestic violence, but still include shocking behavior towards women. For instance, the case of reporter Lisa Olson, who was sexually harassed while working in the New England Patriots' locker room, exemplifies the difficulties for women in a male-dominated world. Exploitation of women is sadly common in the country as a whole, and certainly the world of athletics is no different.

WADE BOGGS ADMITS TO SEX ADDICTION— SUED BY MISTRESS

Major League Baseball received more media attention than normal in summer 1988 when Margo Adams filed a $6 million palimony lawsuit against Wade Boggs of the Boston Red Sox, a four-time American League batting champion. Her claim was that Boggs had essentially breached an oral contract with her when he failed to leave his wife. Boggs admitted having an affair with Adams that stretched over four years, but denied ever promising to leave his wife and family for her. In August 1988 Adams doubled her lawsuit to $12 million, arguing that Boggs inflicted emotional distress on her when he reported to the FBI that she was trying to extort money from him.[1] The embattled Boggs, trying to gain public support, went on television and claimed he felt he was a "sex addict" and that it was a disease. He had apparently diagnosed himself after watching an episode of *Geraldo Rivera* that dealt with the issue of oversexed people. Boggs added that he was cured and had made peace with his family and was moving on with his life.

Adams kept the sex scandal in the papers with a tell-all interview and pictorial with *Penthouse* magazine in spring 1989. The article painted a poor picture of Boggs, suggesting he had issues with white players dating black women. In the article, Adams also said that Boggs referred to Roger Clemens as "Mr. Perfect," and that he believed Jose Canseco could only hit because he was on steroids. Adams received at least $100,000 from *Penthouse* for the story.[2]

The courts eventually dismissed a large portion of her lawsuit. This eliminated the opportunity to collect punitive damages, which meant that she could collect no more than $48,000 if she won the case. This was the amount she lost from taking time off of work to go on road trips with Boggs and his team. A month after that ruling, Adams was arrested at a Nordstrom department store and charged with shoplifting a $258 coat. She pleaded guilty to misdemeanor petty theft. The scandal ended eighteen months after the legal battle began, with the two sides agreeing to an undisclosed settlement that was likely far, far less than what she had dreamed of getting. In 1990 Adams married the man who photographed her for *Penthouse*, and they had a son a year later. Boggs played in twelve consecutive All-Star games and was voted into the Baseball Hall of Fame in 2005. The case demonstrates that many sports fans are loyal to their idols, and that even negative publicity cannot always keep a star from achieving Hall of Fame status.

SEXUAL ASSAULT ROCKS GLEN RIDGE, NEW JERSEY

On March 1, 1989, a group of high school athletes sexually assaulted a mentally disabled girl in the basement of a home in Glen Ridge, New Jersey. The incident shook and divided the residents of Glen Ridge, who had compared their town to a Norman Rockwell painting and cherished the squeaky-clean image of their little corner of small-town America.

Christopher Archer lured the girl with the promise of a date with his brother, Paul, to the basement of a home where twins Kyle and Kevin Scherzer lived. The girl had an IQ of 64 and the mental capacity of an eight year old. The Archers, the Scherzers, Peter Quigley, and Bryant Grober commanded the girl to perform sex acts on herself and on them. All seven would eventually be convicted or enter plea agreements. Another student, Richard Corcoran, would stand trial separately after he made statements incriminating the others. He was the son of a Glen Ridge police lieutenant. The boys used a broomstick and a baseball practice bat to sexually assault the girl.

The young lady did not tell anyone about the rape for several days, but the boys bragged, and rumors of the sexual incident quickly spread through the school and community. The victim eventually disclosed the event to her swimming coach, and seven boys were arrested. Many in the community, however, blamed the victim for the incident, citing previous incidents of sexually inappropriate behavior. Students generally supported the boys, all of whom were athletes and very popular. One student even talked the girl into saying the acts were consensual. Later investigations revealed several other incidents of violence and misbehavior by the accused, including several against the same young lady.

In 1993 the seven defendants were tried for the offenses. The defense aggressively attacked the victim with what the *New Jersey Law Journal* would dub the "Lolita Defense," in which they attempted to paint her as an aggressive seductress and the defendants as the victims. The strategy backfired, as the jury was largely offended by the notion that it was the men who needed protection, as one defense lawyer suggested. The trial was the first in which evidence of rape trauma syndrome was allowed as evidence in a New Jersey court. Four of the men were convicted and three were sentenced to serve some time in detention. Two of the other defendants made plea bargains. Charges were dropped in the case against Richard Corcoran after the parents of the victim decided pursuing the case was not in her best interest. The defendants that were convicted and sentenced have all been released. Corcoran filed and won a lawsuit against the Essex County Prosecutor's Office for malicious prosecution.

Seven years later, Corcoran joined the Army. Police made no fewer than six visits to his home, responding to domestic disturbance calls. He later shot his estranged wife and another soldier (they survived) before turning the gun on himself in a tragedy near Fort Bragg, North Carolina. Corcoran had attended a mandated anger-management class at the post that very afternoon.

The Glen Ridge case became the basis for a 1997 book by Bernard Lefkowitz titled, *Our Guys: The Glen Ridge Rape and the Secret Life of the Perfect Suburb*, which later became a made-for-television movie. For many who read them, the news coverage, book, and movie opened their eyes to the dangers of a culture that permits an "anything goes" mentality when it comes to athletes. Others continue to maintain that this sort of thing can never happen in their backyard.

NEW ENGLAND PATRIOTS SEXUALLY HARASS LISA OLSON

Boston Herald sportswriter Lisa Olson sought a behind-the-scenes resolution when she claimed that players for the New England Patriots sexually harassed her as she conducted interviews in the team's locker room on September 17, 1990. What she got was a highly publicized brawl that largely cast her as out of place in a man's world, followed by threats and harassment from the Patriots' fans.

The event in question took place during a practice-day interview with cornerback Maurice Hurst. Other players gathered around, some naked, and began to fondle themselves and harass her with questions like, "Is that what you want?"[3] The players were later identified as Zeke Mowatt, Michael Timpson, and Robert Perryman. Olson and her editors approached Patriots officials with hopes of a quick resolution, seeking only an apology, but hopes for that were scuttled when the *Boston Globe* broke the story four days later and team owner Victor Kiam foolishly called the complaint "a flyspeck in the ocean" and labeled Olson, "a classic bitch."[4]

The National Football League launched an investigation and appointed Philip Heymann to lead it. The result was a 108-page report that concluded Mowatt fondled himself while making inappropriate comments. Patriots' media relations director James Oldham said he witnessed Perryman gyrating his naked hips behind the reporter and also commenting to her while Timpson joined in. The report also concluded that the players believed Olson was a "looker" and they sought to teach her a lesson. It was important to note, as the battle about whether women should be in the locker room raged, that Olson had attempted to interview Hurst outside, but he wanted to talk inside the locker room instead. NFL commissioner Paul Tagliabue fined the team and the players. The Patriots' fine ($25,000) was taken directly from the team's share of television revenue and Timpson paid his $5,000, according to Tagliabue. The other players, however, never paid their fines, and the league, facing appeals and lawsuits from the athletes, never forced the issue.

When it appeared the incident could not become any uglier, Kiam demonstrated shockingly poor taste by cracking a joke at a banquet attended by about 750 people, honoring Kiam and fourteen others. The comment, which alluded to Olson and the first Gulf War, which was ongoing, suggested that she and Iraqis had all seen "Patriot missiles up close."[5] Kiam apologized, but the damage was done. It would cost him more than an apology, as Olson decided she had had enough of the belligerent owner and filed a civil suit. She named the team, Kiam, Oldham, and the three players in the suit. Citing a legal strategy to save money by avoiding the legal fees of a trial, the team settled the case. Media outlets reported that Olson received between $250,000 and $700,000 or more. The Patriots organization called those figures grossly exaggerated. Olson announced that she would use the money to establish a journalism scholarship at Northern Arizona University, her alma mater, and said that the decision to settle was made in light of her father being diagnosed with cancer.

Olson's life was terribly disrupted in the aftermath of the incident and the enormous media attention it attracted. Over 1,400 news articles were written within two years and countless television broadcasts debated the issue. According to her own accounts, Olson received more than one hundred obscene phone calls and hundreds of pieces of hate mail. Her apartment was broken into twice, and someone wrote, "Bitch, leave Boston or die," in the foyer. Her car tires were slashed and a note was left on the window that warned it would be her neck the next time.[6] She claimed that private investigators were harassing her, hired by Kiam to determine whether she had ever had an abortion and at what age she lost her virginity. To escape the mounting pressure from the harassment and threats, Olson left the country, taking a job in Australia at the *Sydney Daily Telegraph Mirror*. It took her a few years to return to covering sports. Even in Australia, coaches who knew of the scandal harassed her at events she covered.

Sociologists forwarded theories on why Olson suffered such indignities. A study prepared by Mary Jo Kane and Lisa Disch for the *Sociology of Sport Journal* concluded that a woman in the locker room, as a sports writer, "represents a threat so profound that she must be displaced from her role as a social critic of male performance and reassigned to her 'appropriate' role of female sex object."[7] Other female sports reporters acknowledged that when people, male or female, learned of their job, the first question asked tended to be, "So, what's it like in the locker room?"[8]

MIKE TYSON CONVICTED OF RAPE

Heavyweight champion Mike Tyson was known to be exceedingly aggressive, both in and out of the ring. In 1986, at just twenty years old, Tyson became the youngest heavyweight champion ever when he knocked out Trevor Berbick. He defended his title for four years, finally being knocked out in 1990 by James "Buster" Douglas. Over his seven-year career, Tyson had amassed a 41–1 record, with thirty-six knockouts. Estimates were that he earned $100 million in prize money. His career came to a screeching halt when he was accused and then convicted of raping a beauty pageant contestant. The case captured the public attention and split Americans, many of whom became entrenched into either the belief that he was a despicable rapist or that she was a conniving liar who sought to cash in from her encounter with a star athlete. The case was voted the top sports story in 1992 by the Associated Press.

On February 10, 1992, twenty-six-year-old Mike Tyson was convicted of raping eighteen-year-old Desiree Washington in an Indianapolis hotel, where he was a judge for the Ms. Black America pageant and Washington was a contestant. Tyson claimed the sex was consensual. The jury unanimously convicted Tyson, and he was sentenced to ten years in prison, with four of them suspended. In November 1992 the *Washington Times* reported that Tyson had infected Washington with a venereal disease when he raped her. Her attorney did not specify which venereal disease.

Tyson supporters claimed he was falsely accused, and that the case was yet another example of how black men are not treated fairly in the criminal justice system. Democratic representative William A. Crawford of Indiana claimed at a July 1992 rally, "Many people in this city, this state and throughout the nation, myself included, sincerely feel Mike Tyson did not receive a fair trial. No act of force or violence, nor even the explicit or implicit threat of force or violence, was demonstrated or proven in the trial."[9] Another high-profile sup-porter, Nation of Islam leader Louis Farrakhan, pronounced, "Mike liked women; he didn't make no bones about that. Desiree wasn't silly. Desiree was smart."[10] Farrakhan also said the pageant made a huge mistake in inviting Tyson to be a judge and to meet the candidates. "You were bringing a hawk into a chicken yard and the chicken got eaten up."[11]

It was later revealed that Ms. Washington had discussed book and movie deals with advisors prior to the trial, which she had previously denied. Tyson employed high-profile defense attorney Alan Dershowitz to file an appeal in which he maintained Washington's desire to make money provided a motive for her to fabricate the charges. Two of the jurors said Tyson should have been given a new trial, as that information would have made them doubt Washington's credibility. One even said, "In hindsight, it looks like a woman raped a man."[12] Another juror explained she might not have convicted Tyson had she known that Washington "hung out in night clubs since she was 16 and isn't

Mike Tyson curiously smiles and shows his handcuffs as he is transported to prison in Indianapolis, Indiana. He was sentenced to six years for rape of a beauty pageant contestant. Courtesy of AP Photo/Jeff Atteberry.

the innocent young girl presented in court."[13] Washington explained that she had signed a contingency-fee agreement prior to the trial, but did so because she thought that it was to assist her in navigating the media onslaught brought on by the trial, not to make money.

Tyson was released from prison for good behavior after serving three years of his sentence. He remained on probation for four years and was required to undergo psychological counseling as well as perform one hundred hours of community service each year. In June 1995 Tyson settled a lawsuit with Desiree Washington for an undisclosed sum. The settlement was in lieu of a trial in which Washington sought compensatory damages for assault, battery, false imprisonment, and emotional distress. Tyson has continued to maintain his innocence. At a 1995 welcome-home celebration in Harlem, New York, Tyson was asked if he was sorry. Long-time promoter Don King jumped in to respond, "Sorry for what? Come on!" Upon release from prison, Tyson immediately announced he would return to fighting. He also initiated a new charitable foundation for children.[14]

Tyson returned to the ring after his release, but was a shadow of his former self. He also continued to demonstrate erratic, and sometimes criminal, behavior. He famously bit Evander Holyfield's ear during a boxing match, which many argued brought shame to himself and the sport. He later pleaded guilty to misdemeanor assault in 1999 and to cocaine possession and driving under the influence in 2007. Ken Jones of the London *Independent* commented, "Even before Mike Tyson dramatically unified the heavyweight championship by knocking out Michael Spinks in 91 seconds on 27 June 1988, it could be sensed that he was as likely to end up in a penal establishment as the Hall of Fame."[15] Tyson will live in infamy, as much because of his antics as his athletic ability.

MARV ALBERT PLEADS GUILTY TO ASSAULT AND BATTERY

In 1997 fifty-six-year-old sports broadcaster Marv Albert, the voice of the New York Knicks and New York Rangers and the lead announcer for NBC basketball, was charged with misdemeanor assault and battery. Albert had allegedly attacked Vanessa Perhach, a woman with whom he had a ten-year sexual relationship. She said Albert had thrown Perhach on a bed in a Virginia hotel room, bit her on the back more than a dozen times, and forced her to perform oral sex. Perhach alleged that Albert angrily attacked her because she refused to allow another man to join in their sexual activity. Albert's attorneys said Perhach had a history of retribution against lovers and was a chronic liar.[16]

Albert, who was engaged at the time, abruptly ended the trial when he pleaded guilty to the charges. He said he wanted to end the ordeal before it brought more misery to him, his fiancé, and the rest of his family. The two days of testimony featured accounts of Albert's sexual activities, including his penchant for threesomes and his fondness for wearing women's underwear. The plea came one day after another woman, Patricia Masten, came forward to claim Albert had bitten her during a sexual advance. Masten described how Albert had also pleaded with her to engage in three-way sex and pranced around a hotel room in Dallas, Texas wearing a garter belt. She said she ripped off his toupee and ran from the room. Given the nature of the testimony, it was of little surprise that Albert sought a quick end to the trial.

Albert received a twelve-month suspended sentence and was ordered to undergo counseling. The agreement specified that the criminal record would be expunged if Albert did not commit any crimes during the following year. Albert resigned from his sports-casting job at Madison Square Garden (MSG) and was fired from NBC. One year later, Albert returned to his position at MSG. Dave Checketts, president of Madison Square Garden, announced, "He has been very, very loyal to the company. Today, we return the favor."[17] As the voice of basketball to many, Albert's escapades brought negative attention to the sport. Clearly the repercussions were short-lived, however, given that he was able to resume his career almost as if nothing happened. Rather than prompt inquiry into violence against women by professional adults in the sport world, Albert's antics simply made him a laughingstock for awhile.

EUGENE ROBINSON SOLICITES PROSTITUTE—
DERAILS FALCONS

Just before 9 P.M. the night before the Atlanta Falcons took the field to face the Denver Broncos in Super Bowl XXXIII, Falcons safety Eugene Robinson was arrested for soliciting a prostitute in a notorious Miami neighborhood.[18] The self-described Christian had offered $40 to an undercover police officer for oral sex. He was released about two hours later to Falcons general manager Harold Richardson after signing a promise to appear in court within thirty days.

What made the Robinson arrest particularly shocking was that only twelve hours earlier he had been honored by Athletes in Action, a Christian group, with the Bart Starr Award for his exemplary moral character, as recognized by fellow players. Further, as a team leader, he had admonished his teammates to obey the curfew and stay focused on the game. Robinson had a history of charitable work, even winning Man of the Year honors four times in Seattle while he played for the Seahawks, for his work with the Boys and Girls Club and the Union Gospel Mission.

Although Robinson and his teammates initially denied that the arrest was a distraction, there was ample evidence to the contrary. Robinson admitted that he could not sleep after being released. In the game he was badly beaten on an eighty-yard touchdown pass from John Elway to Rod Smith (Denver's longest play of the game), and he missed countless tackles. One Falcons player, demanding anonymity, said, "Instead of getting mentally ready for the Broncos, we were talking about Eugene. The Broncos beat us, but anyone who says that what happened to Eugene was not a factor is lying."[19] Perhaps making the arrest even more scandalous, another teammate said that Falcons players had been going to the notorious Miami neighborhood all week, but Robinson was the only one unlucky enough to get caught.

Beyond the effect on the team, Robinson was tremendously concerned with his family's welfare—a bit too late, some would suggest. The graduate of Colgate University said, "Reputation? I can deal with that. The hurt? My wife? That means much, much more to me. I truly do love my wife. I love her, I love my kids. I'm sorry I had to drag her through that type of deal."[20]

The Falcons had entered the game on a roll, having upset the heavily favored Minnesota Vikings on the road. The 34–19 loss to the Broncos sent the Falcons organization into a tailspin. It would win only seven of its next twenty-four games. Falcons coach Dan Reeves had made an inspirational return to the team earlier in the season only weeks after heart surgery. The loss made him the third NFL coach to never win a Super Bowl after making four appearances. Beyond the immediate impact on his family and on his team, the Robinson case highlights how athletes can get caught up in poor decision making as a result of the culture of entitlement that permeates most professional, and even collegiate, sports.

UNIVERSITY OF COLORADO RECRUITING AND SEX SCANDALS

At the University of Colorado (CU), Lisa Simpson and two other women alleged that several CU football players and recruits gang raped them at Simpson's home during a party in December 2001. Simpson alleged that she and some friends were playing a drinking game at her apartment when approximately sixteen football players and recruits arrived unannounced. The three women filed suits in federal court, contending the university created a hostile environment and used sex to entice recruits. These cases were dismissed. One victim claimed to have lost her soccer scholarship after reporting the incident. She has since dropped her suit. In another incident, former CU recruiting assistant Nathan Maxcey was accused of hiring women from Best Variety escort service to have sex with recruits while they stayed at the Omni Interlocken Resort. Maxcey claimed the charges he made for the services of three girls between June 2002 and July 2003 were for only himself. An adult-entertainment company in Denver allegedly provided strippers for recruiting parties at CU, as well as at Colorado State University, the University of Northern Colorado, and two Texas schools, Rice University and the University of Houston.

Adding to the school's problems, in 2004 former CU football kicker Katie Hnida told *Sports Illustrated* she was abused, molested, and raped while she was on the team in 1999. Elizabeth Hoffman, president of CU at the time, appointed a special assistant to be "the eyes and ears" of the athletic department. Hoffman also asked the Boulder police to investigate Hnida's claims. Campus-based victim's advocates were involved as well.[21] Coach Gary Barnett added fuel to the fire with his comments about Hnida. Barnett said, "Well, it was obvious that Katie was not very good. She was awful, OK? And so, guys, you know what guys do? They respect your ability. I mean, you could be 90 years old, but if you can go out and play, they respect you. Well, Katie was a girl. And not only was she a girl, she was terrible."[22] Barnett was suspended, but not fired for his comments. He later said he made a mistake in making the comments, although to many his apology rang hollow. One day after his suspension was announced, a sixth rape allegation against a football player was made. Barnett claimed he instituted a number of policies to help guide the team, including a 124-page conduct manual. Some players agreed Barnett was a disciplinarian, citing his distribution of wristbands featuring the letters DTRT, for "Do the right thing." One of the allegations was made by a young woman who worked in the athletic department. When she told Barnett that a player raped her, he allegedly told her he would "back his player 100 percent if she took this forward in the criminal process." She claims the player raped her in her apartment, where she told him at least ten times she was not interested in having sex with him.[23]

Other colleges and universities watched the CU case closely. If courts were to determine that CU allowed, even fostered, an environment in which sexual harassment and sexual assault were permitted, the school could be held liable for damages based on Title IX, the federal law requiring gender equity in education programs. Schools are required to take some actions to prevent students from harassment and assault and must take reasonable actions in response once they are given notice of an incident. Katherine Redmond from the National Coalition Against Violent Athletes argued it would be incredible, yet unlikely, if the school were held accountable. "Coaches run these towns," Redmond said.[24] The CU charges were not the first scandal for Coach Barnett. When he was at Northwestern, four of his players were caught in a betting scandal. Barnett, however, was not directly implicated. Nor were the allegations the first scandal at CU. In 1998 a female high school student accused a recruit of sexual assault, and the school also has a history of varied NCAA recruiting violations. Ira Chernus, professor of religious studies at CU commented, "Like every major football school, CU has a big network of 'boosters.' University officials and coaches don't have to arrange or condone special pleasures for recruits. It's all so well organized from outside the university it just runs by itself like a well-oiled machine."[25]

A Congressional subcommittee was formed in February 2004 to investigate the allegations of inappropriate recruiting practices and criminal violations. Colorado governor Bill Owens also appointed the state's attorney general, Ken Salazar, as a special prosecutor to investigate the allegations at CU. Owens also recommended that CU's Board of Regents appoint a prosecutor and a victim's advocate to their investigative commission. The Board did add Jean McAllister of the Colorado Department of Human Services domestic abuse assistance program to their panel. The National Organization of Women (NOW) applauded

Owens for this recommendation. President Hoffman and CU chancellor Richard L. Byyny also made changes to the football team's recruiting practices, prohibiting recruits from staying with players on their visits to campus and from attending private parties. Recruiting visits were shortened from two days to one, with supervision required from the recruits' parents or a designated coach. The curfew for recruits to check in with coaches had been 1:00 A.M., but was changed to 11:00 P.M.

Victim's rights advocates and others were horrified by some of the statements made by panelists on the regent's team. One member, Ms. Lawrence, told a reporter, "The question I have for the young ladies is why they are going to parties like this and drinking or taking drugs and putting themselves in a very threatening or serious position."[26] Barnett was fired in 2005, not because of any of the allegations, rather due to an unsatisfactory win-loss record.

KOBE BRYANT ACCUSED OF RAPE—SETTLES CIVIL SUIT

In her accusation against Los Angeles Lakers basketball star Kobe Bryant, Katelyn Faber alleged Bryant raped her at the Lodge and Spa at Cordillera, a Vail, Colorado resort, where she was employed in 2003. She claimed she went to his room and consensually kissed him before he raped her. The Colorado Supreme Court had rejected the prosecutor's appeal of a lower court decision allowing details of Faber's sex life to be introduced into evidence. One piece of evidence that would have been introduced was DNA showing Faber had sex with another man soon after the incident with Bryant. The criminal case was dismissed after jury selection had already begun. District Attorney Mark Hurlbert told Judge Terry Ruckreigle that Faber no longer wished to participate in the trial, but that this was no reflection on her credibility or the factuality of the charges. Bryant made a public statement after the criminal case was dropped. It read,

> First, I want to apologize directly to the young woman involved in this incident. I want to apologize to her for my behavior that night and for the consequences she has suffered in the past year. Although this past year has been incredibly difficult for me personally, I can only imagine the pain she has had to endure. I also want to apologize to her parents and family members, and to my family and friends and supporters, and to the citizens of Eagle, Colorado.
>
> I also want to make it clear that I do not question the motives of this young woman. No money has been paid to this woman. She has agreed that this statement will not be used against me in the civil case. Although I truly believe this encounter between us was consensual, I recognize now that she did not and does not view this incident the same way I did. After months of reviewing discovery, listening to her attorney, and even her testimony in person, I now understand how she feels that she did not consent to this encounter.

I issue this statement today fully aware that while one part of this case ends today, another remains. I understand that the civil case against me will go forward. That part of this case will be decided by and between the parties directly involved in the incident and will no longer be a financial or emotional drain on the citizens of the state of Colorado.[27]

Discussions of rape and rape myths in cases involving athletes often involve a racial element, as athletes in revenue sports are disproportionately black. While blacks, like any racial group, have diverse opinions about rape, they generally are more likely to doubt allegations against black men given the history of false accusations and horrendous punishments. Numerous polls taken after Bryant was charged with rape indicated racial disparity in assessments of his guilt. Less than 25 percent of blacks surveyed by *USA Today* thought Bryant was probably or definitely guilty, as compared with over 40 percent of whites who did.

Faber filed a civil suit against Bryant seeking compensation for mental injuries, humiliation, and public scorn she received after the June 2003 encounter. The parties settled for an undisclosed amount. During the lead up to the settlement, Faber received hate mail and death threats. One man, Cedric Augustine, sent seventy profanity-laced death threats to both Faber and the prosecutor. He pleaded guilty in March 2005 to one felony count of making interstate threats and was sentenced to nine months in a federal prison. Augustine had also threatened to blow up the Eagle County (Colorado) courthouse in which the trial was to take place. Two others pleaded guilty to making threats against Faber. John Roche was sentenced to four months in prison and a $1,000 fine, and Patrick Graber was sentenced to three years in prison.

Bryant has continued to play for the Los Angeles Lakers. His popularity waned after the rape accusation and was worsened by public feuds with teammate Shaquille O'Neal, who is generally considered among the most likable players in the league, and the highly respected Phil Jackson, who had coached the Lakers to three NBA titles after coaching the Chicago Bulls to six.

Despite the tremendous amount of media attention to the case as it unfolded, it seems to have had little impact on Bryant's career today. His popularity seemed restored by 2007, as sales of his jerseys would attest. Not only was his jersey the most popular in the United States, but it even outsold Yao Ming's in China.

NORTHWESTERN HIGH SCHOOL (MIAMI) COVERS UP SEX CRIME

Northwestern High School in Miami-Dade County has a reputation for success on the gridiron, but also for high dropout rates and low standardized test scores. It is known in South Florida for athletic success above all, and for the tremendous community support that winning garners. Community members say they feel tremendous loyalty to the school and are very protective of it. This culture of protection may be at the root of a scandal involving a star player, sex on the school's bathroom floor, and the ensuing cover-up by school officials.

Antwain Easterling, then eighteen years old and a football star, had sex with a fourteen-year-old honor student and band member on the school's bathroom floor on September 16, 2006.[28] Despite Easterling's claims the sex was consensual, the act was considered statutory rape based on the girl's age. Two other males were arrested along with Easterling and charged with lewd and lascivious battery. A third man, Vincent Shannon Jefferson, twenty-four years old, was arrested on similar charges when the young lady said she had sex with him off school grounds. The scandal continued as school officials knew about and actively covered up the crime, allowing Easterling the opportunity to play in several high-profile football games, including the state title game that Northwestern won. At the time of the incident, Easterling had scholarship offers from Florida, Miami, Rutgers, Wisconsin, and Nebraska, as well as several other schools.[29] Easterling had a newborn daughter from a different relationship at the time.

School officials heard about the incident in October 2006, when the girl's mother spoke to a guidance counselor and two teachers at the school; the guidance counselor told the school's principal and two assistant principals. Principal Dwight Bernard assured the mother the police would be called, but they were not. On December 5, the girl's mother told Officer David Thompson about the incident, and soon after Easterling was charged with lewd and lascivious battery on a minor. Following Miami-Dade School Board policy, he should have been suspended for at least ten days. He was not, nor was he ever disciplined by the school. Rather, Easterling played football for Northwestern three days after his arrest while out on $7,500 bond, helping to lead the team to the state title. He rushed for 157 yards in the team's 34–14 defeat of Lake Brantley High School. A grand jury report released in June 2006 documented that at least seventeen school employees knew about the incident. Easterling has since entered a Diversion program for first-time offenders. Providing he completes the program requirements, the felony arrest will be expunged from his record. He began playing football for the University of Southern Mississippi in fall 2007.

While Easterling has moved on to Southern Mississippi, others involved in the incident have not fared as well. The young lady twice attempted suicide and has been institutionalized.[30] Principal Bernard was indicted on two charges of third-degree felony official misconduct, although his attorney claims he was an easy scapegoat in a culture that operated like a gang.[31] Bernard was fired, along with a number of teachers who also knew of the incident and helped in the cover-up. Athletic director Gregory Killings, who had been with the school since 1983, announced his resignation in July 2007. A grand jury report found that the school district meddled in police investigation of the case, and that superintendent Rudy Crew knew Easterling had been arrested and approved of allowing him to play football. Coach Roland Smith was fired, along with his entire staff, on July 11, 2007. The school had to scramble to find a new coaching staff only weeks before the 2007 season.

In mid July 2007 rumors emerged that Superintendent Crew was considering suspending the entire football team for the 2007 season as a result of the scandal. The district consulted the Florida High School Athletic Association for clarification on the rules and transfer options for players. Crew acknowledged this type of suspension had never occurred before, but said he thought it might be appropriate because "it sends a strong message to all schools that these things need to be dealt with in a timely and appropriate manner."[32] Members of the community were outraged at the suggestion. "For him to go forward with it is ill-advised," said Larry Williams, president of the Northwestern Alumni Association. Williams also commented, "We won't allow our young people to be hurt by a situation that goes on probably at every high school."[33] In addition to the impact on the football team, the highly ranked band would have no one to play for. Typically, games draw sell-out crowds, which would also impact the revenues produced for both Northwestern and the teams they play. In mid July, the football team was ranked first in the nation in a preview by *Rise* magazine. As the season approached, Crew changed his mind and allowed the team to play while serving one-year of probation. The team went undefeated, claiming the Florida state title and finishing ranked first in most national polls.

The cover-up of this case is significant in that it is yet another indicator of the lengths people will go to ensure "their team" keeps its best players active. It highlights the immense support for high school athletic teams in some communities, and it raises important issues of where to draw the line when assigning punishments.

THE LA SALLE UNIVERSITY RAPE COVER-UP

In 2006 La Salle University faced fines and other sanctions for violating a federal law, the Clery Act, requiring universities to report sexual assaults and other crimes that occur on campuses. La Salle officials failed to report alleged sexual assaults perpetrated by members of the men's basketball team in 2003 and 2004. The U.S. Department of Education claimed La Salle should have informed the entire campus community of the assaults. In its report, it alleged La Salle had been negligent in reporting other crime statistics as well. Spokespersons for the university denied any wrongdoing and planned to appeal the department's findings. This would be the first time the Department of Education cited a college for failing to warn students of an acquaintance assault, and only three colleges have been fined in the fifteen years since the Clery Act was passed. The Clery Act, named for Jeanne Clery, requires colleges and universities receiving federal funds to report most types of campus crimes. It was passed after the 1986 rape and murder of Lehigh University freshman Jeanne Clery.

In April 2003 a female student on La Salle's women's basketball team reported to men's basketball coach Billy Hahn and women's coach John Miller that she awoke in her bedroom to find male basketball player Dzaflo Larkai sexually assaulting her. The basketball coaches did not report her claims to anyone in the athletic administration, and she claimed they discouraged her from telling anyone else. The reaction she received from the coaches, she claimed, made her wait fourteen months before she reported the rape. The coaches later claimed they didn't tell anyone because they were honoring her wish that this remain private.

In 2004 a counselor with the university's summer basketball camp told the coach she had been sexually assaulted by two players on the men's team. She claimed La Salle stars Gary Neal and Michael Cleaves sexually assaulted her at a party. Men's coach Billy Hahn investigated the incident and spoke to all parties. He then claimed to have reported the incident to athletic director Tom Brennan late the next afternoon. This time, La Salle alerted the campus community of the assault four days later. The students alleged to be involved were placed on interim suspension. When the alleged victim in the April 2003 case became aware of this incident, she came forward.

In a trial the following fall, Cleaves and Neal were acquitted on all eight counts.[34] The prosecution claimed the woman was sexually assaulted while she vomited in a sink after drinking eight shots of high-proof alcohol. Neal and Cleaves claimed the sex was consensual. The jurors rejected the prosecutor's claim that the woman was too drunk to consent to sex. Defense attorneys argued the woman had made up the charges because she was embarrassed about what she had done. The Philadelphia district attorney dropped the charges against Larkai the following week. In that case, the nineteen-year-old accuser decided she did not want to go forward with the case.

Neal went on to play for Towson State (Maryland) and was the fifth-leading scorer in the nation, averaging more than twenty-eight points per game.[35] Larkai played for Bellarmine University in Kentucky. Cleaves sought reinstatement at La Salle, but was denied. He went on to substitute teach in New Jersey high schools.

In spite of La Salle being sanctioned for failing to report the crimes, Joseph Donovan, a spokesperson for the school, claimed he still believed the school was not required to alert the community in the cases in which the alleged perpetrators were placed on interim suspensions. "We are obligated to let people know if we think there is a danger to someone else. Our contention is, there was no danger to anyone else in the cases where we didn't."[36] Hahn, who had been with La Salle since 2003, resigned after the charges were announced. John Miller, who had been at La Salle for eighteen years, also resigned. Hahn initially found it difficult to get hired as a coach again, but in spring 2007 he signed on as an assistant at West Virginia University under the controversial head coach Bob Huggins.

DUKE LACROSSE PLAYERS FALSELY ACCUSED OF RAPE

Three Duke University lacrosse team members, Colin Finnerty, Reade Seligmann, and David Evans, were indicted for raping a twenty-seven-year-old black female who had been hired to strip at a party in March 2006. The story made national headlines, and the players and team were vilified. Duke cancelled their season, and the coach resigned. By the end, however, it would be the local district attorney, Michael Nifong, who would pay the price, as it became clear that the charges were false, the investigation was a sham, and the players were completely innocent.

The woman claimed three white men pulled her into a bathroom and raped her at the party. DNA tests were run on forty-seven team members. One team member was black and was thus excluded from testing. All the tests came back negative. Prosecutors threatened to press charges for aiding and abetting against the others who were present, hoping to prompt them to provide information.

The lacrosse coach, Mike Presler, who had led the team to the NCAA championship game in 2005, in his sixteenth season at Duke, was forced to resign as the media pressure on the school became suffocating. "It was mass hysteria. People prejudged us, the players, the program. Everybody rushed to judgment that this was true with absolutely no evidence."[37] The media ran with stories about the players and their prior arrests, noting that more than a dozen players had previous convictions, although most were for underage drinking. On April 5, 2006, the Duke lacrosse season was cancelled. Five days before hearing that there was no DNA match to the players, the coach was gone and the season was over.

"The laxers," as they were known in Durham, North Carolina, were young men known to be confident and among the most popular students on campus. While the incident prompted some protests, many on campus, including some females, expressed disbelief that the players sexually assaulted the woman. Rather, they relied on the age-old rape myth, "they could have any girl they wanted, so why would they need to rape anyone."[38] Supporters of the players pointed the finger at Nifong, who they believed pursued the case to endear himself with the black community as he faced reelection.

In spring 2007, after months of being vilified in spite of unwavering claims of innocence, all charges were dropped against Finnerty, Seligman, and Evans. Durham County district attorney Mike Nifong was disbarred for violating rules of professional conduct. The committee found that his handling of the case demonstrated he was not seeking justice, but trying to boost his campaign for reelection. He did not appeal the punishment and resigned in June 2007.

The NCAA granted an extra year of eligibility to the thirty-three team members whose 2006 season was cancelled. Finnerty decided to move on to Loyola College in Maryland and competes for the lacrosse team. Seligman is now enrolled at Brown, and Evans graduated last year and now works on Wall Street. Matt Danowski, who was on the team when the allegations occurred, was voted 2007 Player of the Year. In June 2007, Finnerty, Seligman, and Evans reached a settlement that eliminated the possibility that they could sue Duke University. The players received an undisclosed amount for the coverage of legal fees.

Coach Pressler believed his players all along. Despite his tremendous resume, which featured three Atlantic Coast Conference championships and ten NCAA tournament appearances, he was rejected from several other coaching positions. On August 5, 2006, Pressler was hired as head lacrosse coach at Bryant University, a small Division II school in Rhode Island.

This case was one of the most widely covered in 2006. It evoked a number of issues relevant in society, including race, social class, privilege, and criticisms of the judicial system.

Chapter 5

CHEATING, ACADEMIC FRAUD, AND BOOSTERS RUN AMOK

From copying a classmate's homework to stealing corporate secrets, people of all ages and demographics cheat with regularity. One poll found 74 percent of high school students admitted cheating in the last year.[1] This chapter includes a wide array of cheating that has occurred in sports, and is surely not indicative of the full scope of the problem. Sometimes it is one individual who violates the code of sportsmanship in his or her zeal to win, as in the case of Rosie Ruiz, who faked that she won a marathon after riding the subway for most of the race, or Sammy Sosa corking his bat to hit the baseball even farther.

Cheating transcends the individual athletes, however. It often involves the exact people we entrust with the job of maintaining the integrity of sports, such as coaches, managers, and league or school officials. Illegal recruiting, payments to players, stealing other teams' signs to gain an advantage in baseball and football, and other examples clearly demonstrate that the stink rises to the top far too frequently. Unlike many other sports scandals, which are sometimes treated more lightly than if the same incident occurs outside of sport, the cheating that occurs in sports is often handled with severe punishment to dissuade others from trying to beat the system. Perhaps this is because the incidents are generally not violations of criminal law, but rather violate team, school, or league regulations. In a particularly egregious case involving Southern Methodist University football, a team received the NCAA "death penalty," which set the standard for how significantly a program can be debilitated for trying to cheat to win.

ACADEMIC CHEATING SHOCKS WEST POINT, 1951

Earl "Red" Blaik was hired in 1941 to coach football at West Point. Prior to his hiring, the coach of the Army football team was always a career officer that was assigned to the team for a tour of duty. While Blaik was a former star football player for Army, he had resigned his commission in the early 1920s.

Douglas MacArthur was so impressed with Blaik that he wanted Blaik to be his "aide-de-camp" in the Philippines, but Blaik had already resigned and gone into coaching, so MacArthur selected another Army football player, Dwight Eisenhower. Blaik was coaching at Dartmouth when Army enticed him to return to West Point. Blaik built Army into a national powerhouse because he was allowed to bring in a professional staff. Twenty of his assistants went on to be head coaches, including Vince Lombardi. Blaik became the athletic director and implemented a successful recruiting system. Between 1944 and 1950, the Army Cadets had amassed a record of fifty-seven wins, four ties and only three losses, and had won or shared the national championship twice. They were one game away from winning a third national championship in 1950 before suffering a loss to Navy in the final game. Al Pollard was a stand-out fullback, and going into the 1951 season Army saw him as its next Heisman Trophy candidate. The "Black Knights" (a nickname given to Blaik's football teams) were set to make another run at the national championship.

It all ended in August 1951 when an investigation revealed massive cheating by cadets. Once it was concluded, ninety cadets resigned from the academy, thirty-seven of them football players, because they broke the honor code.[2] The honor code was simple: "A cadet will not lie, cheat or steal or tolerate those who do." Members of Congress voiced their differing opinions, with Senator Fulbright of Arkansas wanting football at West Point suspended, whereas Congressman Potter of Michigan saw the ninety cadets as "victims of athletic commercialism."[3] The system that opened the door for rampant cheating was created in 1947 when enrollment grew to over 2,500 students and cadets were split between two regiments. The school wanted to give each student the same tests, so one regiment would take the test first and then the other regiment would take the test later. This allowed for cribbing, the process of passing along questions or answers, because while the regiments were kept apart most of the time, athletics was one area that brought cadets from both regiments together frequently. When questioned, most cadets involved with the cheating scandal admitted their own guilt, but refused to name other cadets. In the end, for the most part, the only evidence against a cadet was his own admission.

The emphasis on both school and football created a system where upper-class tutors were extensively used. For example, Pollard needed so much help in math he was not allowed to practice until Thursday each week because he needed to spend time with a tutor. He said, "If I hadn't received help I would've flunked out."[4] Bob Blaik, the son of Coach Blaik, was on the football team at West Point, and even though he was an "A" student and ranked sixth in his class, he too was caught up in the cheating scandal because he helped out fellow athletes.

After losing thirty-seven players including a Heisman hopeful and his own son, Coach Blaik was set to resign. He was convinced to stay by MacArthur who, during a two-hour meeting, admonished him not to leave under fire. Blaik continued as Army's coach until 1959, leaving after eighteen years with a record of 121–32–10. Al Pollard went straight into the NFL, while other players enrolled in other universities. Gil Reich, another great player involved in the cheating scandal, enrolled at the University of Kansas and became both an All-American football player and a guard for the basketball team that lost by one point in the 1953 NCAA finals. Reich was drafted by both the Green Bay Packers and the Boston Celtics, but turned them both down and went into the Air Force. After one of the largest single team scandals of all time, Army football was never the same, and the days of Army competing for a national championship have long since passed. Especially significant is the fact that West Point is held up as a bastion of ethics and good character.

THE GIANTS STEAL SIGNS TO WIN 1951 PENNANT RACE

On October 13, 1951, Bobby Thomson of the New York Giants hit one of Major League Baseball's most famous home runs. It was a three-run blast that has been baseball's most replayed moment, memorable for announcer Russ Hodges screaming, "The Giants win the pennant! The Giants win the pennant!" as Thomson rounded the bases. The ninth-inning home run gave the Giants a 5–4 win in the deciding third game of the pennant tiebreaker against the Brooklyn Dodgers. It would be forever known as, "The shot heard 'round the world."

Dodgers' pitcher Ralph Branca would be branded as the guy who gave up the monumental blast. As he watched it head for the outfield fence, he muttered, "Sink! Sink! Sink!"[5] It didn't. Thomson was carried off the field by ecstatic teammates. Footage of the aftermath shows Branca lying on the clubhouse floor, almost lifeless.

The shot concluded baseball's most memorable pennant race. The Giants had trailed the Dodgers by thirteen-and-a-half games on August 11 and closed the gap at a torrid pace. The teams finished with identical records, and the representative to the World Series was determined by a playoff. The first two games were split, allowing Thomson to etch his name into baseball lore with his clutch hit in the deciding game. The Associated Press carried a story in 1962, citing an unnamed source with the Giants, suggesting the Giants' comeback had been aided by stealing the signs that catchers give to pitchers to indicate the pitch they want thrown. That information would then be signaled to the batters, indicating whether they were going to see a fastball or a breaking ball. The story was not accepted as fact for almost half a century.

In January 2000 *Wall Street Journal* writer Joshua Harris Prager officially broke the story. Giants players Monte Irvin, Sal Yvars, and Al Gettel confirmed that the team stole signs. Coach Herman Franks was positioned in the clubhouse above the bleachers and used a military field scope to spot the hand signals delivered by the catchers. He relayed the information to the bullpen with a buzzer system. Backup catcher Sal Yvars then signaled the batters. After beginning to steal signs in late July, the Giants won twenty-three of twenty-eight home games, which, combined with a 29–13 road record over the same stretch, enabled them to close the gap that had seemed insurmountable at mid-season. Yvars, apparently proud of the team's ingenuity, said, "People are always thinking about us getting signs in the Polo Grounds [the Giants' home field]. We were stealing signs on the road. No one writes about that. We were thinking all the time."[6]

Branca reacted to the story by saying, "I've lived with this the last 50 years … I think that's despicable." He continued, "If you steal the signs on the field, that's fine. That's part of the game. But to go off the field, if you have access to something and nobody knows about it, I don't like that very much."[7] Branca had heard that the Giants might have been stealing signs, but never talked about it. "It would have tarnished Bobby's accomplishment, and I didn't want to do that. He still hit the ball. He still hit a home run. I don't want to be a crybaby."[8] Thomson, perhaps protecting his own legacy, claimed that he did not have any information in advance of that fateful pitch. Branca doesn't believe him; referring to the replay he said, "He's like a lion jumping on top of a wounded antelope."[9] Thomson did show compassion for Branca saying, "Years later, now this comes out, maybe this will take some of the pressure he's felt all these years."[10] Both players say they had become very good friends in the years after they were joined by fate, but the confirmation that the Giants had cheated strained the relationship.

After Harris Prager broke the story, baseball historians explored the statistics from the 1951 season to determine how much the sign-stealing scheme helped the Giants. The results were surprising. The Giants actually batted worse at home after they began cheating. The real change in the team that led to the late-season surge was that the team hit better on the road and the pitching was much more effective.[11] Of course, this does not mean that the cheating didn't matter. It is possible the team would have slumped even worse without being able to anticipate pitches. Further, if the scheme helped the team win even one more game, it was enough to get it into a three-game playoff with the Dodgers.

The New York Giants certainly are not the only team in Major League Baseball to steal signs. In 1900 the Philadelphia Phillies stole signs to help post a home record of 45–23, as compared to a dismal 30–40 on the road. The 1940 Detroit Tigers placed sign-stealers in the outfield bleachers, armed with binoculars and a signaling system to tip the batters.[12] The Tigers beat the Cleveland Indians by one game to claim the American League pennant. There have likely been many other sign-stealing conspiracies through the years. It is doubtful, however, that any other ever led to a moment as important to baseball lore as the shot heard 'round the world.

ROSIE RUIZ NEARLY STEALS 1980 BOSTON MARATHON

Sometimes long shots do win races. Perhaps even a major marathon, from time to time. But when twenty-seven-year-old office worker Rosie Ruiz broke the tape at the 1980 Boston Marathon, it appeared to be a result for the ages. She was a complete unknown in marathon running, and her victory would be among the most stunning in sports history. But within days it was revealed to be one of sport's greatest hoaxes. Ruiz had apparently covered the 26.2 mile course in the third fastest time ever by a woman in any marathon, 2 hours, 31 minutes, and 56 seconds. She had broken the Boston Marathon record and beaten 448 other female entrants. And apparently she had hardly broken a sweat. She calmly mounted the victors' platform, alongside men's winner Bill Rodgers, and accepted the medal and laurel wreath. Then, the questioning began.

Immediately there were spectators, competitors, and journalists who were suspicious. She wasn't sweaty or salty enough. She wasn't lean enough. Her running stride was not efficient enough. Her name and race number did not appear on the lists of leaders that were meticulously written down through the first twenty-four miles. And, perhaps most importantly in the moments after the race, she didn't speak the language of the sport. Post-race interviews revealed that she didn't understand common terms used by runners to define simple training principles. She didn't know what *intervals* or *split times* were, which shocked the journalist asking about her training program.

Canadian Jacqueline Gareau was the second woman across the line that day, over ten minutes behind Ruiz. She believed she was the winner when she arrived at the finish. She was followed by her rival, American Patti Lyons. It was Lyons who first voiced doubts: "I never saw [Ruiz]. Do I doubt that she was the winner? I doubt it very much."[13] Further, Lyons added, "Her name wasn't familiar. I never heard of her. I heard I was second all the way. I never saw her at the starting line and we all started together."[14] Bill Rodgers, who won his fourth Boston marathon that day, sadly lost some of his well-deserved attention as the scandal dominated headlines in the following days. His position was immediate and emphatic: "The second I saw her I was skeptical. I know a top runner when I see one."[15]

By the following day, there was blood in the water and the sharks were circling. The race officials could not find any sign that Ruiz had run the race. She didn't appear on the tapes made of the leaders (none of whom remembered seeing her on the course), and eyewitnesses claimed they saw her jump into the race no more than two miles from the finish. Race director Will Cloney was convinced she had cheated. At one point he asked Ruiz, "Should we decide to change the order of finish, would you give the medal back?" She responded, "Would you ask one of your daughters that?" His curt retort was, "No, I wouldn't have to ask one of my daughters that."[16] After eight long days of investigating, the Boston Athletic Association declared Ruiz was a cheat and stripped her of the title. Cloney extended Ruiz an invitation to run in the 1981 Boston Marathon, believing that the result would clear up any questions about her ability as a marathoner. Not surprisingly, she declined.

The controversy surrounding Ruiz's finish raised questions about how she had qualified for the Boston Marathon and her overall pedigree as a runner. Doubts were soon cast on her qualifying performance at the 1979 New York City Marathon, where she had recorded an outstanding finishing time of 2 hours, 56 minutes. As New York City Marathon officials launched an investigation, they quickly found a woman who rode the subway with Ruiz for what would have been the last seventeen miles of the race. Ruiz's result was immediately invalidated.

Ruiz was still defiant almost twenty years later. In an interview for a West Palm Beach paper in 1998, she said she intended to qualify for and run in Boston again. Race director Guy Morse made it clear that she would do no such thing, saying, "We have a policy that anyone who's been disqualified is not invited back for life."[17] Ruiz also intimated in the interview that she still knew she had run the whole marathon and that she still had the winner's medal hidden away.

In 2005 Jacqueline Gareau was granted a chance to enjoy the cheers at Boston that had been stolen from her twenty-five years before. She was asked to serve as the grand marshal for the event. She said, "It was a special feeling out there. I really enjoyed being able to be out there in Hopkinton (the starting point) and soak up the crowd. The way they cheered for me gave me goose bumps."[18] After watching most of the race from a Mercedes, Gareau jumped out and ran the last one hundred meters of the race. She commented, "It was kind of funny they let me run from there, because I was thinking that's what [Ruiz] did."[19]

The life of Rosie Ruiz was rather unfortunate, both before and after the Boston Marathon scandal. In 1973, at the age of twenty, she had a series of blackouts and underwent surgery to remove a tumor from her head. Five years later, a plastic plate was inserted into her head. There has been speculation that these surgeries could be linked to her odd behavior, both in cheating at the marathon and in her firm denial that she did so. Two years after the Boston incident, she was jailed for stealing $60,000 from her employer, a Manhattan real estate company. She returned to Florida, where she would do more jail time, after selling cocaine to undercover agents in a Miami hotel.[20]

Steve Vaitones, the head referee for the 2007 Boston Marathon, commented that people cheat for a variety of reasons. He believed some are trying to meet or exceed personal goals that are out of reach due to insufficient training, or that "they want to finish further up because they are the best runners in their neighborhood and have built a legend unto themselves."[21] Many have speculated that Ruiz never intended to cheat her way into a Boston victory.

Her coworkers had celebrated her "accomplishment" in New York, and her boss offered to pay her way to compete in Boston. She may have just been trying to get a finishing time to justify his expenditure and accidentally jumped into the race too early, not even aware that she was ahead of the top women. Then, as the theory goes, she did not know how to react when she was ushered to the victor's podium, so she just played along.

Some people felt bad for Ruiz at the time. They believed that she didn't mean to win and that she was too scared and embarrassed to tell the truth. These feelings waned as she maintained her innocence. Fred Lebow, the popular director of the New York Roadrunners Club, said in 1981, "I did feel sorry for her when she initially cheated. But when she perpetuated it, I no longer felt sorry. I felt angry."[22] Similarly, a Manhattan lawyer ran in the 1980 New York City Marathon in a shirt that read, "Rosie Ruiz Track Club," with a picture of a subway token on it. When asked if he felt it defamed Ruiz, he answered, "If one doesn't want notoriety, one should not fake marathon races."[23]

Cheating in a major marathon today would be far more difficult than in 1980. Race directors have seen to that through the introduction of new technology that monitors the runners' progress along the course. Also, staggered start times that separate the known contenders from the throng of slower runners make it easier to watch the favorites. Through the use of video cameras stationed frequently along the course, and wire-to-wire media coverage, there is a better record of the events. Computer chip technology made its way into major marathons in the mid 1990s, with products such as ChampionChip offering the means to track each runner via a small disk tied into the shoelaces.[24] At regular checkpoints the runners cross a small mat placed across the road that records their presence. Each chip sends a signal unique to each participant. The Boston Marathon catches about fifteen to twenty cheaters per year with this technology. For the participants, the chips offer the feature of recorded split times, so they can analyze a race to determine how well they paced themselves. Prior to the chip, accurate splits were only offered to top runners. Further, chips show how long it takes the runners to actually cover the course, from start to finish— discounting the time it takes to actually get to the starting line, which can be several minutes in major-city marathons with tens of thousands of participants. When chips debuted in a U.S. marathon, at the 1996 Los Angeles race, William Burke, the L.A. Marathon president commented, "It will be difficult for anyone to pull a Rosie Ruiz in Los Angeles."[25] Although surely Ruiz's scandal was not the only impetus for the creation of the chip, it definitely was a factor.

SOUTHERN METHODIST UNIVERSITY FOOTBALL GIVEN DEATH PENALTY

During the early 1980s Southern Methodist University (SMU) had one of the top football programs in the country. SMU compiled a record of 41–5–1 for 1981–84 that included three Southwest Conference championships. The now defunct Southwest Conference included Arkansas, Baylor, Houston, Rice, SMU, Texas, Texas A&M, Texas Christian University, and Texas Tech during this time. In 1981 SMU went 10–1, but was unable to play in the Cotton Bowl because it had been placed on two years of probation prior to the 1981 season for committing twenty-nine recruiting violations. In 1982 head football coach Ron Meyer left SMU to become the head coach of the New England Patriots and was replaced by Bobby Collins (formerly of Southern Mississippi). SMU's football program continued its dominance as the "Pony Express" of Eric Dickerson and Craig James ran over their opposition. Eric Dickerson broke the Southwest Conference all-time rushing record in 1982 and led SMU to an 11–0–1 record and a final ranking of second in the nation after defeating Pittsburgh in the Cotton Bowl. SMU continued its strong play on the field during the 1983 and 1984 seasons, culminating with a loss to Alabama in the 1983 Sun Bowl and a victory over Notre Dame in the 1984 Aloha Bowl.

On August 16, 1985, the NCAA again placed SMU's football program on probation due to major NCAA violations including cash payments to players. The probation included a ban on bowl games for both the 1985 and 1986 seasons, a ban from televised games in 1986 and 1987, and a reduction in scholarships.

The following year, linebacker David Stanley revealed in a television interview that he was paid $25,000 to sign with SMU in 1983. Stanley also acknowledged that SMU's athletic department made monthly payments to his mother and himself totaling $750, and that the payments continued after SMU was placed on probation by the NCAA in 1985. Two days after the Stanley interview, tight end Albert Reese was suspended pending an investigation into allegations that he was living rent free in an apartment provided by a booster. As the NCAA investigated the new allegations, Southern Methodist University saw its president, athletic director, and the head football coach all resign between November 21 and December 4, 1986. The investigation found monthly payments totaling $61,000 went to thirteen players; the money was provided by a booster who was listed in the 1985 probation as one of several boosters who were not allowed to associate with SMU athletics because of previous payments to athletes that lead to the 1985 probation.[26]

On February 25, 1987, the NCAA handed down the most severe penalty ever for a football program. Southern Methodist University received the so-called "death penalty" for major violations by the coaching and athletic department staffs, which included cash payments to football players while the program was still on probation for previous infractions. The penalty included: the complete cancellation of the 1987 football season; limiting the 1988 season to seven conference road games; the team could not appear on television or in bowl games until 1989; the football team could only have five assistant coaches; and SMU could sign only fifteen scholarship players each year for three years.[27] This is the harshest punishment any football program has ever received to date. Two years prior to the suspension of the SMU football program, the NCAA had passed Proposition 3 at a special convention in Dallas. Proposition 3 allows the NCAA to "suspend a program for up to two seasons if they commit a second major rules violation in a five-year period."[28] The university presidents, who were eager to show that they had control over college sports, passed it by the wide margin of 427–6. SMU was one of the six schools that voted against Proposition 3.

The NCAA allowed the fifty-two scholarship football players from SMU to transfer to other schools without having to sit out a year. This started a chain reaction that saw over 250 college coaches visit SMU over a two-day period in an effort to recruit the SMU players. SMU decided not to field a team in 1988. The loss of two years of football cost SMU around $20 million. The financial impact also immediately impacted contributions to the university totaling $1.5 million less than the prior year, and enrollment figures for incoming freshmen classes dropped.

The fallout from the player-payment scandal did not stop with the players, coaches, and athletic administrators. An investigation revealed that the SMU Board of Governors approved the payments, including Bill Clement, who was then governor-elect of Texas and chairman of the SMU Board of Governors. On March 20, 1987, the SMU Board of Trustees abolished the board of governors, and on June 19 an investigative report by the United Methodist Church's College of Bishops contended that hush money was paid to the athletic director, head coach, and an assistant coach, including a payment of $556,272 to head coach Bobby Collins.[29]

Since the NCAA handed down the death penalty, the football program at SMU has never recovered. Former University of Florida president John Lombardi said, "SMU taught the committee that the death penalty is too much like the nuclear bomb, it's like what happened after we dropped the bomb in World War II. The results were so catastrophic that now we'll do anything to avoid dropping another one."[30] The NCAA has caught other institutions committing rules violations while already on probation, similar to the transgressions at SMU, but has handed down less severe punishments since the 1987 application of the death penalty.

MICHIGAN BASKETBALL PLAYERS TAKE BOOSTER'S MONEY

When Chris Webber, Jalen Rose, Juwan Howard, Jimmy King, and Ray Jackson arrived on the campus of the University of Michigan in fall 1991, they were unlike anything college basketball had ever seen. They were young, talented, and brash. Immediately dubbed the Fab Five, the freshmen superstars took the basketball world by storm with their baggy shorts and high-flying style of play that kids loved and traditionalists despised. They were pioneers in the sense that they dared to bring playground style and antics into the biggest arenas, strutting their way to glory regardless of who disapproved.

Over the course of two seasons, the Fab Five cemented their place in history with an unrelenting style that was part thuggery and part boyish charm, balancing pure athleticism with trash-talking tomfoolery. The Wolverines, with their all-freshmen lineup, won twenty-five games in 1991–92 before losing to an experienced Duke team in the NCAA Finals. They returned to the finals after improving to thirty-one wins the following year, but lost to North Carolina in a game famous for Chris Webber calling timeout when his team did not have any timeouts remaining. In spite of the losses in the NCAA Finals, sales of university merchandise spiked as young fans emulated the new-era stars.

The glory of the Fab Five era would be short-lived. In 1999 it was discovered that Webber, the shiniest star and on-court leader of the team, had been receiving payments from a booster, in clear violation of NCAA rules. Three other players from the post-Fab Five era had also taken money from booster Ed Martin. The payments came to light after the FBI raided several homes in the Detroit area that were connected to a gambling ring that was operating in the Ford motor plants. In Martin's home the investigators found evidence that he had been supplying large amounts of cash to local basketball stars. Martin testified that he had given $616,000 to Wolverines basketball players. Of the Fab Five, only Webber received money, totaling $280,000 and spanning his high school and college years, according to Martin. Martin also testified that he paid $160,000 to Robert Traylor, $105,000 to Maurice Taylor, and $71,000 to Louis Bullock. Martin pleaded guilty to money laundering to conceal profits and avoid taxes and said he expected the payments to gain him favor with the team.[31]

In October 1997 the University of Michigan fired Steve Fisher, who had coached the team through the years that Martin was paying the players. After a seven-month internal investigation, the university concluded that minor violations had occurred under his watch and that the program lacked institutional control. The violations included the coach being at the home of a recruit at the same time that Martin was there in the capacity of a booster. At the conclusion of the NCAA's investigation in 2003, it announced that there was not sufficient evidence against the coach to seek punishment. Fisher went on to coach at San Diego State University.

On November 2, 2002, the University of Michigan announced its self-imposed sanctions. The university submitted a letter to the NCAA that said the men's basketball program would be ineligible for postseason play in 2003, would serve probation for two years, would forfeit all victories from the 1992–93 and 1995 to 1999 seasons, and remove banners from the two Final Four appearances, a National Invitation Tournament banner from 1997, and a

Big Ten Conference Tournament Champions banner from 1998. Michigan also returned $450,000 to the NCAA for money earned for NCAA tournament appearances. The NCAA then applied further sanctions, including that the university could not associate with the players involved for ten years.

Webber initially maintained that he had never received money from Martin and testified that was the case before a federal grand jury. He and his father and aunt were all indicted in 2002 for perjury and obstruction of justice for lying about the money and gifts they received from Martin. The federal case was dealt a blow when Martin died in February 2003. Charges against Webber's father and aunt were dropped when prosecutors said they could not sustain them without Martin's testimony. Facing a trial and possibly from three to ten years in prison if convicted, Webber pleaded guilty in July 2003 to criminal contempt for lying to a federal grand jury. He was sentenced to 300 hours of community service, which he fulfilled by reading to children, and a $100,000 fine.[32] Prosecutors had agreed that incarceration was not appropriate in the case and sought a sizable fine instead. Webber was also suspended for three games by the NBA.

In light of Webber's guilty plea, which included admitting to receiving money while in high school at Detroit Country Day, the Michigan High School Athletic Association asked the school to forfeit all of its games in which Webber had played, including state championships in 1989, 1990, and 1991. School administrators at Country Day said that they would not give back the state titles or the trophies.

In an interview with the Associated Press, Webber said of the Fab Five, "You can't think of Michigan without thinking about us."[33] While that is true, it does not reflect what many think about him and the shame he heaped upon the school. Tom Yeager, speaking on behalf of the NCAA, said of the scandal, "This is one of the most egregious violations of NCAA laws in the history of the organization. In fact, the reputation of the university, the student-athletes and the coach as a result of the basketball team's accomplishments from 1992 through 1998 were a sham."[34] Webber's teammate, Jalen Rose, claimed that the removal of banners and wiping victories from the books would not change whether the team would be remembered. "The one thing about being famous is people forget about you. One thing about infamy, people have to remember you," he said. "And because of that, at the end of the day, what we brought to the game can never be taken away. So we'll never be forgotten."[35]

ZAMBOANGA CITY STEALS 1992 LITTLE LEAGUE WORLD SERIES

In 1992 a Little League baseball team representing Zamboanga City, Philippines, claimed the forty-sixth Little League World Series title with a 15–4 win over Long Beach, California, in the final played in Williamsport,

Pennsylvania. Shamefully, Zamboanga's victory would be short-lived, as a Filipino newspaper revealed that the team was loaded with ineligible players.

Following up on the stories printed in the Philippines, Little League officials determined that eight of the players, beginning during the Far East Regional Series, had been recruited from around the country and put in place of the players who had won at the national level. Some of the replacement players, coming from as far as 700 miles away, did not even speak the most common language spoken in Zamboanga. Little League rules stipulate that all players must have competed in the Little League for the district they represent. To make matters worse, the *Philippine Daily Inquirer* reported that the six players who were truly from Zamboanga were all over-aged imposters, with two of them being fifteen-year-old sophomores in high school. The age limit for Little League participation is twelve. The over-age players adopted the identities of younger players, including cousins and younger brothers. Even their parents joined in the charade. They pretended to be the parents of the players their sons pretended to be.

Eduardo Toribio, who had coached the team to victory in the National Baseball Open, claimed that Manila officials reneged on an agreement that the winner of that tournament would represent the country in the Far East leg of the World Series. He said that the Philippine Sports Commission handpicked the replacement players and, eventually, pushed him out as coach just prior to the championship game. According to Toribio, by the time the team arrived for the final, not even the coaches were from Zamboanga City.

The day after the final game was ruled to be a forfeit, giving the title to Long Beach, California, the top Little League official in the Philippines, Armando Andaya, resigned in protest. He claimed the replacements were made for "justifiable reasons," but failed to elaborate. He maintained that all the players were eleven and twelve years old.[36]

In spite of the scandal, the directors of Little League baseball declined to impose restrictions on teams from the Philippines in the future. According to Luke LaPorta, then the Little League chairman, all teams have to apply for a new charter each year and there would be no restrictions on Filipino teams. He said, "The program is for kids and they didn't do it."[37] The significance of this case is that cheating in sports is so pervasive it has even impacted youth sports. Additionally, the case highlights some of the problems when adults get too involved in activities that are designed for youth.

THE THEFT OF ALBERT BELLE'S CORKED BAT

Albert Belle was having a terrific season in 1994, ultimately posting an outstanding .357 batting average and losing the Major League's batting title by only the narrowest of margins (to Paul O'Neill's .359). His season, however, took a brief setback when he was caught with a corked bat. A teammate then stole the bat out of the umpires' dressing room in a daring scheme worthy of an episode of *Mission Impossible*.

The scandal began when Belle and his Cleveland Indians team was on the road to play the Chicago White Sox. Gene Lamont, the White Sox manager, asked the umpires to confiscate Belle's bat because he suspected it was corked (a process that fills the interior of the bat with cork, which produces more powerful hits of the ball). The umpires complied and locked the bat away in their locker room. During the game the bat was stolen and replaced with another.

Teammate Jason Grimsley would later admit to being the man with sufficient moxie to infiltrate the umpires' locker room to retrieve the bat, which he knew was corked. His plan began with a ground-level survey of the many offices in Comiskey Park, from which he drew a mental blueprint of the facility. He then climbed into the ductwork above the ceiling of the visitor's locker room, flashlight in hand, and made his way through the three-foot-high crawl space. His plan almost ended prematurely when, thinking he was above the umpires' dressing room, he lifted a ceiling tile to find he was above the groundskeepers' room and the groundskeepers were in it! Finding the correct room, he lowered himself down and switched bats.

Unfortunately for the Indians, the switch did not go undetected. Umpire Dave Phillips had photographed the bat prior to locking it away, and he was not amused. He called a press conference the next day to announce the theft of the bat and to demand its immediate return. Security officials even dusted the room for fingerprints and, in the course of their investigation, found the flashlight that Grimsley had left behind.[38] The Indians' management handed over a bat they claimed was Belle's, but further review of the photographs revealed that, this too, was an imposter. Finally, Belle's bat was given back to be inspected. The bat was sawed in half, revealing that it contained an insert of cork. Belle was initially suspended for ten games. The suspension was appealed and reduced to seven games over a six-day period.

LaMont's questioning of Belle's bat begged the question: How did the White Sox know that the bat was corked? The Cleveland Indians claimed that the White Sox used an X-ray machine to scan all of the Indians' bats after the equipment truck dropped them off at Comiskey Park. The White Sox denied that was the case. LaMont simply claimed, "We heard some things."[39]

One possible source for the "things" that LaMont heard could have been pitcher Steve Farr, who had pitched for Cleveland earlier in that same season before moving on to Boston. He told the *Los Angeles Times*, "They had a private woodworking shop in Cleveland. So what happened with Belle didn't surprise me. That stuff had been going on since I was with Cleveland ten years ago. I mean, just a few weeks ago [when Farr was with Cleveland], a guy grabbed someone's bat during batting practice and when his bat broke, cork went everywhere. And that was right in front of the visiting manager."[40] An

American League source later claimed that there was no secret informant, and that Belle gave himself away when he was overheard discussing his secret in the clubhouse at the All-Star Game at Three Rivers Stadium.

Although the White Sox claimed that there was no use of an X-ray machine in this case, using one to examine the competitors' bats is not without precedent. Whitey Herzog, former manager of the St. Louis Cardinals, admitted that his team did exactly that to the visiting New York Mets in 1987. According to Herzog, "We had an X-ray machine at Busch Stadium. When the Mets came into town, we decided to check their bats. We found four of those SOBs using corked bats."[41]

Herzog believed corked bats were rampant in Major League Baseball in that era. He said, "If they really want to stop all this crap, they should have a scanner by the bat rack. I'm telling you, if you checked everybody in baseball, you'd have a whole room full of corked bats. Believe me, the way the ball is flying out this year, you'd be stupid not to check some of these guys. This has been going on for years, but everybody has been talking so much about the ball being juiced, they forget some of these bats are juiced too."[42]

Ironically, Belle found himself in a White Sox uniform only a few years later. After inking a five-year, $52.5 million deal with the team, he was asked about the incident. He replied, "A situation occurred at the end of the season where I think I bumped my head and had amnesia."[43] Beyond the fact that the case demonstrates the asinine activities in which some will partake to win a game, it also is indicative of what went on to be a major issue in baseball—corking of bats.

FSU—FREE SHOES UNIVERSITY

For Florida State University (FSU), a trip to Foot Locker enjoyed by several football players would prove to be more expensive than the players imagined. In summer 1994 *Sports Illustrated* broke the story that agents were trying to secure their relationships with FSU players by offering incentives in the form of cash and gifts, which included a $6,000 trip to Foot Locker for shoes, sweat suits, and sportswear. Raul Bey, a Las Vegas sports agent, flipped the bill for the trip that was also arranged by Paul Williams, a former Tallahassee high school football coach, and Nate Cebrun, also a Las Vegas sports agent.

For seven months, at a cost to FSU of $400,000, outside investigators hired by the university queried how exactly it was that FSU players were receiving such handsome treatment from boosters and would-be agents and exactly who knew what and when. The finding was that in 1993 FSU players violated myriad NCAA regulations by pocketing cash and gifts, but that the coaching staff and school officials committed no wrongdoing. The final report, however, did claim that the problems could have been averted had FSU officials maintained greater oversight. The report claimed, "FSU's coaches and athletics administrators must learn from this case and must make themselves even more sensitive than they were to even the most remote signs or vague rumors of agent activity in and around their program."[44] The investigators refuted the claim made by *Sports Illustrated* that FSU compliance officer Brian Mand was informed of the shopping spree soon after it took place. Just as importantly, the report exonerated linebacker coach Jim Gladden who had been directly implicated as a person with knowledge of the gifts by a former FSU player.

The investigation revealed other illicit benefits to FSU football players, including the offer of free housing from Rick Blankenship, a 1971 graduate and booster. Blankenship was banished from the boosters club by the FSU president. He commented, "I understand President D'Alemberte's position. He has a responsibility to comply with NCAA rules and regulations. Our objectives are the same. We cannot take the same path to them, however."[45]

To lighten, and perhaps avoid altogether, possible NCAA sanctions, FSU punished itself by suspending the offending players from some early season games during the 1994 campaign. In spite of suspending the players, FSU, the defending national champions and a perennial power in the early 1990s, won its first four games by an average score of 45–17. The suspensions, while having no effect on the games, kept FSU in the good graces of the NCAA, which would allow the school to emerge from the scandal essentially unscathed. Virtually the only meaningful punishment for FSU was enduring a few years of recruiting during which prospects wondered if the program would be sanctioned, perhaps through the loss of the right to participate in a bowl game.

Several men were arrested in relation to the activities on the FSU campus. Each was charged with violation of the state's agent registration law. Acting as an agent without registering was a third-degree felony punishable by a maximum of five years in prison. Sentences, however, were light and included a few weeks in jail, probation, and small monetary fines.

The incident would prove to be powerful fuel to the fire of the historic rivalry between Florida State University and the University of Florida. Speaking at the Polk County Gator Club in 1994, Florida head football coach Steve Spurrier asked the crowd of Gators fans, "You know what FSU stands for, don't you? Free Shoes University." Spurrier was entering his fifth season coaching the Gators, and national publications had ranked his team lower in the annual recruiting battle with FSU in four of the five seasons. Asked to explain his comments the next day, he didn't back off: "We've always heard rumors about them. We've always suspected," Spurrier said. "Heck, maybe they're the greatest recruiters in the world. But maybe there are other reasons that those guys go there. Those guys always say they feel 'more comfortable' going to FSU. Well, maybe we're starting to realize what 'more comfortable' means."[46] By the beginning of practice for the 1994 season, Spurrier was prepared to roll out a new joke: "It used to be that I was the most hated Gator in Tallahassee. Now it's the investi-gator!"[47] Florida State coach Bobby Bowden responded,

"The shoes were free, but we've paid a heckuva price for it. So Steve's halfway right."[48]

THE RECRUITMENT OF ALBERT MEANS

As a high school football player, Albert Means was among the best. Several publications called him the best defensive lineman in the country in 1999. He was named to the All-America teams by *Parade*, *SuperPrep*, and *USA Today*. He was strong, fast, and big, at six-foot-four and 340 pounds. He was also for sale to the highest bidder, as his high school coach betrayed his trust and auctioned him off to the college that was willing to pay the most for his services. In the end, the going rate for the superstar player would be $200,000—and an Alabama booster was willing to pay.

Means was a coach's dream: a once-in-a-lifetime defensive blue chipper. He was the kind of player that could ensure job security for a college coach. Thus, the bidding for Albert Means began in 1999 when he and his mother turned over the responsibility of choosing the college Means would attend to his high school coach, Lynn Lang. Unbeknownst to Means, Lang immediately saw dollar signs and pursued them. He asked a University of Tennessee coach for two vehicles, $50,000 to $75,000 in cash, and a house in exchange for persuading Means to become a Volunteer. Lang then successfully played several universities against each other. A University of Alabama assistant coach reportedly referred Lang to a prominent and wealthy booster, Logan Young, the former owner of the United States Football League's Memphis Showboats. It was through Young that the payments, which were to total $200,000, began. Young worked through a middleman to deliver money to the coach, and, just like that, Means had been sold to the Crimson Tide.

Ultimately, Lang's greed was his downfall. While he would drive to practice in his $37,000 Ford Explorer (Eddie Bauer model) and brag about the size of his score, he cut his assistant coach, Milton Kirk, out of the deal. Kirk would later blow the whistle. He claimed he did it not out of vindictiveness, but out of concern for Means. "Here's a kid that had done everything we asked him to do and then here's a grown person who's going to take advantage of a kid who's already coming from a disadvantaged situation. I couldn't live with that," Kirk said.[49] There was no question, however, that Kirk intended to gain financially from the scheme and blew the whistle when it was clear that Lang was putting him off.

In the fallout that followed, the NCAA placed the University of Alabama on probation for five years, which included the loss of twenty-one football scholarships over three years, and a two-year ban from bowl appearances. Lang pleaded guilty to racketeering conspiracy for accepting a total of $150,000 and cooperated with prosecutors in the case against booster Logan Young.[50] During Lang's testimony, he indicated that eight schools offered to buy

Means's services, including Memphis, Tennessee, Arkansas, Mississippi, and Michigan State. Three schools (Alabama, Georgia, and Kentucky) actually handed out money. Lang also testified that Means had never passed the ACT that made him eligible to play at Alabama. Rather, an imposter had taken the test under his name. Lang was sentenced to two years probation and 500 hours of community service. Similarly, Kirk entered a guilty plea to a conspiracy charge and was sentenced to three years probation and 200 hours of community service.

Logan Young was convicted in February 2005 on charges of conspiracy to commit racketeering, crossing state lines to commit racketeering, and arranging bank withdrawals to cover up a crime. He was sentenced to six months in prison, followed by six months of home confinement. He was free pending an appeal when he died at home in 2006, just over a year after being convicted. Many speculated, and media outlets even reported, that he had been murdered, possibly in connection to the scandal. Those stories were false. Investigators determined that he died from a fall down the stairs, during which he struck his head on an iron railing. As he stumbled around the house, he left a terrible and bloody scene that led to the early speculation of foul play.

The Albert Means recruiting scandal was important in that it brought to light that top high school prospects truly can be bought, which many had suspected. Further, as one sports columnist suggested, it begged the question, "If schools have become that aggressive when it comes to a lineman such as Means, what must they be doing to acquire star quarterbacks, running backs and receivers?"[51]

Means transferred after one season at Alabama to the University of Memphis and was immediately eligible to play. The NCAA waived the normal one-year residency requirement that would have forced Means to sit out a year. NCAA spokesman Wally Renfro said the NCAA's Administrative Review Subcommittee reviewed the case and considered what was best for the player in light of the fact that he knew nothing of the payments that Lang had received. Means missed one season at Memphis due to academic issues, but returned to complete his eligibility. He was not drafted to play in the National Football League.

TENNESSEE FOOTBALL ACADEMIC FRAUD ACCUSATIONS

In late September 1999 ESPN.com reported on incidents of possible academic fraud by athletes and their tutors at the University of Tennessee (UT). The scandal was particularly damaging given that it came on the tail of one of the football program's greatest moments—claiming the 1998 national title. ESPN.com reported that academic programs coordinator Robin Wright informed tutor program supervisor Gerald Dickey and associate athletic director Carmen Tegano about several plagiarism cases involving football players. According to ESPN, none of the information was passed on to the proper campus authorities charged with investigating such claims. Four football players were immediately suspended (Leonard Scott, Reggie Ridley, Keyon Whiteside, and Ryan Rowe) until the university could review the allegations. Two football players who had transferred, and one women's basketball player were also named. Linda Bensel-Meyers, director of composition for the UT English department, issued a statement claiming "the acts of plagiarism appeared to be institutionally mandated by the athletic department."[52] A former Tennessee wide receiver, Tory Edge, supported Bensel-Meyers's claim by saying, "Not with every tutor. But you get some guys who come up there just bleeding orange. They don't care; they just want to be around the football team."[53] The report set forth a chain of events that placed the University of Tennessee in the media spotlight for possible academic fraud, and resulted in several internal and external investigations that continued for over two years.

The university, lead by UT attorney Ron Leadbetter, conducted a probe into the allegations of academic fraud that included an interview with Bensel-Meyers. She claimed, however, that the interview prevented open discussion and that Leadbetter did not want her to bring in files that backed up the claims that academic fraud was commonplace in the tutoring program. Leadbetter's investigation concluded with the university finding that no tutors wrote papers for athletes and there was no cover-up of NCAA violations. Some faculty members expressed concern about the investigatory process. John Finger, head of the history department, commented, "I think it's ridiculous to think that the university, as tied to the athletic department as it is, could come up with a completely objective assessment of the situation."[54]

In December 1999 the NCAA conducted an inquiry into the university's investigation. The NCAA also concluded that the University of Tennessee was not violating any NCAA rules in its academic assistance of athletes. Bensel-Meyers was interviewed by NCAA investigators, but, just as with the university's investigation, she claimed the NCAA investigators also did not want to see her records that exposed the academic problems at the university.

In April 2000, Bensel-Meyers released summaries of some of the records she had compiled. The records were from thirty-nine athletes, of which most were football players and included all of the starters from the 1999 season. The summaries showed twenty of the players were on academic review multiple times, and thirty players had a total of 105 cases of grade changes after they were initially entered by professors. Two players each received eleven grade changes and two other players had failing grades changed to an "A." The report summaries also showed that one athlete was placed on academic review ten times in five years at UT (the University of Tennessee's academic review is instituted when a student's grade-point average falls below 2.0). In May 2000 Bensel-Meyers handed over the records of the thirty-nine athletes to a faculty committee that was charged with investigating specific allegations of academic fraud in the athletic department.

Through the media, UT responded by disputing Bensel-Meyers's claim that most of the thirty-nine athletes never bothered to declare majors, but it did not address her other, and more serious, allegations. The NCAA returned in August 2000 to investigate the issue of grade changes, and this time Bensel-Meyers was able to share her information regarding players she alleged were "academically suspect" because of the tutoring program and claims of plagiarism, grade changes, and using the learning disabilities guidelines liberally to avoid academic eligibility issues. For her efforts to protect the academic integrity of the institution, Bensel-Meyers received death threats, had her office broken into, and was harassed in malls and grocery stores. She even believed her phone had been tapped. Her appearances on *20/20*, HBO's *Real Sports*, and ESPN outraged the Volunteers' faithful fans and caused many of her colleagues to distance themselves.

Bensel-Meyers filed a complaint with the Federal Bureau of Investigation (FBI). The FBI failed to find any violation of federal law, but the threats against her stopped. According to Bensel-Meyers, she knew her phone was tapped when she received a call from an alumnus who offered unsolicited information. After hanging up, the caller received a call from someone who knew the allegations he had just made.[55] The FBI did not say whether Bensel-Meyers's phone calls had been monitored, but the university claimed it did not monitor employees' calls.

In the end, both the NCAA and the Southeastern Conference cleared the University of Tennessee of any violations under the basic argument that neither body has any "authority over academics" nor do they "police academics."[56] Robin Wright, who authored the memos initially used by ESPN to break the story, left Tennessee in January 1999 for a position at Stephen F. Austin University, where she runs the award-winning and nationally-recognized academic assistance and resource center. On July 1, 2003, Linda Bensel-Meyers resigned from the University of Tennessee and accepted a faculty position at the University of Denver. She continues to be active and influential in the movement to protect the academic integrity of higher education. The case brought up important issues regarding the quality of education for student-athletes. This issue remains important today, as scholars and sports fans regularly assess graduation rates, grade-point averages, and even the majors selected by student athletes as at least partial indicators of a university's commitment to creating not just athletes, but *student*-athletes.

UNIVERSITY OF MINNESOTA ACADEMIC FRAUD

On March 10, 1999, the *St. Paul Pioneer Press* reported that Jan Gangelhoff, a former employee in the academic counseling department at the University of Minnesota, claimed she had written hundreds of assignments and assisted in other course work, including research papers and take-home tests, for at least twenty men's basketball players at the University of Minnesota. Gangelhoff reported that she received $3,000 and was told it came from coach Haskins. The report came out one day before the Gophers were set to play in the first round of the NCAA basketball tournament. A few hours before tip-off, university president Mark Yudof declared four players ineligible for the first-round game against Gonzaga, pending an investigation. The players were starters Kevin Clark and Miles Tarver and reserves Antoine Broxsie and Jason Stanford. The Gophers lost to Gonzaga, 75–63.

The same day, another former employee accused head coach Clem Haskins of asking him to do course work for a player in 1986. As the accusations piled up, former player Russ Archambault claimed Haskins gave him hundreds of dollars between 1996 and 1998, when he was kicked off the team for missing curfew. Melissa Burns, a former academic counselor for the basketball program, came forward to report that she had quit because she had suspicions of cheating by players. She claimed officials disregarded her concerns, and that Coach Haskins "intimidated her." Next, Elayne Donahue, the former head of academic counseling, said that faculty members were pressured to help assist the team in keeping players eligible to play. This included changing grades and issuing grades before completion of the work. She also claimed Haskins gave free tickets to a faculty member to secure eligibility of players.

The investigation initially focused on Alonzo Newby, the academic counselor for the men's basketball team and the man Gangelhoff named as the person who handed her the $3,000.[57] In June 1999, Newby was fired because he had refused to talk to investigators during the university's independent investigation.

The university and Haskins also reached a settlement in June 1999. The university agreed to buy out his contract for $1.5 million because officials felt they did not have enough direct evidence to fire Haskins with cause. However, the university sued to recover the $1.5 million after the investigation turned up a copy of a check made out to cash for $3,000 from Clem Haskins, and he admitted to paying Jan Gangelhoff. When the two sides finally settled the case, Haskins was required to return $850,000 of the $1.5 million.

Once the smoke cleared from the academic-fraud scandal, several high-ranking administrators were also left without jobs. McKinley Boston, the vice president for student development and athletics, athletic director Mark Dienhart, compliance director Chris Schoemann, and men's senior associate athletic director Jeff Schemmel all did not have their contracts renewed. Boston and Dienhart resigned shortly after the final report on the investigation was released because they had failed to catch the academic fraud. Among the reasons the academic fraud went unnoticed was that in 1994, Haskins requested a reorganization of academic counseling. Academic counselors for men's basketball would report directly to the athletic department, while all other sports had their academic counselors reporting to the university's academic counseling department.

The NCAA placed the Gophers on probation for four years and reduced the number of scholarships allowed. The punishment was considered light because the university already had self-imposed penalties including sitting out the postseason the previous year. The NCAA also required the school to alter the team's records from the 1993–94 season to the 1998–99 season, forfeiting every game played in those seasons. The team was stripped of its 1997 Big Ten Championship win, Voshon Lenard was stripped of his career scoring record, and Haskins was stripped of all victories over his last six seasons. Literally overnight, Haskins's record at the University of Minnesota went from 240–165 to 111–294. Unfortunately, this was not the last allegation of academic fraud at the college level.

DANNY ALMONTE STARRED IN LITTLE LEAGUE, TWO YEARS TOO LATE

Danny Almonte was like a man playing with boys when he took the mound in the 2001 Little League World Series. He threw heat that the batters had little hope of putting a bat to. Through the tournament, Almonte used seventy-miles-per-hour fastballs, striking out forty-six of the batters he faced, allowing only three hits and one run. In the regional finals he threw a no-hitter, and then he bettered that with the first perfect game in the Little League World Series since 1957. It would be revealed that Almonte's success was tainted, however, as he was two years older than the competition that he toyed with. The Rolando Paulino All-Stars team, who many called the Baby Bombers, was disqualified from its third-place finish (Almonte did not pitch in the game the team lost), and his records were stricken from the books.

Almonte had moved from the Dominican Republic to the Bronx, New York, where he began to play Little League in 2001. Almost immediately he was dogged by accusations that he was too old. Parents from two opposing teams were so confident that he and his teammates were too old that they hired private investigators to look into the matter. Neither found conclusive evidence. However, reporters for *Sports Illustrated* did find that Almonte's father had registered a questionable birth certificate in 1994. That discovery led to a full investigation.

Sonia Rojas Breton, Almonte's mother, claimed he was born in 1989 and produced a handwritten and photocopied birth certificate to prove it. She claimed he had been born at home. Just ten blocks from her house in Moca, the official records office had a birth certificate showing his birth year as 1987 and that he had been born in a nearby hospital. Almonte's mother claimed all records but hers were false. After an investigation, Dominican public officials disagreed and charged his father with falsifying a birth certificate.

Compounding the Almonte scandal was that it was more than just a case of a forged birth certificate. Little League rules require players to represent a team in at least six games prior to June 15 to be eligible to play on an All-Star team. Almonte had not even lived in the Bronx long enough to satisfy this requirement. School officials in the Dominican Republic certified that he was finishing the seventh grade there and up to June 15 was taking final exams. That meant not only had his father cheated the system, but also that there were conspirators with the local Little League who attested that Danny had played in games that he did not. He wasn't even in the country when they were played.[58] This prompted one sports columnist to write, "That's the part I can't understand. I've seen plenty of parents who thought nothing of bending the rules to give their kids an edge. But the depth of collusion in this case, the sheer number of people who willingly lied and the audacity of their deceit, is simply unbelievable."[59]

Little League officials were more inclined to place the blame for the Almonte scandal on the adults involved than to blame the player. Felipe de Jesus Almonte and league founder Rolando Paulino were both banned from Little League for life. "Clearly, adults have used Danny Almonte and his teammates in a most contemptible and despicable way," said Stephen D. Keener, the president and CEO of Little League Baseball.[60] As of 2004, Almonte reported that he no longer spoke to his father.

The Almonte scandal was indicative of how one name can become synonymous with a form of cheating and a player can go from hero to goat overnight. A teammate of Almonte, catcher Francisco Pena, was also in school in the Dominican Republic through June, making him equally ineligible to have played, but his name never made the headlines. Even years after the incident, Almonte made back page headlines when, at eighteen and a high school senior, he married a thirty-year-old hairdresser. From time to time stories continued to make the papers about Almonte's success as a high school pitcher and then subsequent struggles as a minor league ballplayer, and his surprising failure to be drafted by a Major League Baseball team in 2006. In an interview in 2004, Almonte commented that he learned some life lessons from the scandal. Sadly, he expounded, "I feel now like I don't trust everybody like I did before. The people I trusted wronged me."[61]

SAMMY SOSA'S CORKED BAT

Chicago Cubs star Sammy Sosa, one of the most prolific home run hitters in Major League Baseball history, was caught cheating with a corked bat against the Tampa Bay Devil Rays in June 2003. Sosa had gained fame as the man who battled and ultimately lost to Mark McGwire in the home run race of 1998. Sosa had enjoyed a tremendous reputation, with one columnist calling him a "quintessential good guy … a lovable slugger with an infectious smile."[62] The corked bat changed all that. Like McGwire, Sosa's accomplishments were already suspect as a result of the steroid problems that plagued the sport when his bat shattered and umpires found the cork.

Cork inside a baseball bat helps players hit the ball farther. Corking a bat is a violation of baseball's rules, and several players have been suspended from Major League Baseball when their bats splintered and cork spilled out, including Albert Belle, Wilton Guerrero, Chris Sabo, Billy Hatcher, and Graig Nettles.

Sosa was suspended for seven games and came back to hostile fans who booed him when he was on road trips. They called him "Corky" and waved signs calling him "Scammy Sosa." To his credit, Sosa just kept smiling and swinging and never showed a surly reaction.

Sosa offered an explanation and apology for the incident: "I use that bat for batting practice," Sosa said. "It's something that I take the blame for. It's a mistake, I know that." He went on to explain that he had the bat to put on a show for fans during batting practice and accidentally took it into the game.[63] Many doubted his story and believed the real explanation was that the slugger was coming back from an injury and was mired in a slump, recording only two hits in fifteen at bats since coming off the disabled list. In his favor was the fact that he had broken hundreds of bats and none before had been corked. His other bats were confiscated and X-rayed. None were revealed to have been corked. Regardless, the corked bat incident has remained as a stain on Sosa's reputation.

UNIVERSITY OF GEORGIA ACADEMIC FRAUD

The University of Georgia suspended assistant men's basketball coach Jim Harrick Jr. pending an investigation on February 28, 2003. One day prior, ESPN televised an interview with former University of Georgia basketball player Tony Cole, in which he claimed that he had some of his bills paid by and received academic help from Harrick Jr. Cole accused Harrick Jr. of paying over $1,300 in hotel and phone charges before Cole enrolled at the University of Georgia. Cole said the coach completed junior college correspondence courses for him and gave him a passing grade in a class taught by Harrick Jr. Cole never attended the course. Cole did not leave the University of Georgia basketball team on good terms. After being charged with aggravated assault with intent to rape, he was dismissed from the team. The charges were later dismissed. Harrick Jr. held the position of assistant under his father, Head Coach Jim Harrick.

Within days the University of Georgia suspended Harrick Jr. and never renewed his contract. The move took his father by surprise. Only one day before he had told reporters that "we don't do work for people, nor do we give them money. Do we make mistakes? Yeah. Will they find something minor? Maybe." He made it clear that he thought an investigation would vindicate his son and the program.[64] The *Atlanta Journal-Constitution* reported that Charlie Tapalian, a booster, was the source of the money Cole received to pay his bills. Cole produced a Western Union receipt for the $300 with the sender named as "Jim Harrick."

Within days the university suspended Harrick Sr., and declared two starting players ineligible because of academic fraud that involved the Coaching Principles and Strategies of Basketball class taught by Jim Harrick Jr. It also banned the basketball team from competing in both the Southeastern Conference (SEC) tournament and the NCAA tournament, a move that cost the university hundreds of thousands of dollars (their share distributed by the SEC). The actions by the University of Georgia received praise from NCAA president Myles Brand, who said, "I want to compliment President Mike Adams for his leadership and his rapid, strong response to the situation in the face of tremendous pressure," and, "I think we are starting to see a very important trend. I think the system is working."[65]

Harrick Jr.'s Coaching Principles and Strategies of Basketball course had three basketball players in it. Each received an "A," but never attended the class. Not that it mattered much. Harrick Jr. had made attendance optional for all students and gave a final exam that included such questions as: How many halves are in a college basketball game?

On March 27, 2003, Jim Harrick Sr. resigned as head basketball coach of the University of Georgia after reaching a settlement with the university. This was the third time in Harrick Sr.'s twenty-three-year coaching career that he left a program under a cloud of suspicion. Harrick Sr. was previously at UCLA, where he was fired for lying on expense reports. He then coached at the University of Rhode Island, where allegations of academic fraud among players surfaced. Under the agreement, the University of Georgia paid Harrick Sr. $254,166, the balance due for 2003.[66] After leaving the University of Georgia, Jim Harrick Sr. temporarily retired from coaching and became a basketball analyst. He returned to coaching in 2006 with the Bakersfield Jam, a team in the NBA's Developmental League.

INELIGIBLE PLAYER BRINGS DOWN ST. BONAVENTURE

The St. Bonaventure men's basketball program grabbed national headlines in March 2003, when the Atlantic 10 Conference determined that center Jamil Terrell, a transfer student, had been playing in spite of being academically ineligible. The scandal grew after the team refused to play its final two games, costing the university $120,000 in fines.[67] By the time the dust settled, the coaches and university president were gone, the athletic director's contract was not renewed, lawsuits were filed, and the chairman of the board of trustees committed suicide.

In 2002 St. Bonaventure athletic director Gothard Lane attempted to prevent the impending scandal by alerting the university president and then two members of the board of trustees that a new transferred player, Jamil Terrell, was ineligible. Terrell had earned a welding certificate at his community college, but did not have the requisite associate's degree. President Wickenheiser, whose son was the assistant coach who had recruited Terrell, personally approved the transfer and cleared Terrell to play. Lane was sure that he was correct that Terrell was ineligible. Unconvinced by Wickenheiser's response, he contacted the two board members. They declined to get involved, and the university would pay a heavy price.

The Atlantic 10 Conference stripped the team of six victories and banned it from postseason play for violation of transfer rules.[68] NCAA investigators determined that Wickenheiser was to blame, as he had authorized Terrell to play despite the objections from Lane and the compliance staff. Citing lack of institutional control, the NCAA cut two of the team's scholarships for 2004 and 2005 and reduced the opportunities for coaches to go on recruiting visits.

As the scandal wore on, Wickenheiser resigned, coach Jan van Breda Kolff was dismissed, and in spite of his attempts to enforce the eligibility rules, Lane's contract was not renewed. The most stunning tragedy related to the scandal was the suicide of the chairman of the board of trustees, Bill Swan, in August 2003. Swan, an alumnus who had dedicated his life to the university, had worked to usher the school through the scandal, ousting the president and briefly running the university. His effort to see the school through the storm was scuttled when the university released the results of its investigation, which claimed Lane had informed Swan and trustee Jim Gould about his eligibility concerns and Wickenheiser's response. Lane had forwarded the trustees copies of e-mails in which Wickenheiser stated that Terrell was eligible, in his estimation, and that there would be no further discussion of the matter. Declining to get involved, Swan told Lane that it "was an internal issue and that R. Wickenheiser would be accountable if the conclusions set forth in the email to Lane were erroneous."[69] Swan was vilified by the local media and via e-mails from alumni, and he was viciously attacked on Internet chat sites for his reluctance to get involved and avert the scandal. In particular, postings on a site called Bonnie Bandwagon attacked Swan, which profoundly affected him, according to his wife. "Bill was annihilated," Ann Swan recalled. "He went into a shell.... He felt as if his morals, values and his soul had been attacked."[70] The week before Swan hanged himself in the basement of his home, he asked his wife if she had seen the Internet. After the suicide, she recalled one post on the site that read, "Every time Bill Swan opens his mouth, he hangs himself."[71] Swan left a short note that, in part, apologized for the pain he caused St. Bonaventure University.

Claiming he was wrongfully dismissed and libeled, Coach van Breda Kolff sued the university for $21.5 million. An investigation conducted by the university had concluded that the coach did not know the player was ineligible, but asserted that he should have attempted to determine the player's status after questions were raised. The suit was settled in 2005 for an undisclosed amount. Van Breda Kolff was an assistant with an NBA team in 2003–4 and then directed basketball clinics in Nashville.

Gothard Lane sued the university, claiming he became a scapegoat after the NCAA became aware of the ineligible player. The suit, which sought $1 million for defamation, claimed university officials made false and malicious public comments about him after the scandal made national news. "They said I violated NCAA rules," Lane said, "[but] I was the one trying to stop them from violating NCAA rules."[72] The university settled for an undisclosed amount in 2006. Lane claimed he was vindicated by the settlement and the public admission by the university that he had not violated any NCAA rules. "I don't know how many athletic directors have confronted their president and told him he was wrong. Then I went over his head to two trustees."[73] Lane was out of work for over two years and was rejected from over eighty positions. He finally found work in October 2005 as director of championships for the Eastern College Athletic Conference.

The NCAA sanctions, coupled with players transferring out of the program, significantly hurt the team. In 2003–4 the team won only seven games, the fewest in over a decade. The poor play continued for years. Anthony Solomon, who was hired to replace van Breda Kolff and clean up the program, was fired in March 2007 after posting a 24–88 record over four seasons. The team lost nineteen or more games in each of his seasons. He had caused a controversy of his own by accusing fans of not supporting the team, and he was booed off the court at his last home game. At its lowest point, some Atlantic 10 officials wondered whether the team even should have continued to be a part of the conference. The NCAA probation ended on July 14, 2006, returning some measure of hope to the Bonnies faithful.

SPYGATE—NEW ENGLAND PATRIOTS BUSTED FOR SPYING

The New England Patriots were caught red-handed videotaping the New York Jets defensive coordinator signaling plays to his defense during the first game of the 2007 football season. The Patriots won the game in a rout. The practice, which allowed the Patriots to change its play via a last-second audible, gave its offense "a great advantage," according to one former NFL defensive coordinator. Not only was the videotaping illegal, but the league had issued a memo to clarify that teams must not do it. New England Patriots coach Bill Belichick claimed that he had a different interpretation of the rule. NFL commissioner Roger Goodell made it clear that Belichick's interpretation was unequivocally wrong. Belichick never explained how he misinterpreted the rule that read, "No video recording devices of any kind are permitted to be in use in the coaches' booth, on the field or in the locker room during the game."[74] The incident quickly became known as Spygate, and Belichick was dubbed "Belicheat" by some sports columnists.

Curiously, it was former Belichick assistant, Eric Mangini, who blew the whistle. He had left the Patriots, against Belichick's wishes, to become head coach of the Jets. Many wondered if Mangini knew of the Patriots' chicanery because he had participated in it while coaching with New England, and, if so, had cheating helped him earn a head-coaching position before turning thirty-five? Regardless, he was more than willing to order Jets security to wrestle the camera away from the Patriots' employee who had kept it aimed directly at his defensive coordinator.

Goodell fined Belichick $500,000 and the Patriots $250,000. He also stripped the team of a first-round draft pick for the following season. As rumors circulated that the Patriots also stole audio signals from opponents, Goodell ordered the team to turn over all evidence of its videotaping program. He promptly had all of the evidence destroyed. Given the commissioner's record of doling out severe penalties to players, many thought Belichick deserved a suspension from one game, if not several, in addition to the fine. Belichick offered an apology but, oddly, refused to say what he was apologizing for and consistently declined to discuss the incident, much to the consternation of the media members who peppered him with questions about it over the next several weeks.

Beyond the penalties levied by the league, Belichick lost considerable credibility with the fans. He had won three Super Bowls as head coach of the Patriots, and another two as defensive coordinator with the New York Giants under Bill Parcells. All of the titles became instantly suspect. Some players who had lost Super Bowls to the Patriots acknowledged that they questioned their losses. Pittsburgh wide receiver Hines Ward said he believed his team lost out to the Patriots' use of inside information in 2002, and Philadelphia cornerback Sheldon Brown found it suspicious that every time Patriots quarterback Tom Brady changed a play in the 2005 Super Bowl it was a perfect call. The reigning league MVP, LaDainian Tomlinson, said that the Patriots live by the motto, "if you're not cheating, you're not trying."[75]

In a classic example of unconditional love in sports, the Foxboro fans gave Belichick a standing ovation as he ran onto the field the week after Spygate. After dismantling the San Diego Chargers, his players hugged him and team owner Robert Kraft presented him with the game ball. Former players and team officials from around the league also showed support for Belichick. The Chargers' general manager, A. J. Smith, called Belichick an "outstanding football coach" and "a master of strategy."[76] Only time will tell how significant Spygate will be in shaping the legacy of a coach who is almost certain to be a Hall of Fame inductee.

Chapter 6

RACIST AND OTHER REGRETTABLE COMMENTARY

Contrary to some perceptions, racists don't just parade around in the wee hours of the night donning white sheets. Nor is racist commentary restricted to hushed tones or sentences that begin with, "I'm not a racist, but ..." Sometimes, and quite shockingly, racist comments are spewed by those who have a platform on television and radio programs and are paid to make insightful comments. Some of the "insight" reveals shocking ignorance on the part of the commentators, who generally believe they are simply being provocative or speaking a truth that few dare to speak. From Al Campanis and Jimmy the Greek to Rush Limbaugh and Don Imus, the comments have often been directed at black athletes and their abilities, or perceived lack thereof.

There are also those who could best be described as equal-opportunity offenders, targeting minorities in general, homosexuals, and anyone else they perceive to be different from themselves. Marge Schott, Reggie White, and most notably Major League Baseball player John Rocker famously verbally attacked racial and ethnic minorities, as well as people based on religious differences and sexual orientation. Given the light punishments athletes and others involved in sport tend to receive for offensive behavior, it is somewhat surprising that commentators who have made ludicrous comments tend to be sanctioned fairly significantly. Many have lost their jobs, been fined, suspended, and publicly scorned—although, as with so many scandalous people in the sports world, they are typically quick to bounce back.

AL CAMPANIS CLAIMS BLACKS LACK "NECESSITIES" TO MANAGE

Forty years after Jackie Robinson broke Major League Baseball's color barrier when he suited up for the Brooklyn Dodgers, the real progress that blacks had made in the sport would be overshadowed by the unfortunate comments of a member of that same Dodgers organization. The Dodgers, since signing

Robinson in 1947, had been considered one of the most liberal and progressive teams in the sport. Thus, it was shocking when executive president Al Campanis suggested, on ABC's *Nightline* with Ted Koppel, that black players lacked the necessities to move into management and front office positions. The comment came during an episode dedicated to the topic of Jackie Robinson breaking baseball's color line that aired on April 7, 1987. Koppel had asked Campanis to explain the lack of blacks in front office and managerial positions. Campanis replied, "I don't believe it's prejudice. I truly believe that they may not have some of the necessities to be, let's say, a field manager, or perhaps a general manager."[1]

Campanis apologized the day after his comments aired. Dodgers' team president, Peter O'Malley said, following the apology, that Campanis's job was absolutely not in jeopardy. Campanis had been with the Dodgers organization since 1947, the same year Jackie Robinson was signed. But by the next day, public outcry and criticism from political and civil rights leaders made it clear that Campanis had to go. He resigned under fire two days after making the comments. O'Malley said, "Comments given by Al Campanis are so far removed from what the organization believes that it is impossible for Al to continue his responsibilities."[2] Regarding his promise of the day before, that Campanis's job was safe, O'Malley said, "The reflection of a good night's sleep after a hectic day yesterday helped me conclude that this was the appropriate, proper, and right thing to do."[3]

Major League Baseball Commissioner Peter Ueberroth appeared on *Nightline* the day after the incident. He refused to address Campanis by name, saying, "There can be benefit from what I think is a very unfortunate set of remarks by somebody that was maybe thinking a little bit in the past or a lot in the past. Obviously the individual does not speak for baseball. He spoke for himself. He does not speak for the Dodgers as I think the Dodgers proved very clearly today."[4]

When Campanis made his comment, there had only been three black managers in Major League Baseball history, and there were none working at the time. Frank Robinson had been fired from the San Francisco Giants in 1984. Between 1984 and 1987 there were thirty managerial openings. None went to black candidates.

Frank Robinson, who became baseball's first black manager in 1975, saw that some good could come from the comments and the attitudes they revealed. "I was upset, but I didn't get angry. I was happy because it brought it out in the open from a high-ranking official from behind closed doors. Everyone suspected it for years, but when it was mentioned or brought up, everyone always denied it."[5] Similarly, the comments were seen as an opportunity to push for a healthy change in baseball by the NAACP, which threatened to shut down Major League Baseball with demonstrations both inside and outside of stadiums if owners refused to create affirmative action policies to address the dearth of blacks in management positions. NAACP executive director Benjamin Hooks said that he did not believe demonstrations would be necessary, given that the owners were already embarrassed by the scandal.

JIMMY "THE GREEK" SNYDER CLAIMED SLAVERY CREATED BLACK ATHLETES

Jimmy Snyder, better known as Jimmy "the Greek," was a gambler and football personality who appeared on the *CBS* football program *The NFL Today* for twelve years as a betting analyst. Born Demetrios Georgios Synodinos in Ohio, in 1956 Jimmy the Greek moved to Las Vegas where he established his reputation for being able to pick winners in the weekly wagering on National Football League games.

It was during a videotaped luncheon interview for a Washington-area local television show that Jimmy the Greek made racist comments that would cost him his job and reputation. On a show dedicated to the progress of blacks in society, Jimmy the Greek said, "[Blacks are] bred to be the better athlete.... This goes all the way back to the Civil War when, during the slave trading, the owner, the slave owner, would breed his big black to his big woman so that he would have a big black kid, see? That's where it all started."[6] He went on to cite such "evidence" as claiming that blacks have larger thighs than whites, and other such preposterous and unfounded claims. He also suggested that the only hope for white players was in outworking or outthinking the black players because they were outclassed athletically.[7] The show aired on Martin Luther King Day in 1988.

Jimmy the Greek went on to take the position that the only thing left for whites in sports is coaching. "If they take over coaching like everybody wants them to, there's not going to be anything left for the white people; I mean, the only thing that the whites control is the coaching jobs."[8] When media members questioned him about his comments, he said, "I want you to listen to everything that was said and then you make your own decision as to what I said that was so wrong."[9]

CBS fired Jimmy Snyder almost immediately. Snyder retired to a quiet life, but continued to write a betting column for a Las Vegas newspaper. He died in 1996 at the age of 76.

MARGE SCHOTT OFFENDS EVERYONE, EMBARRASSES BASEBALL

Marge Schott took over the Cincinnati Reds, baseball's first professional team, in December 1984. She told the press she bought the team as a Christmas present to herself and to keep the team from leaving Cincinnati. Schott was owner during the team's 1990 World Series Championship. During her fifteen-year tenure with the Reds, she was not known for her bubbly personality or her tact. It is rumored she settled a player's contract dispute by flipping a coin. Former marketing director for the Reds, Charles "Cal" Levy claimed in a 1992 deposition that he had heard Schott refer to outfielders Eric Davis and Dave Parker as "million-dollar niggers." The deposition was part of a lawsuit filed by Tom Sabo, who claimed he was fired as team controller because he disagreed with Schott's unwritten policy of not hiring blacks. Sabo lost the suit. Levy also claimed Schott owned a Nazi swastika armband and that he once overheard her say, "sneaky goddamn Jews are all alike." The *New York Times* quoted former Oakland Athletics front-office staff person Sharon Jones as saying that Schott had made similar comments in front of several baseball owners. Jones said Schott commented in a conference call, "I once had a nigger work for me. He couldn't do the job, I had to put him in the mail room and he couldn't even handle that. I later found out the nigger couldn't read or write. I would never hire another nigger. I'd rather have a trained monkey working for me than a nigger."[10]

Schott was suspended from everyday control of the Reds in 1993 and fined $25,000. Many Cincinnati officials felt Schott's comments reflected a broader race-relations problem in the city, where approximately 38 percent of the population at the time was black. Hank Aaron, baseball's career home run leader and the second-highest ranking black executive in Major League Baseball at the time, argued Schott's comments were as severe as the gambling problems of former Reds' manager Peter Rose. "You don't need people like this in the league," Aaron said.[11]

Suspension did not deter Schott. Upon her return to the league, she continued to use racial and ethnic slurs and even praised Adolf Hitler in an interview. Schott again enraged the public in 1994 when she said her players could not wear earrings, because "only fruits wear earrings." For that remark, Schott was reprimanded by baseball's Executive Council and was asked to make a donation to charity.[12] In a 1996 television interview, Schott commented that Hitler was "good in the beginning" but "went too far."[13] In a 1996 issue of *Sports Illustrated*, Schott made this comment about Asian Americans: "Well, I don't like when they come here, honey, and stay so long and then outdo our kids. That's not right." The reporter also said Schott imitated Japan's prime minister Kiichi Miyazawa in a "cartoonish Japanese accent."[14] Baseball commissioner Bud Selig called Schott's comments about blacks and Jews, "the most base and demeaning type of racial and ethnic stereotyping."[15] Schott was suspended again from 1996 to 1998. She apologized for her comments in May 1996, saying, "Let me take this opportunity to set the record straight. I do not and have never condoned Adolf Hitler's policies of hatred, militarism and genocide. Hitler was unquestionably one of history's most despicable tyrants."[16]

Umpire John McSherry tragically passed away in April 1996, when he was scheduled to umpire the Reds' opening day game. Schott quickly scribbled a sympathy card and sent it with flowers to the umpires' dressing room. It would seem to be a nice gesture, until it was learned that the flowers were a gift to her from the team's television affiliate and she simply recycled them. To make matters worse, Schott said she felt "cheated" because the game had to be postponed. In the same year, Schott fired Manager Davey Johnson because she did not approve of him living with his girlfriend before they were married.[17]

Under pressure from the league, Schott sold controlling interest of the Reds in October 1999. After that, she rarely appeared in public. When she did, it was generally to announce donations to the Cincinnati Zoo or other area charities. A chain-smoker, Schott was hospitalized in spring 2004 for breathing problems. She passed away at age 75 in March 2004. Barry Larkin, who was on the team from 1986 until the time that Schott died, remembered her fondly. He said, "I think people are remembered for the good things they do when they are gone. Now that she's gone, they will remember the parties she had to raise money for kids, her involvement in the zoo, her giving to minority groups. She gave to minority programs before her racist comments came out."[18] Although Schott had been denounced for slashing the Reds' promotions and marketing, she was applauded by fans for keeping ticket prices the lowest in the league and for selling $1 hotdogs. It stands to reason that her disgusting comments will have more to do with her legacy than her willingness to sell a cheap hotdog.

FUZZY ZOELLER DISPARAGES YOUNG TIGER WOODS

As Tiger Woods was putting the final touches on his runaway victory at the 1997 Masters Tournament, fellow professional golfer Fuzzy Zoeller was making racially insensitive remarks about Woods to a group of journalists gathered in a prominent interview area just off the eighteenth green. As the twenty-one-year-old superstar was polishing off the field in record fashion, Zoeller said, "That little boy is driving well.... So you know what you guys do when he gets in here? You pat him on the back and say, 'Congratulations and enjoy it,' and tell him not to serve fried chicken next year. Got it?" He then began to walk away, stopping to add, "Or collard greens or whatever the hell they serve."[19] The remarks were regarding the Champions Dinner, which precedes the tournament with the previous year's champion selecting the menu. Woods, who is primarily African American and Asian American, said that he was not particularly surprised by the comments and that, "Over time I think we will all see that it's an incident that was good for golf. But it's going to take some time to understand it."[20]

The tape of the comments was not broadcast for a week. CNN included the footage in its weekly show *Pro Golf Week* in a feature on the impact that Woods would have on the game as the first minority to win a major tournament. Once CNN ran the footage, other stations picked it up and it was a

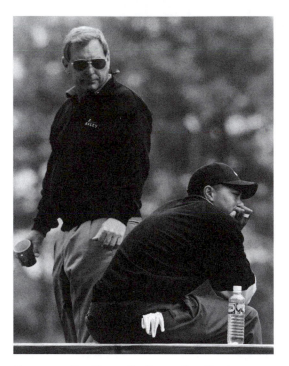

One year after Fuzzy Zoeller made offensive comments about Tiger Woods at the Masters, the two made an uncomfortable pairing in the second round in 1998. Courtesy of AP Photo/Elise Amendola.

fixture in the news for several days. The question remained: Why had no other news outlet carried the story immediately? It was clear that the interview involved many reporters (an ESPN microphone can be seen in the footage). CNN maintained that it was not protecting Zoeller and simply did not believe the footage belonged as one of many post-tournament sound bites. Rather, CNN chose to wait and put the comments in the context of a show dealing with the race issue. This did not address the troubling fact that numerous journalists heard the comment and none included it in post-event stories.

After the initial program aired, Zoeller apologized profusely and attempted to contact Woods several times. Woods did not immediately return his calls. He saw the comments as a racial incident and not as an innocent joke, and sent a message by taking several days to accept Zoeller's apology. The delay, according to some golf insiders, caused some resentment among his fellow professionals who generally liked Zoeller. The fallout did not end with the apology. Zoeller was stripped of his corporate support, as Kmart and Dunlop retracted his endorsement deals.

Sensing that the controversy needed closure, Woods agreed to meet with Zoeller at a tournament a month later. Over a twenty-minute lunch, they worked to clear the air. Woods maintained that he had a problem with the tone that was used and that he did not take the comments as a joke, but he was willing to put the event in the past. Zoeller said, "The cloud's off my head," and likened the lunch to a Catholic confession.[21] Unfortunately, he also said, "The only thing I'm upset about is that I had to buy his lunch,"[22] which was yet another poor attempt at humor and indicated that he still did not grasp the gravity of the situation.

One year later, Zoeller had escaped his pariah status as far as sponsors were concerned. Daiwa golf clubs, Sport-Haley clothes, and Ocean Waves sunglasses all were willing to pay forty-six-year-old, good-old-boy Fuzzy Zoeller to endorse their products. Ocean Waves president Kevin Carlson said that it was not difficult to partner with him, explaining, "He made a comment that was taken completely the wrong way."[23] Carlson offered no explanation for how the comments should have been taken, but did describe Zoeller as "a fun guy and a kidder."[24]

The comments remained a hot topic at the Masters one year later. Zoeller resented the media for carrying the story, saying, "I didn't write it up. You're the ones who buried me and I appreciate it."[25] As Zoeller apparently realized that his career would be defined by the controversy, he admitted, "It will never die."[26] Woods also had blamed the media for keeping the issue alive.

At the 1998 Champions dinner, Woods selected cheeseburgers, grilled chicken-breast sandwiches, French fries and milk shakes. Bob Goalby, 1968 Masters Champion, said that if they served cheeseburgers he would walk out. He didn't follow through on the threat. A more recent comment, made by Golf Channel commentator Kelly Tilghman, a friend of Woods, received similar media outcry. The difference was that Tilghman immediately apologized for saying younger players' only chance of beating Woods was to lynch him.

REGGIE WHITE, THE MINISTER OF DEFENSE, GETS OFFENSIVE

Reggie White was among the finest defensive players to ever play professional football, at one time holding the record for quarterback sacks in a career. He was also an ordained minister, leading to his moniker, "the minister of defense." He retired from the National Football League after the 1998 season, after helping the Green Bay Packers win a Super Bowl in 1997 but then losing to the Denver Broncos in the following year's title game. White had spent eight years buoying the defense in Philadelphia before accepting a free agent contract with the Packers. He intended to transition into broadcasting as a football analyst with CBS as the sun set on his playing career.

White's plans to be a broadcaster were scuttled by a speech that he delivered for Wisconsin State legislators on March 25, 1998. In the speech, which stretched to an hour, White condemned homosexuality as a sin and a personal choice. He claimed that homosexuals could not compare their struggle to the civil rights movement because their struggles were essentially self-imposed and a result of a sinful lifestyle. He added his belief that homosexuality, which had "run rampant," was a sign of an increasingly Godless country and that homosexuals struggling for rights actually offended him.

White went on to say that blacks "like to dance," Hispanics "can put 20 or 30 people in one home," Native Americans excelled at "sneaking up on people," whites "do a good job with building businesses," and Asians "can turn a television into a watch."[27]

As his comments created a public outcry, White issued an apology saying he never intended to slight anyone and admitted that his examples might have been "clumsy and inappropriate." His apology was qualified, however, by saying that he would not apologize for "standing on God's word."[28]

The minister of defense was branded with a new nickname in the aftermath of the speech: the minister of offense. He lost the opportunity to work for CBS, which issued a press release saying it "doesn't accept bias from its announcers of any kind."[29] While most NFL players were mum on the issue, some outspoken players were critical. Minnesota Vikings running back Robert Smith was quoted in the *Minnesota Star Tribune* as saying, "I find many of Reggie's comments incredibly ignorant. His statements on gays are embarrassing and speak to how little he knows about issues outside of religion."[30] White read Smith's comments in the presence of journalists. When he finished he looked up, clearly upset, and said only, "I have no comment."[31]

In July 1998 White appeared in his Packers uniform in a full-page advertisement in *USA Today* headlined, "Toward an open debate on homosexual behavior" and under his picture it read, "In defense of free speech." The $63,000 ad was paid for by a coalition of fifteen Christian groups. The NFL was not pleased that White appeared in uniform, and a Packers spokesman said, "He is speaking as an individual."[32]

White returned to the playing field with the Carolina Panthers in 2000, but was a shadow of his former self. During the preseason he said that he stood by the comments he made in the 1998 speech. He explained that he did not have anything personal against homosexuals in particular, but rather that he believed homosexuality is a sin and that he hates all sin. Regarding the comments about ethnic groups, he said, "The thing I was trying to bring across is we do have differences. God didn't create us all to be the same. Within all of our communities, all of us as different races and different ethnic groups, we have something to offer one another."[33]

Reggie White died suddenly of a respiratory condition on December 26, 2004, at the age of forty-three. In the few years between his second retirement and his passing, White had moved away from organized religion. He spent time learning Hebrew and studying the roots of religion. He wrote a book in which he questioned black leaders, asking why they didn't do more to build businesses in black communities and accusing them of being self-serving.

JOHN ROCKER EXPOSED VIA *SPORTS ILLUSTRATED* ARTICLE

When asked whether he would ever play for a baseball team in New York City, Atlanta Braves pitcher John Rocker responded, "I would retire first. It's the most hectic, nerve-racking city. Imagine having to take the [Number] 7 train to the ballpark, looking like you're [riding through] Beirut next to some kid with purple hair, next to some queer with AIDS, right next to some dude who just got out of jail for the fourth time, right next to some 20-year-old mom with four kids. It's depressing."[34] This was only the beginning of the hateful comments that Rocker made for a December 1999 *Sports Illustrated* article. He went on say that the thing he most disliked about New York City was the foreigners. "I'm not a very big fan of foreigners."[35] He then disparaged women, Asians, Russians, and Hispanics. Then he started in on his own

Six months after making disparaging comments about New York and its people, John Rocker faced the wrath of Mets fans at Shea Stadium. Matt Campbell/AFP/Getty Images.

teammates, calling one player a fat monkey and blaming reserve shortstop Ozzie Guillen for losing the fourth game of the National League Championship the previous season. Whether Guillen made a poor play mattered little in light of the fact that Rocker broke a long-honored code that players do not publicly blame teammates for losses.

Although Rocker admitted during the interview that he is not particularly intelligent, he did have a gift for sports. As a high school player he could fire a ball over ninety miles per hour and drew many pro scouts to games. The Braves drafted him in 1993, and he was a project, enjoying some success but throwing wildly at times. He eventually switched from starter to relief pitcher, and it was in that capacity that he became a major leaguer. His loud mouth immediately commanded as much attention in the clubhouse as his arm did on the mound.

As Jeff Pearlman noted in his *Sports Illustrated* article, a teammate of Rocker's made a comment in the aftermath of the NLCS Game 4 loss that would prove to be prophetic. Mike Remlinger, a more seasoned player, said, "The thing is, baseball is a game of humility. You can be on top one minute, as low as possible the next. When you're young, you don't realize it. But sooner or later you learn—we all do. Be humble."[36]

Rocker would learn soon enough. His ninety-seven miles-per-hour fastballs and 104 strikeouts had him the toast of the town the previous season. But he became an instant pariah when the *Sports Illustrated* story hit the newsstands. The Major League Baseball community was shocked. His teammates distanced themselves. The people of New York were irate. Even the rock-and-roll band Twisted Sister asked the team to cease using its song ("I Wanna Rock") to introduce Rocker when he entered a game.

Saying that Rocker had "offended practically every element of society," Commissioner Bud Selig suspended him until May 1 of the 2000 season.[37] The players association appealed the decision, and arbitrator Shyam Das reduced the suspension to the first fourteen days of the regular season and a $500 fine (it was initially $20,000!).

While he tried to mend fences with teammates, Rocker was less interested in maintaining a relationship with the author of the article. Rocker went after Pearlman, verbally confronting him outside the Braves' clubhouse early in the season, causing teammate Brian Jordan to call Rocker a "cancer."[38] His apologies to teammates did not all fall on deaf ears. Randall Simon, who was the target of the "fat monkey" comment said, "I looked at him in the face and he showed me that he really meant that he regretted what he said.... I really accepted his apology. I forgive him for what he said."[39] After Rocker met with and apologized to the team, manager Bobby Cox announced to the media that "They're giving John Rocker the greatest opportunity in the world to turn this around. They were terrific."[40]

In late June 2000 Rocker returned to New York to face the Mets and its fans, which were not so prepared to forgive. Rocker figured that it could not hurt to ask. He prepared a statement, which officials for both clubs arranged to show via video on the stadium JumboTron just before the game commenced. The fans booed wildly. There was so much concern for Rocker's safety that he had been transported from the hotel to the ballpark in a New York Police Department van. The game was staffed by 450 more uniformed and plainclothes police than normal, and a wooden canopy was constructed to cover the Braves' bullpen. Rocker spent the early innings of the game hidden away in the Atlanta clubhouse.

Rocker never had another season like 1999. He remained with the Braves only through 2001 and then was traded to the Cleveland Indians, then the Texas Rangers. In 2003 he played a few games for the Tampa Bay Devil Rays, but was released from the team. In an ironic twist, Rocker ended up trying to scratch out a paycheck in minor league baseball with the Long Island Ducks of the Atlantic League in 2005. While with the Ducks, he reflected on his comments, saying, "I don't have any ill feelings [toward New York], and it would be nice to think that the New York people can be as mature as I think I am now and bury the hatchet and move on."[41] He was released from that team after only two months.

Rocker currently promotes the Speak English Campaign, which seeks the "sustainment of the American heritage and American culture." In 2007 Rocker was implicated in a steroids scandal when his name showed up on the client list of Applied Pharmacy, a company raided in connection with a nationwide investigation into illegal steroid sales. The pitcher, who had been amazingly muscular throughout his career, denied any knowledge of an illegal prescription. The story is ongoing.

ESPN HIRES RUSH LIMBAUGH—EMBARRASSMENT SOON FOLLOWS

Fans of the National Football League across the country recognized the quality of play and leadership that Donovan McNabb brought to the field as he led the Philadelphia Eagles to consecutive National Football Conference Championship games in 2001 and 2002. In 1999, in recognition of his ability, he had become the first rookie to start for Philadelphia since 1991. He earned a spot in the Pro Bowl in 2000 and 2001. By 2003 fantasy football gurus, who care more about stats than skin color, were touting him as one of the finest quarterbacks in the league. Thus, it was shocking that ESPN's newly hired football analyst, conservative talk show host Rush Limbaugh, would claim that McNabb was, in essence, a fraud who was propped up by a supportive media.

It was September 8, 2003, on ESPN's *Sunday NFL Countdown*, that Limbaugh said, regarding McNabb and the Eagles making consecutive trips to the NFC title game: "The media has been very desirous that a black quarterback do well. There is a little hope invested in McNabb, and he got a lot of credit for the performance of his team that he didn't deserve. The defense carried this team." He would go on to say that McNabb hasn't "been that good from the get-go," and that the credit he received was due to "a little social concern in the NFL."[42] Limbaugh's cheap-shot comments came at a time when the Eagles had started the season 0–2, with losses to the defending Super Bowl champions (Tampa Bay) and the eventual champions (New England), and McNabb nursing an injured thumb and still recovering from a broken leg.

Limbaugh's comments were particularly preposterous considering the media has been far more likely to subject black quarterbacks to greater scrutiny than white quarterbacks, and has never been known to give them a free pass for poor play. *USA Today* columnist Ian O'Connor wrote, "Imagine that. For decades young black athletes had been told they couldn't run the huddle, couldn't manage the offense, couldn't lead the team, and here was Limbaugh decreeing that black quarterbacks had an unfair advantage over their white peers because the media had been "very desirous" of evening the field."[43]

McNabb chose to take the high road regarding the Limbaugh comments. He didn't have to say much, as the firestorm that ensued demonstrated that many commentators and football fans were itching to respond for him. Limbaugh would resign his position with ESPN almost immediately. Meanwhile, McNabb let his play do the talking. He led the Eagles to twelve wins over the remaining fourteen regular season games, and a playoff win over the Green Bay Packers before losing to Carolina in the NFC Championship.

Limbaugh's comments certainly did not represent the first challenges that Donovan McNabb faced as a black quarterback. As a high school player he was heavily recruited by colleges, but not to play quarterback. McNabb's coach at Mount Carmel High School, Frank Lenti, tried in vain to convince recruiters that he could throw the ball, but they wanted him as a wide receiver, running back, or multiposition player. Stereotypes that black players could play speed positions but not lead the team as quarterback had persisted throughout the history of football, in spite of some success earned by those granted the opportunity to pursue it. "When those recruiting analysts said Donovan was a fine athlete who couldn't play quarterback in college, that really upset him," Lenti said.[44] All the recruiters ignored Lenti, in spite of his nine state championships and head-coaching record of 228–36—except for the recruiters from Syracuse and Nebraska, that is. Those schools had the foresight to offer McNabb a scholarship and the chance to play quarterback. McNabb chose to attend and star at Syracuse based on their strong communications program.

Given the immense pressure faced by black players (and certainly quarterbacks), a group of former black NFL quarterbacks, including Warren Moon and Doug Williams, started a group called "The Field Generals" to act as a support system for current players. According to Williams, who was the first black quarterback to win a Super Bowl, "As a quarterback—I don't care who you are—there's going to be some of those days. As a black quarterback, sometimes they're a little tougher."[45]

DON IMUS TAKES CHEAP SHOT AT RUTGERS
BASKETBALL PLAYERS

Can the word *ho* be a term of affection? Is "nappy-headed" a derogatory way to describe black people? More than a public debate over semantics, the comments shock-jock Don Imus made about the Rutgers University women's basketball team in 2007 prompted national discussion over the limits of free speech.

The Rutgers women played for the NCAA national championship in April 2007. One day later, Imus was talking with his producer on air during his *Imus in the Morning* radio show about Rutgers' loss to Tennessee. The Rutgers players were referred to as "nappy-headed hos." Imus also snickered as executive producer Bernard McGuirk, drawing on the Spike Lee movie *School Daze*, compared the women's title game to "the jigaboos versus the wannabes."[46] A storm of criticism emerged from around the nation. Imus issued an apology two days later. Rutgers president Richard McCormick called the comments "unconscionable." Initially, Imus was suspended for two weeks from WFAN and MSNBC. Amidst calls from the National Association of Black Journalists, as well as black leaders Al Sharpton and Jesse Jackson, CBS fired Imus. In addition, program sponsors, including General Motors, Procter & Gamble, and American Express, announced they did not wish to be associated with a show that spewed racist and sexist comments. Imus accepted his punishment, saying, "I've been dishing it out for a long time. Now it's my turn. I get that."[47] He also met with the team and its coach, C. Vivian Stringer, to issue them a more personal apology. One of the players, Kia Vaughn, described how Imus's words impacted her: "I'm a woman. I'm someone's child. It hurts. It hurts a lot. Unless they have given this word a new definition, this is not what I am."[48] Vaughn filed a suit against Imus and NBC Universal, CBS Corporation, and others, citing slander and defamation. She later dropped the suit, saying that she desired to concentrate on her studies and basketball training.

Anita DeFrantz, an Olympic medalist, president of the Amateur Athletic Foundation of Los Angeles, and chairperson of the International Olympic Committee's Commission on Women In Sport, commented, "Here we go again—a prominent media person using sex and skin color to insult an innocent group of women. As an African-American, the message I got from Imus' words could not have been more clear: The Rutgers athletes didn't deserve to be on the floor. They were subhuman, after all, because their skin is dark. Things white and light are always right; this is the message that is constantly being given through the media in this country. It's time for us to seriously consider why. And it's time for it to stop."[49] Other female sports leaders expressed that Imus's comments reflected a broader problem with the media: when there is coverage of female sports, it is often either highly sexualized or trivializes the participants.

Imus's defenders claimed he was simply exercising his right to freely speak, and that the nature of his show was to inflame the public. They claimed Imus was an "equal-opportunity" offender, not a racist or sexist, because he has always been willing to insult pretty much anyone.

Imus pursued a wrongful termination suit against CBS, seeking the remaining $40 million on his five-year contract. He claimed that the language of the contract demonstrated that he had been hired to be irreverent and to provide controversial programming. The suit was settled in his favor. Imus's absence from the radio would be short lived. After settling with CBS, he sought a new contract and opportunity to return to the air. Imus found a new home with ABC and returned to the air in December 2007.

Chapter 7

POLITICS, COLLUSION, STOLEN VICTORIES, AND OTHER ODDS AND ENDS

his chapter is dedicated to scandals that defy easy classification. It captures the wide variety of sports scandals and includes an array of problematic and shocking situations. The intersection of sport and civil rights, extreme forms of hazing, race and religious discrimination, false accusations, bribery, and questionable decisions by referees, judges, and coaches are all included. Some things hover between appalling and laughable, like when Mississippi State coach Jackie Sherrill castrated a bull in an attempt to motivate his team. Other situations are far more serious, such as the false accusations leveled against Richard Jewell for the bombing of the Atlanta Olympics and the hazing that occurred among hockey players at the University of Vermont. The lengthy and scandal-ridden career of basketball coach Bobby Knight is included as well. Even the most ardent college basketball fan will likely be surprised by the number of times Knight has been at the center of controversy on his march to the all-time wins record in NCAA Division I basketball.

MUHAMMAD ALI VERSUS THE U.S. MILITARY

As a child, Cassius Marcellus Clay was considered undisciplined and belligerent. Growing up in a tough neighborhood, he began to channel his aggression, which was matched by his verbal boasts, at age twelve, when a white Louisville policeman, Joe Martin, took him under his wing. Never stellar in the classroom, Clay devoted himself to amateur boxing. He appeared in 108 bouts between 1955 and 1960, winning six Kentucky Golden Glove titles, two National Amateur Athletic Union (AAU) championships, and two National Golden Glove titles. An especially notable win was the gold medal in the light heavyweight division of the 1960 Summer Olympics in Rome. This win was different, as it showcased Clay on the international scene. It was also different because Clay returned from the Games a changed man.

Clay expected to be welcomed as an American hero when he returned from the Olympic Games. Instead, he returned to bitterly segregated Louisville. According to one story, he was refused service at a Louisville diner, where he appeared wearing his gold medal. Enraged, he left the restaurant and threw the medal in the Ohio River.

Not long after, Clay began his professional career as a heavyweight, winning a six-round decision over Tunny Hunsaker. He went on to win his next eighteen fights, fifteen of them by knockouts. On February 25, 1964, Clay fought Sonny Liston for the heavyweight championship. Liston was a huge favorite against the twenty-two-year-old Clay. Never intimidated, Clay boasted to the media the week before the match and, delivering on all he promised, knocked Liston out in the seventh round.

Within a short time of being crowned heavyweight champ, Clay announced he had joined the Nation of Islam and changed his name to Muhammad Ali. Over the next two years, he defended his title in nine matches. He became an outspoken critic of race relations in the United States and an activist for black pride. Ali explained, "We've been brainwashed. Everything good is supposed to be white. We look at Jesus, we see a white with blond hair and blue eyes. We look at all the angels; we see white with blond hair and blue eyes."[1]

In 1967 Ali's title was revoked when he refused induction into the U.S. military. When he appeared at the U.S. Veterans Administrative Office in Houston to hear "Cassius Clay—Army" announced, he did not move an inch. Outside, fans yelled, "Draft beer, not Ali!"[2] He claimed to be a minister of the Nation of Islam, and thus service would violate his religious principles.[3] Ali's famous quote, "I ain't got no quarrel with the VietCong.... No VietCong ever called me Nigger," perhaps best summed up his feelings. Ali also commented, "I'm expected to go oversees to help free people in South Vietnam, and at the same time my people here are being brutalized and mistreated, and this is really the same thing that's happening over in Vietnam." At the time, blacks represented 11 percent of the American population but 30 percent of the casualties in Vietnam.[4] He later explained, "I never thought of myself as great when I refused to go into the Army. All I did was stand up for what I believed."[5] The leading sportscasters of the time, including Jimmy Cannon, Red Smith, and Arthur Daley, all denounced him for his decision. Many in the public were critical as well, although even if he would have served he would not have been on the battle lines. Ali had been offered a service position entertaining the troops with boxing exhibitions.

Ali was sentenced to a five-year prison term and a $10,000 fine, which he had expected. In addition, state boxing commissions revoked his license to fight. He equated going to jail with the civil rights struggle, commenting, "I have said it once and I will say it again. The real enemy of my people is here.... I have nothing to lose by standing up for my beliefs. So I'll go to jail, so what? We've been in jail for 400 years."[6] His attorney's appeals, which ulti-mately reached the U.S. Supreme Court, kept him out of a prison cell.

Although the Supreme Court did not officially reverse his conviction for draft evasion until 1971, Ali began fighting again in 1970. The Supreme Court's unanimous decision held that the Justice Department was incorrect when it denied Ali's religious conviction and his conscientious objector status. In the United States, applause was mixed with derision, as many saw Ali as a traitor to his country. Across the world, boxing fans celebrated. Others who felt the war in Vietnam was unjust rejoiced as well.

Ali knocked out several opponents to gain the opportunity to fight Joe Frazier and regain his title, but suffered the first loss in his professional career when he dropped a fifteen-round decision. In October 1974 Ali regained the title in a heavily promoted fight in Kinshasa, Zaire, against George Foreman. He peppered the press with artful phrases predicting his win, including, "Float like a butterfly, sting like a bee. His hands can't hit what his eyes can't see." In his fight against Foreman, Ali showed off his famous "rope-a-dope" move. He then defended his title ten times in the next four years, including a fifteen-round revenge victory against Joe Frazier in the Philippines. On February 15, 1978, Ali lost the title to Leon Spinks, but then regained it from Spinks seven months later. He was the only fighter to win the heavyweight crown three times.

Although Ali announced his retirement from boxing in June 1979, he chal-lenged Larry Holmes for the title less than a year later. On October 2, 1980, Holmes dealt Ali the worst defeat of his career. He was, by one definition, "far over the hill—several hills," when he signed on to fight twenty-seven-year-old Jamaican Trevor Berbick on December 11, 1981. Berbick won in a unanimous decision, and went on to win the heavyweight title.

Ali is known as an innovator, not just for his quick hands, agile footwork, and ability to absorb punch after punch, but for his ability to enlist the media as a competitive strategy. According to one source, "Ali elevated the language of ridicule into an art form."[7]

In 1988 a federal judge dismissed a $50 million lawsuit filed by the former heavyweight champ four years earlier, alleging he had been unlawfully denied conscientious objector status during the Vietnam War and was wrongfully stripped of his title in 1967. Ali alleged the government unlawfully arrested, detained, and seized him, and that his speech and expression were unlawfully restrained. The judge determined the claims should have been made years prior.

Ali has suffered physically since his retirement. He is afflicted with Parkin-son's disease, a neurological condition that causes tremors, loss of balance, memory problems, and confusion. Doctors have determined the Parkinson's is due to the repeated blows to the head he endured. These announcements have prompted many in the medical world, and even some in boxing, to call for mandatory use of headgear or for the complete elimination of the sport. Despite these challenges, Ali went on to be a goodwill ambassador for the United States. He met with Saddam Hussein in 1990 in an effort to forestall the Persian Gulf War, and was a spokesperson for Operation USA in Rwanda in 1996. In 1996 he was selected to run the final leg of the torch relay to light the Olympic flame at the Atlanta Games.[8] Today, Ali is held up as an icon, although many forget his importance as a civil rights activist.

TOMMIE SMITH AND JOHN CARLOS—THE BLACK POWER SALUTE

Although it was just one part of black athletes' movements in the 1960s, when Tommie Smith and John Carlos took the medal stand in Mexico City at the 1968 Olympics, their black-gloved fists raised, the nation was alerted to the fact that athletes too were involved in civil rights struggles. In fall 1967 amateur black athletes, led by professor Harry Edwards of San Diego State, formed the Olympic Project for Human Rights (OPHR) with the intent of boycotting the 1968 games. The OPHR had three basic demands: that boxer Muhammad Ali's title, stripped when he refused to go to Vietnam when drafted, be restored; that the U.S. Olympic Committee remove the current head, Avery Brundage, who was known to be a white supremacist; and that South Africa and Rhodesia be uninvited from the games in a gesture of black solidarity against apartheid. Edwards promoted the boycott, arguing that black Americans should refuse "to be utilized as 'performing animals' in the games."[9] He commented, "What value is it to a black man to win a medal if he returns to the hell of Harlem? They are only being used to further the racist attitudes of the U.S.A."[10] Fairly quickly, many athletes rejected the full boycott, contending they had worked their whole lives for the chance to compete in the games.

Smith and Carlos took the medal stand on the second day of the games. Smith won the 200-meter gold, setting a world record in the process, and Carlos earned the bronze. Silver-medalist Peter Norman of Australia, a white athlete, joined them in the protest. Smith said that he and Carlos informed Norman of their intentions so he wouldn't be embarrassed. In an interview thirty-nine years later, Norman commented, "I told them, sure, that I certainly supported their cause, but as it turned out, it would have looked ridiculous if I had raised my fist, too. John asked if I'd wear a button that said, 'Olympic Project for Human Rights' and I did."[11] As the U.S. flag rose up the flagpole and The Star-Spangled Banner played, Smith and Carlos bowed their heads and raised their fists in a black-power salute. Although it is rarely acknowledged, the two men also wore no shoes to protest black poverty and beads on their necks as a symbol against lynching. The crowd booed as they left the podium. At a press conference after the event, Smith explained, "If I win, I am an American, not a black American. But if I did something bad then they would say 'a Negro.' We are black and we are proud of being black."[12] He also said, "It is very discouraging to be in a team with white athletes. On the track you are Tommie Smith, the fastest man in the world, but once you are in the dressing rooms you are nothing more than a dirty Negro."[13]

Only hours later, Brundage had stripped Smith and Carlos of their medals and kicked them out of Olympic village, saying, "They violated one of the basic principles of the Olympic games: that politics play no part whatsoever in them."[14] Across the nation, others were critical of Smith and Carlos' actions. The *Los Angeles Times* called it a "Nazi-like salute." A Chicago sportswriter called the two men "storm troopers."[15] Boxer George Foreman waved a miniature American flag after he won the gold, which many perceived as a rebuke of Smith and Carlos. Foreman claimed the flag had nothing to do with them, and that he always carried a flag to let people know he was American. Other athletes supported OPHR's movement. The crew team, all-white, issued a statement of support. And, despite the fact that women were virtually left out of the movement, the women's 4 x 100-meter relay team dedicated its gold medal to Smith and Carlos. Later in the games, Lee Evans, who helped found OPHR, set a world record in winning the 400 meters. On the stand, he wore a black beret. Smith and Carlos received death threats when they returned to the United States.

During his career, Smith set an amazing eleven world records, either as an individual or as part of a relay team. The 1968 Olympic record was not his first world record, nor his first civil rights protest. After Smith set his first world record in spring 1965, he joined one hundred other people in a civil rights protest walk from Sunnyvale to San Francisco, California.

After the Olympic games, Smith got a job at a car wash while he finished his degree at San Jose State. He also played in two games for the Cincinnati Bengals, and eventually earned a master's degree. Both Smith and Carlos went on to be high school track and field coaches. Smith also coached track and was assistant athletic director at Oberlin College in Ohio, then a coach and teacher at Santa Monica College in California. Smith wrote a book titled *Silent Gesture*. It chronicles his life, starting from growing up one of twelve children who worked in cotton and grape fields. Throughout the book, Smith discusses his confidence that the protest was the right thing to do, although he expresses deep regret that public reaction to the protest caused his mother's premature death and broke up his first marriage. He also disputes some of the most popular stories about the incident, saying that he still has his gold medal and that he was never a member of the Black Panthers, as was widely alleged. In 2005 San Jose State granted Smith an honorary doctorate. He has publicly denounced those athletes caught using steroids or other performance-enhancing drugs, calling them "an insult to the playing field in all sports."[16] Carlos continued to be active in civil rights and other forms of protest. He has spoken out publicly against the war in Iraq. In an interview thirty-seven years later, Carlos explained, "It was the revolt of the Black man. Athletics was my occupation. I didn't do what I did as an occupation. I raised my voice in protest as a man."[17] Carlos explained that only the less fortunate praised them for their efforts when they returned from the games. Businessmen and black political caucuses, he said, never embraced him or Smith.

San Jose State unveiled a statue honoring Smith and Carlos in 2005. At the unveiling of the statue, which does not contain an image of him, Peter Norman commented, "There is often a misunderstanding of what the raised fists signified. It was about the civil rights movement, equality for man.... The issues are still there today and they'll be there in Beijing."[18]

USSR VERSUS U.S. BASKETBALL—TRY, TRY AGAIN

The United States Olympic basketball program entered the 1972 Summer Olympics with a perfect record. From the introduction of basketball as an Olympic sport in 1936, the United States had not lost a single game. The United States selected its Olympic team from its top amateurs every four years and they played only a handful of exhibition games to prepare. Conversely, the Soviet Union put together a full-time team that played almost 400 games before the Olympics. Their meeting in the 1972 Olympic finale became one of the most famous games in Olympic history, noted for an outcome that remains in dispute.

The United States opened the Munich Olympic Games by easily handling its first seven opponents. Tragically, terrorists attacked the Israeli Olympic team and killed eleven of its team members, temporarily delaying the Games. Once the Games resumed, the United States won its eighth game, a thirty-point victory over Italy, to advance to the gold-medal game against the Soviet Union.

The Soviet team was stiffer competition than the United States had faced throughout the Games. The Soviets led for most of the game and had the Americans down by ten points with less than ten minutes to play. The United States, with strong play from guard Kevin Joyce, fought back. With ten seconds left, Doug Collins stole the ball and was fouled on his way to the basket. With three seconds on the clock, Collins made both free throws to give the United States the lead for the first time at 50–49. The events that followed would go down in history as the most controversial in Olympic basketball.

After Collins made the second free throw, the Soviets put the ball in play, but the referees stopped the game with one second remaining. The Soviets argued they had called timeout between Collins's two free throws. The referees reset the clock to three seconds. To this day, there has never been consensus as to whether the timeout was legally called. The Soviets in-bounded the ball again, and the horn blew, apparently indicating the end of the game and an

American victory. The referees ordered the teams back on the court, however, claiming the clock had not been properly restored to three seconds before the play. The third and final time the Soviets in-bounded the ball, Alexander Belov caught the full-court pass and made the winning shot as time expired. The stunned Americans stood in disbelief. Forward Mike Bantom said, "It was like they were going to let them do it until they got it right."[19]

The United States filed a formal protest with the International Basketball Federation that day, but the five-member panel did not overrule the result. The panel split down cold war lines, with three communist bloc members voting for the Soviets and the other two voting for the Americans. The United States basketball team refused to accept its silver medals, and to this day they lay unclaimed in a vault in Switzerland. Team captain Kenny Davis said, "We felt like they just did something to us that was illegal and we didn't know any other way to protest than to say that you're not about to get us to show up to take that silver medal."[20] Doug Collins expressed his feelings about the controversial game: "It was sort of like being on top of the Sears tower in Chicago celebrating and then being thrown off and falling 100 floors to the ground."[21] Kenny Davis has gone as far as placing a clause in his will that his wife and children "can never, ever receive that medal from the '72 Olympic games."[22]

MAJOR LEAGUE BASEBALL COLLUSION CASES

In January 1986 Major League Baseball's Players Union announced that it would formally charge the owners of the teams with collusion because of the lack of competing offers to free agents during the winter. At that time, twenty-eight free agents had signed contracts; twenty-six of the players had signed with their previous teams because they did not receive a single offer from any other team in Major League Baseball. In September 1987 Tom Roberts, the arbitrator in the collusion case between the players and owners, found that "baseball owners conspired to destroy free agency after the 1985 season" in violation of the collective bargaining agreement.[23]

In total, the grievance involved sixty-three players, including notable players such as Kirk Gibson, Donnie Moore, Carlton Fisk, Phil Niekro, Joe Niekro, and Butch Wynegar—none of whom received a single offer from another ball club. Kansas City appeared to have an interest in Gibson. However, after the owners meeting in October and the general managers meeting in November 1985, the Royals dropped its interest in the All-Star outfielder.[24] Gibson's agent claimed the collusion cost his client between $3.5 and $4 million.

The Players Union brought a second collusion grievance against the owners for their actions during the 1986 off-season. George Nicolau was named as the arbitrator of Collusion Case II after the owners dismissed Roberts, who heard the first case. Testimony in Collusion Case II revealed agreements between owners, going back to 1983, to cap offers to free agent players. A third collusion case was filed against the owners for their actions during the 1987 off-season and the creation of an information bank that kept records of offers clubs made to free agents, allowing every ball club to see what others were offering free agents. Arbitrator Tom Roberts handed down the financial penalties of Collusion Case I, which amounted to $10.5 million. The owners were also found guilty of collusion in both Collusion Case II and Collusion Case III. In December 1990 the players and owners reached a settlement covering all three cases, totaling $280 million.

All told, over three hundred players were impacted by the three years of collusion between the owners. As a result of the settlement, each team was responsible for paying almost $11 million. In 1990 the average payroll for an MLB team was only $16.5 million, and three teams had payrolls that were less than $11 million.

Marvin Miller of the Players Association said, "I think it may be the worst sport scandal in history, It's disgraceful ... disgraceful and not enough has been said or written about it."[25] Miller believed the collusion by MLB owners was so far beyond the famous 1919 Black Sox scandal because that involved eight players and one series, while the collusion scandal was a methodical conspiracy among all owners, general managers, and the commissioner to steal money from over three hundred players over a three-year period.

ROY JONES JR. ROBBED OF GOLD MEDAL

For three rounds of boxing, American Roy Jones Jr. dominated Park Si-Hun, his South Korean opponent, in the gold medal bout in the 156-pound division at the 1988 Olympics in South Korea. Computerized analysis had Jones out-punching Park by an astounding 86–32 margin. Nearing the end of the second round, Park was given a standing eight count, the boxing version of a timeout, which allows a battered fighter to regain his composure. Every objective viewer of the fight knew that it was a clear and definitive victory for the American. All that remained was to raise his hand in victory.

Shockingly, it was Park's hand that was raised instead. Jones thought it was a mistake, saying, "I thought they'd announced the wrong corner."[26] In spite of Jones's overwhelming dominance in the ring, the fight had indeed been awarded to the South Korean. Two judges, a Soviet and a Hungarian, had scored Jones as a decisive winner. Two others, from Uruguay and Morocco, scored it for Park. The fifth scored it a draw, but gave Park the nod for aggressiveness. The Moroccan judge, Hiduad Larbi, said that he voted for the Korean to appease the Korean fans, in spite of agreeing that Park was dominated in the fight. He said, "The American won easily. So easily, in fact, that I was positive my four fellow judges would score the fight for the American by a wide margin. So I voted for the Korean to make the score only 4–1 for the American and not embarrass the host nation."[27]

There were, however, other more sinister theories to explain the event. The U.S. coach, Ken Adams, suggested there was a payoff to the judges to vote for Park. He claimed that prior to the fight he had witnessed somebody who he described as "a Korean" showing some gold, wrapped in a rag, to two boxing officials, one of whom worked the Jones fight. Adams admitted that he did not see if the officials took the gold.

Regardless of whether money or gold changed hands to rig the outcome of the fight, international boxing has a history of dubious outcomes to fights and Adams knew this could be a factor prior to the Olympics. Sitting in the Olympic village days before the opening ceremonies, Adams had commented that the haul of gold medals for American boxers depended on several factors including "if everybody gets a fair shake."[28] Sports reporters who covered boxing at the time heard whispers that the Korean would win if he could just stay standing through three rounds. Throughout the fight a fan screamed at Jones, "Don't let it get to the judges! Don't let it get to the judges!" Then, after the third round, the same fan was heard saying, "You let him off the hook."[29]

In spite of the egregious robbery of the gold medal from Jones, Park initially defended his title publicly, saying in a news conference that there "was a little home-ring advantage," but he maintained that he won the bout and that his toughest fight had actually been against an Italian fighter.[30] He would later, however, acknowledge that Jones was the rightful winner. While there certainly were Korean boxing fans who celebrated the result, there were other Koreans who were ashamed and embarrassed by it. In fact, fifty Korean monks journeyed to the Olympic village to apologize to Jones before he left the country. Almost immediately after the fight, Olympic officials recognized Jones with an award for being the outstanding boxer of the Games.

Jones initially considered boycotting the medal ceremony. Even after accepting the silver medal, he questioned his own actions. "I guess I was trying to show everybody that we [the United States] can win well, and we can lose well."[31]

The three judges who handed Park the fight were suspended for two years by the International Amateur Boxing Association (IABA). The IABA president, Anwar Chowdry said, "We have to punish these officials for contravening the regulations during the boxing tournament in Seoul."[32]

The United States Amateur Boxing Federation (USABF) appealed the result of the fight based on the admission of the Moroccan judge that he did not score the fight properly. The appeal was dismissed for not coming within the thirty minutes allowed after the result was announced. The USABF representative pressed the issue, given that there was no time limit for incidents of fraud. The executive committee voted 11–2, with fifteen abstentions, to reverse the decision, but the general-secretary, East German Karl-Heinz Weir, ruled that the decision would stand. Olympic boxing did, however, change the rules that govern scoring to include computerized scoring methods that force the scoring to be more transparent and to keep viewers apprised of the score as fights progress.

Roy Jones Jr. was welcomed home with a series of medal presentations from friends and family who created at least fifteen gold medals to bestow on the real champion. Coworkers of his father, Roy Jones Sr., gave him a medal inscribed, "A Solid Gold Medal for a Solid Gold Champ." Jones went on to have an outstanding professional boxing career, amassing over fifty wins and holding titles in four divisions. He was voted the "Fighter of the Decade" in 1999 by the Boxing Writers Association of America.

Jones's name resurfaced in discussions of Olympic scandals in 2002 when, at the Salt Lake City Winter Olympics, South Korean short track skater Kim Dong-Sung was disqualified for cutting off competitors, which effectively handed the gold medal to American hero Apolo Anton Ohno. Some believed that replays did not support that Kim's actions merited disqualification, and Korean skating fans claimed it was payback for the debacle in the Jones fight. In the world of sports, as in many other institutions, paybacks are hell.

STEINBRENNER BANNED FROM BASEBALL

On July 30, 1990, Major League Baseball Commissioner Fay Vincent banned legendary New York Yankees owner George Steinbrenner from further management of his team. The surprising decision resulted from a relationship Steinbrenner had with Howard Spira, a known gambler, in which the owner paid for negative information regarding one of his own players, Dave Winfield. Steinbrenner had been at the helm of the Yankees for over seventeen years and was the most recognized owner in the sport.

Through Steinbrenner's testimony and other evidence, Vincent determined the owner had violated Major League Baseball's Rule 21, dealing with conduct not in the best interest of the game. Further, Vincent said that the testimony revealed "a pattern of behavior that borders on the bizarre."[33] The crux of Vincent's issue with Steinbrenner was that the owner had maintained the relationship with Spira, without alerting the commissioner, over a period extending for months, with the purpose of gaining information about Winfield through a private investigation. Winfield and Steinbrenner had been locked in an ongoing dispute, and Steinbrenner was likely seeking leverage through whatever means possible. Steinbrenner's relationship with Spira culminated with a payment of $40,000 to the known gambler. During the testimony, which produced 372 pages of transcripts, Steinbrenner offered a variety of reasons for the payment, ranging from charity to extortion, neither of which swayed Vincent. He was convinced that Steinbrenner intended the payoff to create distance between himself and Spira, whom Steinbrenner had no further use for and considered a potential source of embarrassment.

Steinbrenner likely underestimated Vincent when he went into the hearings and attempted to use patronizing tactics and flattery to control the proceedings. For example, Steinbrenner said to Vincent, "I think you know how I feel about you, and maybe I should have sought advice and come to you as a friend." To this, Vincent curtly replied, "Not as a friend. As commissioner."[34] Through these types of exchanges, Vincent concluded that Steinbrenner did not "appreciate the gravity of his conduct."[35]

In the decision, which both Vincent and Steinbrenner agreed to, the owner was allowed to maintain a partial ownership of the team (reduced to below 50 percent), but he was not to have a part in the management or day-to-day operations of the club. At the time, Steinbrenner said he had agreed to and accepted the arrangement and would not apply for reinstatement after a year, as the league rules allowed, nor would he mount a legal challenge against the decision. In fact, Steinbrenner went so far as to say, "I'm very happy it was resolved. I'm very satisfied with the resolution."[36]

One day after being ousted, Steinbrenner named his son, Hank Steinbrenner, as his successor, under strict guidelines that the father not confer, consult, advise, or communicate, directly or indirectly, with the son or any other Yankees officials on matters regarding the management of the team. Naturally, this begged the question of how such a mandate could be enforced. The Yankees had to submit in writing (every six months to the American League president) that no such interference occurred. Anyone caught violating the terms of the agreement faced a ban from baseball.

The banishment of George Steinbrenner was short lived. By 1991 he wanted back in. Vincent said he would not even consider the matter as long as three lawsuits filed against the commissioner and Major League Baseball were active. Not surprisingly, the suits began to drop away. The timing of Steinbrenner seeking readmission was likely not a coincidence. Just prior, Howard Spira had been convicted of trying to extort $110,000 from Steinbrenner and was sentenced to twenty-two months in prison.

A mere thirty months after he was exiled, Steinbrenner was allowed to return to Major League Baseball. The owner who had changed managers eighteen times immediately voiced support for the current manager, Buck Showalter, and other front office employees. Showalter remained as manager for several seasons before being forced out in favor of Joe Torre. Steinbrenner's return to the stadium was frantic as he tried to navigate a throng of fans. As one reporter wrote, "Steinbrenner was hailed like a conquering war hero, not a man who was suspended from baseball."[37] Such was the crush of reporters that it took him over an hour to move one hundred yards from the entrance gate to the playing field. He responded to the attention by saying, "I knew there would be a lot of attention. It makes me feel good. I'd rather get shoved around a little bit than not have anyone here."[38] Perhaps the best indicator of the impact of this case can be seen in the references made to it on the all-time most popular sitcom, *Seinfeld.*

JACKIE SHERRILL VERSUS THE BULL

As a head football coach, Jackie Sherrill could win games. After an unsuccessful year at Washington State, Sherrill was 50–9–1 at Pittsburgh, including three consecutive 11–1 seasons, from 1977 to 1981. Then he was 52–28–1 at Texas A&M from 1982 to 1988 before departing under a cloud of suspicion that led to two years of NCAA probation for the school for, among other issues, unethical conduct and lack of institutional control.

As Sherrill began anew at Mississippi State after a few years away from coaching, perhaps he was looking for some extra motivation to help his players turn around the moribund program. After a 7–5 debut for Sherrill in 1991, the team sought to open the 1992 season on a high note, but faced the perennial power Texas Longhorns, ranked thirteenth in the country prior to the September 5 game. According to columnist William C. Rhoden, "Sherrill apparently became dismayed because his team did not know the difference between a bull and a steer."[39] So, he decided to have a bull castrated in front of his team, right there on the Mississippi State practice field. Apparently this was intended as a metaphor—that his team would castrate the Longhorns on the following Saturday. Asked how this was intended to motivate his players, the coach answered, "That's everybody's different perception."[40]

It seemed that not everyone found the motivational tool to be useful or appropriate. Within days a complaint was filed with the state chapter of the Animal Rescue League. The Mississippi State University president, Donald Zacharias, said the act was "inappropriate and contrary to the educational ideals" of the university. At a weekly news conference, Coach Sherrill said, "If this incident was in any way not perceived as proper by those who love Mississippi State, then I apologize."[41] For the MSU faithful, the apology was probably not necessary. They were thrilled their team had upset Texas by a score of 28–10.

Bill Conlon, a regular on ESPN's *The Sports Reporters* (a popular show at the time), suggested Mississippi State fans consider a new cheer: "2-4-6-8 ... who we gonna castrate?"[42] Perhaps this case was important only for how bizarre it was, as the authors are unaware of other coaches dismembering live animals as a motivational tactic. We have, however, heard of other nefarious plots to fire up a team, even at the high school level, so it's possible Sherrill proved to be a role model for some, however unsavory.

MAHMOUD ABDUL-RAUF WON'T STAND FOR NATIONAL ANTHEM

Denver Nuggets player Mahmoud Abdul-Rauf caused a national stir during the 1995–96 National Basketball Association season when he cited his religious conviction as precluding him from standing for the national anthem before any of the season's first sixty games. Born Chris Jackson, he changed his name in 1993 as a reflection of his conversion to the Islamic faith. His new name means, "elegant and praiseworthy; most merciful, most kind," which is fitting for a man who said that he "was never a head case, never known to be a hassle, boastful or impolite."[43] He acknowledged that the perception of him changed through the controversy, with fans seeing him as a villain. Prior to the controversy, Abdul-Rauf was best known for his ongoing battle to overcome Tourette syndrome, which causes uncontrollable tics, body movements, and involuntary speech.

Abdul-Rauf would stay in the tunnel or stretch during the national anthem. The firestorm began when he was asked to explain his beliefs and he responded that the flag is "a symbol of oppression, of tyranny."[44] He was suspended by the league for violating a rule calling for players to stand in a dignified posture during the anthem. After missing one game and having his pay docked $31,707, the player and league reached a compromise. Abdul-Rauf would stand for the anthem and would engage himself in personal prayer. When asked if he was standing for the anthem, he explained that he was "not standing for it, I'm standing while it's being played."[45]

Sports fans learned more about Islam as a result of the controversy, which led many to wonder whether there was a negative effect on his play due to his observance of the holy month of Ramadan, during which he fasted from sunrise to sundown for thirty days late in the NBA season. Abdul-Rauf became a lightning rod for fans and commentators who felt his choice was an affront to the American flag. Controversy increased as other professional athletes were asked to comment. Professional golfer Mike Sullivan fueled the fire when he said, "I don't think they should suspend him. I think they should shoot him."[46]

After compromising with the league, Abdul-Rauf returned to action on the road against the Chicago Bulls and was booed every time he touched the ball. He had a solid game in spite of the distraction, scoring nineteen points in only twenty-one minutes. One fan yelled a racial obscenity at him as he left the court. He was visibly supported by his teammates, several of whom hugged and patted him at the end of the anthem. Following the season, the Nuggets traded him to the Sacramento Kings. The controversy followed him to Sacramento, as fans continued to taunt him. On one occasion he was woken in the middle of the night when a man telephoned to sing the national anthem at him.

Abdul-Rauf's interpretation of his faith was not universally shared by Muslims. Mohamed Jodeh, president of the Colorado Muslim Association, stressed that the Islamic faith does not prohibit people from standing for the national anthem. "There's no conflict between standing for the anthem and Islamic thinking," he said.[47]

After missing the last three months of the 1997–98 NBA season with illness and injury, Abdul-Rauf went to Turkey to finish his basketball career.

BOMBING OF ATLANTA OLYMPICS—RICHARD JEWELL WRONGLY ACCUSED

Atlanta's dream Olympiad was forever marred when a bomb exploded on July 17, 1996, during the Centennial Olympic Games. After the explosion at Olympic Park, Richard Jewell, the security guard who had spotted the bag containing the bomb and moved people away, was hailed as an overnight international hero. Just as quickly, when it was leaked that he had been questioned as a suspect, he became the target of a reckless and vicious media witch hunt.

The pipe bomb, filled with nails, detonated at the park that served as an area for meeting and celebrating throughout the Olympics. It killed one person and injured 111 others. The tragedy would have been far worse had Jewell not acted as he was trained, rapidly evacuating the area after identifying the threat. The *Atlanta Journal-Constitution* first carried the story that he was a suspect and the media frenzy began. Jewell was labeled as an attention seeker who planted the bomb himself and used it as an opportunity to play the role of hero. Newspapers called him "a simpleton security guard, a failed cop from Bumpkinville, a roly-poly loser, a beefy nobody,"[48] and "the village Rambo."[49] Columnists made up names for Jewell, such as "Una-Bubba," as they suggested "his arrest was imminent; the noose was tightening around his neck."[50] One forensic psychologist even said that Jewell "sounds like someone who craves excitement the way an arsonist does."[51]

The *Atlanta Journal-Constitution* cited unnamed law enforcement sources in its front page article that said Jewell "fits the profile of a lone bomber."[52] Media around the world carried images of the FBI carrying bags, presumed to be evidence, out of Jewell's home. In an attempt to get Jewell to give up his rights to an attorney, the FBI tried to trick him into participating in a video about responding to bomb scenes. Then, eighty-eight days after beginning the pursuit of Jewell as a suspect, the FBI cleared him of any wrongdoing.

Jewell launched a wave of legal action against a variety of media outlets for libel. He secured settlements from NBC, CNN, the *New York Post*, and ABC. He also reached a settlement with his former employer, Piedmont College. After he was named as a suspect, the president of the college had described him as "erratic," an officer who wrote "epic police reports for minor infractions,"[53] and a "badge-wearing zealot" who should be investigated.[54] Settlements ranged from a reported $5,000 with ABC to $500,000 from NBC for remarks made by Tom Brokaw.

When Jewell's lawyer was asked if Jewell would lose public sympathy by pursuing lawsuits, he responded, "The working people of this country don't have any problem at all with Richard Jewell taking down these damned big shots for what the hell they did to him."[55] Jewell also sued the *Atlanta Journal-Constitution*. Among the evidence against the paper were taped depositions in which four of the copy editors said they had problems with the story and had alerted superiors about potential libel issues. Jewell faced an uphill battle in the suit when a court ruled that he was a public figure after he was hailed as a hero, meaning he would have to show the paper not only published a falsehood, but also acted with actual malice, meaning the publishers knew the information was false or acted with a reckless disregard for the truth.

The Olympic Park bombing was actually committed by Eric Rudolph, a white supremacist, backwoods survivalist. He had been in the U.S. military, but had dropped out of the Army Special Forces when he became disturbed by the number of minority soldiers he had to spend time with. Rudolph committed a string of bombings in the Atlanta area, including a 1997 abortion clinic attack and another a month later at a lesbian nightclub. In 1998 he bombed another abortion clinic, this time in Alabama, killing an off-duty police officer and maiming a nurse. Rudolph disappeared into the mountainous backwoods of North Carolina after fleeing from his home in the small town of Murphy. He managed to elude capture for over five years, living in the hills of Appalachia. He was on the FBI Top Ten Most Wanted list and had a $1 million bounty on his head. Finally, in 2003, a rookie policeman in Murphy made a routine arrest of a man loitering around the trash bins behind a supermarket; the disheveled man was Rudolph. He had been hiding in the area for years with the help of sympathetic locals who supported his antiabortion position. Rudolph pleaded guilty in 2005 to committing four bombings in a deal that spared him the death penalty but ensured he would never be released from a maximum-security prison. Jewell was among the people in the Atlanta courtroom when the plea was entered. He sought to bring closure to his own experience and to support the victims and their families.

On the tenth anniversary of the Olympic Park bombing, at a ceremony in Atlanta, Georgia, governor Sonny Perdue set the record straight regarding Richard Jewell. "His actions saved lives that day. He did what he was trained to do. Mr. Jewell, on behalf of the people of Georgia, we want to thank you for keeping Georgians safe and doing your job during the course of those games," he said.[56] Jewell responded, "I never sought to be a hero. I have always viewed myself as just one of many trained professionals who simply did his job that tragic night. I wish I could have done more."[57]

In August 2007, at the age of 44, Jewell passed away in his home. He had been suffering from failing health and was on medical leave from work. He had spent the previous three years working as a deputy sheriff for the Meriwether County Sheriff's Department. After the Olympic Park bombing fiasco was behind him, he worked for several small-town police departments. He never talked about being accused of the bombing unless he was prompted about it, according to friends and coworkers. At the time of Jewell's death, his lawsuit against the *Atlanta Journal-Constitution* was still unresolved.

UNIVERSITY OF VERMONT HOCKEY CANCELLED
AFTER HAZING INCIDENT

University of Vermont (UVM) president Judith Ramaley imposed the death penalty on her own university's hockey team in January 2000 after hazing among team members came to light. The atrocious acts against walk-on goalie Corey La Tulippe and other freshmen players in fall 1999 included performing the "elephant walk," in which the players paraded naked while holding each other's genitals. The severe sanction was intended to deter athletes, both at UVM as well as across the country, from future acts of hazing, which was already a hot topic in athletics.

Coach Mike Gilligan, a sixteen-year veteran at the school, announced the remainder of the season would be cancelled on January 14, 2000. The Division I team, competing in the Eastern College Athletic Conference, had fifteen games left on its schedule. The decision to cancel the season was shocking, as hockey is to Burlington what football is to Lincoln, Nebraska. In the fall, the team held an initiation party at which nine freshmen recruits were told to perform the elephant walk and to drink excessively, and most were in a drunken stupor by the end of the evening. La Tulippe first reported the incident, claiming that among other things the freshmen were told to do push-ups while dipping their genitals into glasses of beer. They were then told to drink the beer. He claimed another freshman had been blindfolded and fondled by strippers while the older players watched and laughed.

Not only was the team punished for hazing, but also for stonewalling the university's internal investigation. "It looks like everybody has lied," Gilligan told the players.[58] As news about the hazing incident broke, members of the faculty expressed concern about how the university would punish the students who were involved. "This is a state that has always turned a blind eye to what the ice hockey team has done," said Jean Richardson, an associate professor of environmental studies and president of the university's faculty senate.[59] In the weeks that followed the cancellation of the hockey season, Gilligan refused to resign, despite pressure to do so. He also met individually with the players and spoke with their families. He brought in counselors to help the team work through their anger and frustration, and, to the surprise of many, he urged the university to maintain the players' scholarships. The Cats also held informal practices throughout the cancelled part of the season.

Long-time athletic director Rick Farham cautioned all student-athletes about the dangers of hazing. "Doing things like stupid racism, dressing up in goofy clothes, whatever it is. You wouldn't think college students would be doing stuff like that. And I know, from talking with other coaches, administrators and students from other colleges, that it's just not UVM. What appears to be fun and games for 15 minutes can turn into a travesty."[60] Throughout the entire scandal and aftermath, Gilligan maintained he knew nothing about the party or any hazing. Farham also defended Gilligan, maintaining there is no way the coach would have encouraged his athletes to haze each other.

An investigation by university officials acknowledged that certain officials were not forthcoming with information even after campus police inquired about rumors that hazing had occurred. During the investigation, La Tulippe was interrogated about his involvement in the incident and asked about accusations that he had urinated on a teammate in the shower in high school, as well as exposed a swollen and bruised testicle to women. He allegedly did not dispute those claims, although it is difficult to see their relevance to the hazing situation.

Many members of the team completed various community service projects during the summer following the cancelled season, to the satisfaction of some Burlington residents and to the dismay of others. Of the twenty-one players from the 1999–2000 roster, eighteen returned to play for the team in 2000–2001. Players felt as though the incident had received enough attention. Jerry Gernander commented, "What happened is something I wouldn't wish on anyone, but we served the time. And now it's our turn to shine on the ice."[61] Evidently UVM hockey fans were quick to forgive, as the team received a two-minute standing ovation before it even took the ice for its first game back.

On February 10, 2001, under tremendous pressure from the UVM board of trustees, President Ramaley resigned. Her resignation was tied to budgetary woes at UVM, as well as her handling of the hazing situation. The university suffered from the scandal. According to David Nestor, the vice president for student affairs, there was an estimated 5 percent decline in Vermont students enrolling at the university in the following year. The Vermont legislature passed a law prohibiting hazing. The university committed to holding workshops on hazing for all student-athletes, and got involved with the NCAA to develop a policy on hazing.

NOTRE DAME HIRES, THEN FIRES, GEORGE O'LEARY IN RESUME DEBACLE

When George O'Leary was named to fill the opening as head football coach at Notre Dame in 2001, he had twice been honored as Atlantic Coast Conference coach of the year. He had even been national coach of the year in 2000. He had earned those awards. Unfortunately, he also laid claim to having a master's degree and three years of college playing experience at the University of New Hampshire. Those were distinctions he had not earned. The falsifications on his resume were revealed within days of him accepting the job at Notre Dame. He had attended New Hampshire for two years and never played a game. He later took two graduate courses at Stony Brook in New York, but was far from a degree. He resigned five days after accepting what he had considered a dream job.

The inaccuracies had resided on O'Leary's resume for decades, stemming from his attempts to break into the extremely competitive world of coaching. Once the information was included on his resume, it seemed to take on a life of its own, following him from job to job and never being omitted. They were finally uncovered when a reporter sought to contact some of O'Leary's old teammates for comments regarding his acceptance of the Notre Dame position. The ordeal sparked a national debate about credential fraud. Coaches across the country scrambled to update their biographies, clearing up any potential inaccuracies. At Georgia Tech, which had been embarrassed by the O'Leary scandal, a new assistant football coach was forced to resign when he admitted that he had not played football and baseball at Florida State as his profile suggested. Another Georgia Tech coach listed a master's degree, which he was really six credits short of earning. He was allowed to keep his job because an oversight committee determined he had worked diligently to correct the information.

Like there is for so many good football coaches, there was a safety net in place to limit the devastation of O'Leary's fall. He apologized, resigned without a fight, and then moved on to the NFL's Minnesota Vikings where he was a defensive line coach and then defensive coordinator over two seasons. The Vikings' head coach, Mike Tice, had been a high school quarterback under O'Leary. From there he moved back into college football as head coach for the struggling program at Central Florida. To his credit, O'Leary quickly turned the program around, snapping a seventeen-game losing streak (the longest in the nation at the time), and then leading the team to a postseason appearance in 2005. He earned the Conference USA Coach of the Year Award in the process.

While coaching the Vikings, O'Leary addressed the issue thusly, "I made a stupid, stupid mistake, and I paid a dear price for it. My mother used to say, in her Irish Catholic way, 'God never closes one door unless he opens another.' I said to her, 'Well, he slammed this one pretty good, Mom.'"[62]

SALT LAKE CITY BRIBES WAY TO OLYMPIC GAMES

The Olympic Games have faced, and survived, a wide variety of scandals since reemerging in 1896. Most notable have been political boycotts, cheating by participants and judges, and performance-enhancing drug use. But none threatened the future of the Games like the Salt Lake City bid scandal. The power to determine which potential host city will win the right to the Games, and the economic windfall that comes with it, lies in the hands of 115 people. The scandal revealed that some of the 115 voters could be, and were, bought.

Marc Holder, who was the longest-serving member of the International Olympic Committee, levied the charge that votes were bought and sold. He did not, however, place the blame on the potential host cites. Rather, he asserted that the cities were blackmailed by unscrupulous International Olympic Committee (IOC) members. "For us, Salt Lake City was a victim of blackmail and not a villain. The real villains are the agents who put the cities in awkward positions using blackmail."[63] He claimed that one agent told the bid cities that no city had won the games in fifteen years without his help.

An independent investigation of the Salt Lake bid reported, among other things, that one IOC member from the Republic of Congo received over $250,000, that the children of IOC members were enrolled at the University of Utah, with the bid committee paying the bills (although there were no records of a scholarship fund ever recorded), and that apartments and other living expenses were paid for the children of IOC members. The list went on to a tune of over $800,000 in illicit payments in cash, educational, medical, and travel expenses to fourteen IOC members. Salt Lake City was granted the games in an unprecedented first ballot vote in 1995.

The investigation into how Salt Lake City secured the Olympic bid revealed that this was no isolated incident. IOC members had been showered with gifts when Atlanta sought the Summer Olympics bid for 1996. Charlie Battle, who was senior vice president of international relations for the Atlanta Committee, admitted that the $200 gift limit set by the IOC was completely ignored. He said that as Atlanta pushed for the bid, his committee showered IOC members with gifts including golf clubs, trips, and even a bulldog for a Cuban official who had mentioned that he had always wanted one. Battle expressed that he felt no regrets, and that the culture of soliciting an Olympic bid supported lavish gift giving and entertainment.

As Nagano was vying for the 1998 Winter Games, Japanese corporations contributed $20 million toward the construction of an Olympic Museum in Lausanne, Switzerland. It was a pet project for IOC president Juan Antonio Samaranch. Nagano was granted the Games, outmaneuvering Salt Lake City, which many felt had a stronger bid. Perhaps those who dreamed of a Salt Lake Games learned from the experience and applied the lesson in its successful bid.

In the wake of the scandal, the IOC voted new measures into place to restore the public's faith in the system. Among the measures were: banning IOC members from accepting expense-paid trips to bid cities; reducing the age limit for members from eighty to seventy; changing membership from life terms to a reelection process; and restricting the terms that future IOC presidents could serve. Regardless of these changes, allegations of various forms of cheating occurred in subsequent games as well. The stakes are simply too high, it seems.

ALABAMA FIRES MIKE PRICE BEFORE HE COACHES A GAME

In May 2003 Alabama fired head football coach Mike Price before he ever coached a game for the Crimson Tide. Price had coached Washington State for fourteen seasons, amassing an 83–77 record with five bowl appearances, prior to accepting the high-profile Alabama position. He coached Alabama through spring practice before an unfortunate night in April when Price became heavily intoxicated at a topless bar in Pensacola, Florida. Media accounts of the night's events varied, and rumors circulated the Alabama campus almost immediately. The common thread of the stories was that Price drank heavily, showered dancers with money, and took women back to his hotel room.

Price claimed he was blindsided by his firing. A week after the incident he met with Alabama athletic director Mal Moore, president Robert Witt, and sports information director Larry White. He said, "I was told to go on being the head coach and fulfill my head coach duties as the coach at Alabama. I went to banquets, was recruiting, and played a golf tournament."[64] Even when Price was called to attend a board meeting, he believed his job was safe. He prepared an apology, but was never allowed to deliver it. As he waited outside the boardroom for several hours, his fate at Alabama was sealed. As President Witt left the meeting, he told Price, "People like you and me don't get second chances," and then he walked to a press conference and announced Price's firing.[65] Price learned he was fired at the same time as the assembled media members. A faculty panel denied an appeal, rejecting his request for a hearing. Price sued the school, claiming he had been assured he would not be fired and that he would have an opportunity to tell his side of the story. The suit was dismissed because he had never signed his seven-year, $10 million contract.

Days after the firing, *Sports Illustrated* ran a story on Price's night at the topless club. The story claimed he had sex with two women in his hotel room. Price responded by suing the author, Don Yaeger, and Time, Inc., which owns *Sports Illustrated*. He sought $20 million, claiming he was defamed and slandered by the story. He admitted he had been heavily intoxicated, but denied that he had sex with anyone. Although *Sports Illustrated* stated that it stood behind the story, the case was settled after the courts denied the magazine the right to protect its confidential sources. The 11th U.S. Circuit Court of Appeals ruled that Alabama law protected newspapers and broadcast news, but not magazines.

After the settlement was reached, Price called a news conference at which he claimed to feel vindicated, and through a media release he called it a "great victory." Time believed his comments violated the terms of the agreement and sought to have a court dismiss the charges, thereby throwing out the settlement. The settlement had allowed each side to make only limited public comments about the deal. The sides later agreed to a second settlement.

Price was hired to coach at the University of Texas–El Paso (UTEP) in December 2003. UTEP president Diana Natalicio said, "We know Mike Price is a man who has been humbled by a highly public mistake. He paid dearly for that grievous error in judgment, and all of us believe he has earned the opportunity to restart his career."[66] Price said, "When something you love has been taken away, it really hurts. It hurt so much that now I know that coaching was my true calling."[67] He immediately turned around the Miners' program, posting an 8–4 record his first year, earning a national ranking during the season, and leading the team to a bowl game. The team won eight more games and again played in a bowl in his second year. The Miners had posted three consecutive two-win seasons before Price was hired. As was clear from other scandals, it seems those involved in sport get more second (and third, and fourth, etc.) chances than does the average Joe. But, this type of case has drawn attention to the issue of moral turpitude, and whether athletes and coaches can and should be punished for activities that, although not necessary unlawful, prompt negative attention.

BARTMAN INTERFERES WITH FOUL BALL, CUBS LOSE

On October 13, 2003, the Chicago Cubs were five outs away from advancing to the club's first World Series since 1945. It was Game 6 of the National League Championships and the Cubs were ahead three games to two in the series with the Florida Marlins and led 3–0 in the game's eighth inning. Cubs' pitching ace, Mark Prior, had only given up four hits in the game and was making it look effortless. It seemed nothing could stop the Cubs. Then, Marlins second baseman Luis Castillo hit what would become one of the most famous foul balls in Major League Baseball history.

As the ball headed down the left field line bound for the stands, Cubs outfielder Moises Alou raced toward the wall, intent on making a dramatic catch. As the ball descended into the fans, each hoping to catch a souvenir, Alou reached the pinnacle of his leap, glove outstretched. Coming between Alou's glove and the ball were the hands of longtime Cubs fan Steve Bartman. As the ball disappeared into the seats, Alou reacted angrily, as did the Cubs faithful. The twenty-six-year-old financial analyst was showered with abusive taunts, spit, peanuts, and beer. Fearing that he would be attacked, security escorted him out of the ballpark. He pulled his jacket over his face as he left.

The Cubs proceeded to implode, allowing eight runs in the inning and losing the game. In the final game of the series, the Marlins pounded Cubs starter Kerry Wood, scoring seven runs in the first six innings. The Marlins moved on to the World Series. The Cubs were left to wonder what could have been.

The morning after Game 6, Bartman released a statement saying, "I had my eyes glued on the approaching ball the entire time and was so caught up in the moment that I did not even see Moises Alou, much less that he may have had a play. Had I thought for one second that the ball was playable, or had I seen Alou approaching, I would have done whatever I could to get out of the way and give Alou a chance to make the catch." And with that, Bartman tried to move on.[68] Unfortunately, Cubs fans were not prepared to let that happen. Bartman received threatening phone calls, and police had to be stationed outside his house. For days, news crews camped out on his lawn, which was shown on television, raising concerns for his safety. Media helicopters circled overhead, hoping to catch a glimpse of the man who, unfairly, had become Chicago's public enemy number one. Bartman literally had to go into hiding. As the media blitz continued, Major League Baseball commissioner Bud Selig called Bartman to offer his support. The Cubs organization and former Cubs star Rick Sutcliffe publicly expressed support for the unfortunate fan.

Two days after Game 6, the *Chicago Sun-Times* named Bartman on its Web site and other media outlets followed suit. Chicago's Mayor Richard Daley blasted the media, expressing that it would be to blame if a deranged fan hurt the young man. Asked about a society that would vilify a fan, he responded, "What does it say about you media people? Don't worry about society. What about you? You would not print your editor's name, address and telephone number.... You'd be fired tomorrow."[69]

Florida Marlins fans sent gifts to Bartman. He dedicated them all to the Juvenile Diabetes Research Foundation because he was a big fan of Ron Santo, a former Cubs player afflicted with diabetes. Santo was thrilled that Bartman and others used the mishap to draw attention to the disease and said, "I feel bad for Bartman. He was not the reason we lost that ballgame."[70]

As weeks passed, the Bartman story would not die. Halloween followed the event by mere weeks and Bartman's ensemble was a popular costume, replete with Cubs hat, sweatshirt, earphones, and glasses. *Saturday Night Live* did a Bartman skit. Online auction site eBay featured a variety of themed items, most of which could only be described as anti-Bartman, such as a mock-up photo of him holding a torch to the Hindenberg.

Contrary to popular belief, Bartman did not leave the stadium with the ball. It was picked up by Jim Staruck, a lawyer who had been seated behind Bartman. Staruck auctioned off the ball. It went for $113,824.16 to Harry Caray's restaurant. After paying auction fees, Staruck collected about $90,000 in pre-tax dollars, which he planned to dedicate to his child's education. Staruck gave none of the windfall to charity.

The restaurant planned a demolition of the ball and hired Oscar-winning special effects coordinator Michael Lantieri to make sure the ball was destroyed in spectacular and safe fashion. The ball was drilled and packed with enough explosives to launch it at 8,000 feet per second. It was blown apart inside a transparent and bulletproof box. The event was covered live by MSNBC, CNN and ESPN. It was billed as a fundraiser for the Juvenile Diabetes Research Foundation, and Harry Caray's donated thousands of dollars. Over $1 million in cash and in-kind gifts and corporate donations went to the charity because of the event.

After the ball was exploded, some of the remains were purchased by Hallowed Ground, a company that makes specialty T-shirts to commemorate events. The company used a patented process to put finely ground bits of the ball into a silk-screening ink for Bartman Ball shirts. A portion of the proceeds from each sale was donated to the Juvenile Diabetes Research Foundation.

One year later, Moises Alou said that he did not blame Bartman; "I don't blame the fan. Everybody wants a souvenir. There's no manual that says how you should act when a foul ball is coming your way."[71] By the 2004 season, the ushers at Wrigley Field could identify the seat with a quick glance at a ticket and identified it as "the Bartman seat." At least eleven Cubs stickers adorned the Bartman seat, like flowers placed on a gravesite.

BASKETBALL COACH PARTIES WITH RIVALS' STUDENTS AFTER LOSS

Larry Eustachy was the successful and popular coach at Iowa State University from 1998 to 2003, leading the team to an appearance in the Elite Eight in 2000. His coaching reign ended when, after a loss against the Missouri Tigers in 2003, he appeared at a fraternity party at a Columbia, Missouri, apartment complex. Still wearing the black mock turtleneck that he coached in, Eustachy was photographed by a University of Missouri student while he drank a can of beer and kissed young women on the cheeks and was kissed by them in return. The story prompted widespread discussion by sports columnists on the topic of coaching behavior and the lack of role models in sports.

One week after the embarrassing photos appeared in the *Des Moines Register*, Eustachy resigned amid stories that this was not the only party he attended and that there was an emerging pattern of behavior. Photos of the coach at a Manhattan, Kansas, party emerged from the night of a 2002 loss to the Wildcats. He initially vowed to fight for his job, but in the end determined that he would be best served by stepping down and seeking help for his alcohol dependency. He also focused on mending fences with his wife and two sons. He turned down an offer to join an NBA coaching staff, which came days after his resignation.

Eustachy was paid $1.1 million per year, making him the highest-paid state employee in Iowa. He had been voted Big 12 coach of the year in 2000 and 2001 after his team claimed the league titles. He added the Associated Press national coach of the year award in 2000. During Eustachy's five years at Iowa State, he compiled a 101–59 record and boasted a 260–145 record over thirteen seasons as a head coach. But his record of success would not be enough to save his job. The Iowa State basketball program was already feeling the heat from an assistant coach, Randy Brown, who had been charged with having child pornography on his work computer, and from two players being charged with alcohol-related offenses. The photos were more than the university community could stand. Iowa State athletic director Bruce Van De Velde said the event brought "profound embarrassment" to the school. Van De Velde suspended the coach and recommended that he be fired. On the same day, Eustachy admitted he had an alcohol addiction.

Eustachy took full blame for the scandal as players, boosters, and fans fought to save his job by vilifying the president and athletic director. He said, "President Geoffroy is not the problem. Bruce Van De Velde is not the problem. I've created this situation and I'm holding myself totally accountable, and we move on."[72] Iowa State and the coach agreed to part ways, with Eustachy receiving a $960,000 settlement that Geoffroy said, "supports Mr. Eustachy and his family in his struggle with alcohol," while it "allows our basketball program to move forward."[73] Eustachy entered a thirty-day rehabilitation program at Hazelden in Minnesota and sat out the 2003–4 season.

As he resigned, Eustachy vowed he would get his life in order and return to coaching, and the basketball community rallied around him. In an interview conducted a year later, Oklahoma coach Kelvin Sampson, a best friend to Eustachy, said, "Our country was built on second chances," and, "Sometimes we have to have catastrophe in our life to make us see what's important."[74] Sampson suggested that in his year away from coaching, Eustachy had successfully reconnected with his wife and boys and was ready to coach again. It did not take long for a university to offer him the opportunity. Southern Mississippi came calling in 2004 and Eustachy jumped at the opportunity to redeem himself. After two lackluster seasons, his team won twenty games in the 2006–7 season.

BOBBY KNIGHT

Dean Smith had spent his entire coaching career at the University of North Carolina and had amassed a total of 879 career wins. No coach had won more games at the helm of an NCAA men's basketball program. Smith was known for his humility and character. Smith's record was broken by a far-more controversial coaching figure, Bobby Knight. In a career that stretched over forty years at Army, Indiana, and Texas Tech, Knight bullied his way to the record, winning his 880th game on January 1, 2007.

As Knight approached the record, sports columnists called him, "the last of the coaching cavemen," an "ogre under the bridge," a "serial moron,"[75] a "lout," and a "serial violator of protocol."[76] They decried his behavior as boorish, raging, bullying, and antisocial. While Knight and Smith shared a tremendous ability to win basketball games, the sports media suggested that they shared little else. Smith was considered a gentleman. Knight was called a "rageaholic" by Linda Alis, a behavior specialist who appeared on ESPN to discuss Knight's erratic behavior while he coached at Indiana University (IU).[77]

A partial list of Knight's career controversies includes the following events, many of which appeared on a *Sports Illustrated* timeline on its Web site in 2004:

In 1979 he was sentenced in absentia to six months in jail after he was convicted of hitting a police officer as he prepared the U.S. team to play in the Pan American Games in Puerto Rico. In 1987 the government of Puerto Rico dropped efforts to have Knight extradited to serve the sentence.

In 1981, following an Indiana win over Louisiana State University, Knight had an altercation with an LSU fan and allegedly shoved him into a trash can.

In 1983 he cursed Big Ten commissioner Wayne Duke, who was seated in the press box at an IU game. Knight stood at mid court and yelled insults regarding the officiating of the game. He was publicly reprimanded.

In 1985 he famously threw a chair across the court at Assembly Hall while an opposing player shot a free throw. He was ejected and suspended for one game. He publicly apologized.

In 1986, after being given a technical foul for shouting at officials, Knight kicked a megaphone and berated the IU cheerleaders for disrupting a free throw that his player was shooting.

In 1987, as his team was en route to the NCAA title, he banged his fist onto the scorer's table in a rage. The NCAA assessed him a $10,000 fine.

In 1987, with his team trailing badly in an exhibition game against the Soviet Union, he pulled the team off the court and refused to let them finish the game after he was ejected for arguing with a referee. He later apologized.

In 1988, after failing to be voted into the Basketball Hall of Fame, Knight called it, "a slap in the face" and later asked to not be renominated. He was anyway and was voted into the Hall in 1991.

In 1988, during an interview with Connie Chung on the subject of stress, he commented, "I think if rape is inevitable, relax and enjoy it." A protest march ensued on the IU campus.

In 1991 Knight refused to shake hands with Illinois coach Lou Henson after a game. Henson later called him a "classic bully" and suggested that he thrives on intimidating others.

In 1992, brandishing a bullwhip, Knight pretended to whip Calbert Cheaney, a black player on his IU team. The event drew national attention and protest from the NAACP.

In 1993 Knight pulled his son, Pat Knight, from a game and appeared to kick him. He claimed he had kicked the chair his son was sitting on.

In 1994 Knight head butted player Sharon Wilkerson on the sideline of a game. At the conclusion of the season, after Senior Day, Knight recited a poem to the crowd of Indiana University faithful: "When my time on Earth is gone, and my activities here are past, you can bury me upside down, and my critics can kiss my ass!" to thunderous applause.

In 1995 and 1998 he was fined by the NCAA for mistreating an NCAA tournament media liaison and an officiating crew. The fines were $30,000 and $10,000, respectively.

In 1999 Knight accidentally shot a hunting companion, Thomas Mikunda, causing wounds that were not life threatening. Knight failed to report the accident and was hunting without a license. His friend sued him for negligence and claimed that Knight pressured him to lie about the incident so it would not affect his employment at IU. The case was dismissed when the parties reached an out-of-court settlement.

In 2000, after former player Neil Reed claimed the coach choked him during a 1997 practice, IU investigated and a videotape of the incident was found. Other incidents that came to light included Knight attacking an IU sports information director, as well as a former assistant coach. Knight also threw a vase near an athletic department secretary. He was suspended for the first three games of 2000–2001 and was subjected to a zero-tolerance policy. He was fined $30,000 for actions that then IU president Myles Brand called, "abusive, uncivil, and embarrassing."[78] Knight violated the policy when he grabbed an IU student who addressed him as "Knight." Brand announced that Knight would no longer serve as the school's basketball coach.

In 2003, having been hired at Texas Tech, Knight participated in an ESPN interview and used profanity in a tirade about his relationship with former player Steve Alford, who was coaching at Iowa. Alford was taking part in the interview.

In 2004 Knight had a very public altercation with Texas Tech chancellor David Smith at a grocery store in Lubbock. When he broke the wins record in 2007, Knight used the stage to commend Texas Tech's new chancellor, saying, "What an improvement you are."[79]

On the verge of the record, Knight was asked in a conference call whether he would be remembered more for his antics or revered for his three national titles and other successes. He responded, "What you might think doesn't bother me in the slightest. How's that for an answer?" He then hung up.[80]

Knight's Texas Tech Red Raiders defeated the New Mexico Lobos 70–68 in Lubbock to give him the record. "We're part of history," declared junior guard Martin Zeno.[81] The postgame celebration included blaring Frank Sinatra's "My Way" at United Spirit Arena. It was a fitting song, of course. Knight, fighting back his emotions, said to his players, "If you guys still love me after everything I say to you and everything I put you through, that's a hell of a compliment."[82] In the postgame press conference, Knight was asked if he had any regrets, as the song suggested. "Sure. Just like the song, I have regrets," he replied. "When I look back on it, I don't think my way was all that bad."[83] There seemed to be disagreement from the sports writers, many of whom used their columns to openly begin rooting for Duke's Mike Krzyzewski to break the record so it could again be held by an honorable coach.

NOTES

CHAPTER 1

1. Carter, Russell. (1979, August 11). Tomjanovich: It felt like "Scoreboard fell on me." *Washington Post*, p. C5.

2. Huff, Donald. (1979, August 7). Jury selected to hear Kermit Washington case. *Washington Post*, p. D5.

3. Ryan, Bob. (2000, June 8). His name linked to "contact" but Washington should be known for project, not punch. *Boston Globe*, p. D1.

4. Hamilton, W. (1994, January 15). Three held in assault on Kerrigan. *Washington Post*, p. A1.

5. Ibid., p. A1.

6. Howard, J. (1994, January 28). Harding admits knowledge of plot after the attack. *Washington Post*, A1.

7. Leibovich, L. (1998). The mystery of O. J. Simpson. Salon. Retrieved July 12, 2007, from www.salon.com/media.

8. Bodenrader, T. (1997, June 30). Bite of the century: Chomp at the bit—glove cutter gets himself an earful. *Boston Herald*, p. 102.

9. Brunt, S. (1997, June 30). Holyfield more than a mouthful for Tyson. *Globe and Mail* (Toronto), p. C12.

10. Johnstone, D. (1997, December 28). The "ear that was": Bizarre biting runaway best story winner. *Sunday Star Times* (Wellington, New Zealand), p. B2.

11. Views on a champ, a chomp, a chump. (1997, June 30). *Austin American Statesman*, p. D8.

12. Ibid.

13. Ibid.

14. Ibid.

15. Whicker, M. (1997, June 30). Call him ear-responsible: Tyson delivers punchline to the joke that is boxing. *Orange County Register*, p. S7.

16. Reusse, Patrick. (1997, December 14). Iron Mike unmasked: The world was shocked when Mike Tyson bit a piece of Evander Holyfield's ear, but trainer Teddy Atlas was not surprised—he knew Tyson would opt for easy way out. *Star Tribune*, p. C4.

17. Ibid.

18. Whisler, J. (1997, November 9). Post-bite therapy hasn't helped Tyson. *San Antonio Express-News*, p. 5C.

19. Ibid.

20. Ibid.

21. Steinmetz, Matt. (1997, December 2). Sprewell suspended for Carlesimo attack—Warriors chokes, punches his coach. *Seattle Times*, p. C1.

22. Wise, Mike. (1997, December 7). Pro basketball: A suspended player, a shaken league. *New York Times*, Section 8, p. 1.

23. Steinmetz. (1997), p. C1.

24. Lopresti, Mike. (1997, December 4). NBA could soon choke on its troubles. *USA Today*, p. 3C.

25. Wise. (1997), Section 8, p. 1.

26. Ibid.

27. Gearan, J. (1997, December 5). Is league's penalty excessive? *Telegram and Gazette* (Massachusetts), p. D1.

28. Isola, Frank. (2004, November 4). Spree backpedals: Says media distorts position. *Daily News* (New York), p. 76.

29. Convicted NFL player says he didn't know victim well. (2001, February 14). Associated Press. Retrieved July 12, 2007, from LexisNexis Academic database.

30. Fryer, J. (2001, April 6). Triggerman in Carruth shooting sentenced to 40 years behind bars. Associated Press. Retrieved July 12, 2007, from LexisNexis Academic database.

31. Convicted NFL player. (2001).

32. Ibid.

33. Heath, T. (2001, January 23). Carruth sentenced to almost 19 years: Appeal is likely in shooting death. *Washington Post*, p. D1.

34. Paul, K. (2000, November 8). McSorley's verdict: One year. *Boston Globe*, p. E4.

35. Podell, I. (2000, February 23). McSorley suspended after attack on Brashear. Associated Press. Retrieved July 16, 2007, from LexisNexis Academic database.

36. Ibid.

37. Ibid.

38. Ibid.

39. Allen, K. (2000, March 8). McSorley faces charge of assault. Incident opens new debate over sports leagues "policing own." *USA Today*, 1C.

40. Ibid.

41. Lewis murder charges dropped: Ravens star accepts misdemeanor charge, will testify. (2000, June 5). CNN/Sports Illustrated [online version]. Retrieved September 11, 2007, from sportsillustrated.cnn.com/football/nfl/news/19/06/04/lewis_agreement.

42. Litke, Jim. (2001, January 24). Lewis unrepentant over Atlanta stabbings. *Post-Tribune* (Gary, IN), p. C4.

43. Roughness: Lewis pitching slam bam video doesn't do much for his image, or the NFL's either. (2002, November 24). *Post Tribune* (Gary, IN), p. C2.

44. Ibid., p. C4.

45. Lewis avoids civil trial. (2004, May 3). *Milwaukee Journal Sentinel*, p. 3C.

46. Roughness: Lewis pitching. (2002).

47. Williams guilty of four charges: Ex-player acquitted of manslaughter. (2004, May 1). *Charleston* (West Virginia) *Gazette*, p. 3B.

48. Ibid.

49. Brennan, John. (2007, July 17). Part of 911 call tossed: Judge issues rulings for Jayson Williams retrial. *The Record* (Bergen County, NJ), p. A03.

50. Soshnick, Scott. (2005, January 13). Williams joins minors while awaiting retrial. *National Post*, p. S5.

51. Moore, David Leon. (2003, April, 18). Stunned family, friends of Dennehy rip Bliss: Secretly recorded tapes reveal plot to say Dennehy dealt drugs. *USA Today*, p. C03.

52. Ibid., C03.

53. Moore. (2003), p. C03.

54. Ibid., p. C03.

55. Maher, J. (2005, June 24). NCAA spares death penalty for Baylor: Beleaguered program to lose nonconference schedule for a year. *Austin American Statesman*, p. D2.

56. Moore. (2003).

57. Hanna, Bill, and Caplan, Jeff. (2004, May 12). Baylor, basketball player's mother settle lawsuit. Knight Ridder Tribune News Service. Retrieved August 28, 2007, from ProQuest database.

58. Biggane, B. (2004, March 12). *Palm Beach* (Florida) *Post*, p. 1C.

59. Ibid.

60. Bertuzzi back on the ice after long suspension. (2005, August 16). Associated Press. Retrieved July 16, 2007, from LexisNexis Academic database.

61. Ibid.

62. Moore surprised Bertuzzi cleared to play. (2005, August 11). Associated Press. Retrieved July 16, 2007, from LexisNexis Academic database.

63. Vample, R. (2006, August 16). Artest does community service in Detroit, part of brawl sentence. Associated Press. Retrieved August 9, 2007, from LexisNexis Academic database.

64. Zirin, D. (2005). *What's my name, fool?* Chicago: Haymarket Press, p. 172.

65. Dunn, S. (2007, August 7). Punter's interview with police highlights day 6 of attempted murder case. *Greeley* (Colorado) *Tribune* [online version]. Retrieved August 12, 2007, from LexisNexis Academic database, para. 14.

66. Ibid., para. 20.

67. Ibid., para. 7.

68. Killion, Ann. (2007, August 20). Michael Vick experience was a horror show. Knight Ridder Tribune News Service. Retrieved August 22, 2003, from ProQuest database.

69. Red, Christian. (2007, August 21). With Vick plea, dog bites man: Reverses field, agrees to accept Fed deal. *Daily News* (New York), p. 48.

70. Michael Vick timeline. (2007, August 21). *Times-Picayune* (New Orleans), p. 7.

CHAPTER 2

1. Sullivan, Robert. (1985, May 20). In Pittsburgh, the party may soon be over. *Sports Illustrated*, p. 34.

2. Lidz, Franz. (1985, June 10). Embarrassing evidence. *Sports Illustrated*, p. 15.

3. Met testifies of "romance" between players and drugs. (1985, September 6). *Seattle Times*, p. D2.

4. Smizik, Bob. (1985, September 15). Baseball and Pirates on trial, and they're losing. *Seattle Times*, p. C3.

5. Lacayo, Richard. (1985, September 23). The cocaine agonies. *Time*. Retrieved September 18, 2007, from time.com/time/printout/0,8816,959943,00.html.

6. Bodley, Hal. (2004, March 4). Ueberroth took action in 1986 cocaine scandal. *USA Today*. Retrieved August 30, 2007, from usatoday.com/sports/baseball/columnist/bodley/2004-03-04-bodley_x.htm.

7. Bias reportedly suffered three seizures before help called. (1986, October 17). United Press International. Retrieved July 11, 2007, from LexisNexis Academic database.

8. Bias's death shook Maryland. (1987, June 5). United Press International. Retrieved July 11, 2007, from LexisNexis Academic database.

9. Dunham, W. (1987, June 10). Driesell: Cocaine comment misinterpreted. United Press International. Retrieved July 11, 2007, from LexisNexis Academic database.

10. Ibid.

11. Jenkins, S. (1987, June 5). Driesell: Acquittal helps Bias' reputation. *Washington Post*, p. G3.

12. Ibid.

13. Bias grand jury blasts Maryland's athletic department. (1987, February 27). United Press International. Retrieved July 12 from LexisNexis Academic database.

14. Bias's death shook Maryland. (1987).

15. Brubaker, B. (1986, August 17). Drug use by players may lead to more surveillance by NBA. *Washington Post*, p. B1.

16. Fainaru-Wada, Mark, and Williams, Lance. (2006, December 24). From children to pros, the heat is on to stop use of performance enhancers. *San Francisco Chronicle*, p. A1.

17. Williams, Lance, and Fainaru-Wada, Mark. (2005, October 19). Short prison terms for BALCO defendants: Judge blasts steroid dealer for continuing to protect his superstar drug clients. *San Francisco Chronicle*, p. A1.

18. Corbett, Sara. (2007, August 19). The outcast. *New York Times*, p. 60.

19. Ibid.

20. Ibid.

21. Drew, Jay. (2007, September 21). CEO: Landis ruling a relief. *Salt Lake Tribune* [online version]. Retrieved September 21, 2007, from ProQuest database.

22. Pells, Eddie. (2007, September 21). Landis' bid to retain Tour title fails: Arbitration panel upholds DQ. *Chicago Sun-Times*, p. 83.

23. Landis has more to say on Web site. (2007, September 26). *Washington Post*, p. E2.

24. Connolly, Dan. (2007, August 9). Is Bonds fit for crown? With no. 756, Barry Bonds stands alone atop the home run list. But he begins his reign facing some king-sized doubts. *Baltimore Sun* [online version]. Retrieved August 8, 2007, from LexisNexis Academic database.

25. Dabe, Chris. (2007, August 9). Is Barry Bonds a home run king? A cheater? It's all about … perceptions. *Beaumont* (Texas) *Enterprise*. Retrieved August 11, 2007, from LexisNexis Academic database.

26. Bonds gets call from Bush, ripped by tabloids. (2007, August 9). Associated Press. Retrieved August 11, 2007, from LexisNexis Academic database.

27. Collier, Gene. (2007, August 9). It's history: The chase is over: Bonds hit no. 756—while many points are moot, the debate over the San Francisco slugger's status has only just begun. *Pittsburgh Post-Gazette*, p. D1.

28. Klapisch, Bob. (2007, August 9). Hank strikes out: Aaron's video tribute doesn't mask his insincerity toward baseball's all-time lie king. *The Record* (Bergen County, NJ), p. S01.

29. Connolly. (2007).

30. Springer, Steve. (2007, August 8). Bonds slugs home run no. 756 to pass Aaron. *Los Angeles Times*, p. A1.

31. O'Neill, Dan. (2007, September 18). Fashion maven seeks input on future of 756th home run ball. *St. Louis Post-Dispatch*, p. D2.

CHAPTER 3

1. Cook, William A. (2005). *The Louisville Grays scandal of 1877: The taint of gambling at the dawn of the National League.* Jefferson, NC: McFarland & Co.

2. Ibid.

3. Linder, Douglas. (2001). The Black Sox trial: An account. Retrieved August 30, 2007, from www.law.umkc.edu/faculty/projects/ftrials/blacksox/blacksoxaccount.html.

4. Italie, Hillel. (1989, September 3). Black Sox gambling scandal was part of times. *Houston Chronicle*, p. 7.

5. Linder. (2001).

6. Ibid.

7. Daly, Dan. (2007, July 24). Not exactly a novel concept: Donaghy scandal like NFL in '46. *Washington Times*, p. C1.

8. Lomax, Michael E. (2002). "Detrimental to the league." Gambling and the governance of professional football, 1946–1963. *Journal of Sport History 29*(2), p. 303.

9. Fignone, Albert J. (1989). Gambling and college basketball: The scandal of 1951. *Journal of Sport History 16*(1), p. 44–61.

10. Goldstein Joe. (2003, November 19). Explosion: 1951 scandals threaten college hoops. ESPN Classic [online version]. Retrieved August 30, 2007, from espn.go.com/classic/s/basketball_scandals_explosion.html, para. 36.

11. Isaacs, Neil D. (2001). *You bet your life: The burdens of gambling.* Lexington: University Press of Kentucky.

12. Tulane star confesses he was paid by coaches. (1985, April 5). *Seattle Times*, p. E1.

13. Tulane scandal: 8 indicted, coaches quit. (1985 April 5). *San Francisco Chronicle*, p. 69.

14. Lovinger, Jay. (2002). *The gospel according to ESPN.* New York: Hyperion, p. 75.

15. Ibid., p. 76.

16. Neff, Craig, and Lieber, Jill. (1989, April 3). Rose's grim vigil: As gambling charges—and the media—engulf him, Pete Rose awaited his fate. *Sports Illustrated*, p. 52.

17. Brioso, Cesar, and Barzalai, Peter. (n.d.). The Rose Scandal. *USA Today* [online version]. Retrieved September 21, 2007, from usatoday.com.

18. Lieber, Jill, and Neff, Craig. (1989, July 3). The case against Pete Rose. *Sports Illustrated*, p. 20.

19. Voisin, Ailene. (1993, June 5). Mike's mess: Jordan says book's claims "preposterous"—Bull breaks his silence, denies gambling losses. *Atlanta Journal-Constitution*, p. D1.

20. Ibid., p. D1.

21. Brubaker, Bill. (1993, October 9). Jordan is cleared in probe: No betting violations uncovered by NBA. *Washington Post*, p. G1.

22. Lane, Wendy E. (1995, December 18). "I'm Back"—Jordan returns and rules again. Retrieved August 16, 2007, from LexisNexis Academic database.

23. Bisher, Furman. (1993, October 15). Maybe Jordan's decision wasn't totally his own. *Atlanta Journal-Constitution*, p. C1.

24. Attner, Paul. (1993, October 18). Retired or just tired? In retirement, Michael Jordan may find the challenge he needs: To reclaim his position as the best ever. *The Sporting News*, p. 29.

25. Ibid., p. 29.

26. Jordan tells "60 Minutes" he was "stupid" about gambling. (2005, October 19). Associated Press. Retrieved August 16, 2007, from LexisNexis Academic database.

27. Dedman, Bill. (1998, December 4). College football: 4 are indicted in Northwestern football scandal. *New York Times*, p. D1.

28. Gerstner, Joanne C. (1998, December 14). Northwestern cases: It "can happen anywhere"—time, academic focus temper "embarrassment." *USA Today*, p. 10C.

29. Mueller, Mark, Crittenden, Jules, and Ford, Beverly. (1996, November 14). Suspended BC player says betting more widespread. *Boston Herald*, p. 34.

30. Ryan, Bob. (1996, November 7). BC will pay the price for inexcusable acts. *Boston Globe*, p. E1.

31. Ex-Arizona State player writes about point-shaving. (1998, November 5). Associated Press. Retrieved June 13, 2007, from LexisNexis Academic database.

32. Ibid.

33. Miller Eric, and Wagner, Dennis. (1997, December 7). ASU's player gambling debt tied to point-shaving scandal. *Pittsburgh Post-Gazette*, p. D15.

34. Okimoto, Jolyn. (1999, June 22). Five men sentenced in college basketball point-shaving scandal. Associated Press. Retrieved June 13, 2007, from LexisNexis Academic database.

35. Rushlo, Michelle. (1999, November 16). Former ASU player sentenced to one year for point shaving. Associated Press. Retrieved June 13, 2007, from LexisNexis Academic database.

36. O'Keeffe, Michael. (2000, May 22). Seeking another shot: Isaac Burton, NBA hopeful. *Daily News* (New York), p. 67.

37. Wesch, Hank. (2002, November 2). Pick six betting scandal is cup of worms: Racing officials from N.Y. to Arcadia aim to restore confidence. *San Diego Union-Tribune*, p. D1.

38. Fitzgerald, Jim. (2003, March 21). Pick six defendants sentenced. *Times Union*, p. C3.

39. Eng, Richard. (2003, March 28). Pick six tales add to racing's rich lore. *Las Vegas Review-Journal*, p. 9C.

40. Fitzgerald. (2003), p. C3.

41. Finley, Bill. (2003, October 29). Winner of the pick six may now go to a track. *New York Times*, p. D2.

42. Anderson, Rick. (2003, December 10). Neuheisel returns the kick. *Seattle Weekly*. Retrieved August 11, 2007, from seattleweekly.com/2003-12-10/news/neuheisel-returns-the-kick.php.

43. Korte, Tim. (2005, February 8). Neuheisel lawyer explores UW's different accounts of why coach was fired. Associated Press. Retrieved July 11, 2007, from LexisNexis Academic database.

44. Withers, Bud. (2005, January 11). Lawsuit vs. UW headed to trial: Neuheisel suing for wrongful termination—Attempt to have case dismissed fails. *Seattle Times*, p. D1.

45. Ibid., p. D1.

46. Ibid., p. D1.

47. Korte. (2005, March 8).

48. Ibid.

49. Anderson. (2003, December 10).

50. Jasner, Phil. (2007, August 21). Reffing degrading: Two former striped shirts say officiating needs overhaul. *Philadelphia Daily News*, p. 70.

51. Dilbeck, Steve. (2007, August 17). Whole truth shall set NBA free. *Daily News* (New York), p. S1.

52. Perkins, Dave. (2007, August 21). If NBA ref sings, Stern will hang. *Toronto Star*, p. S1.

53. Telander, Rick. (2007, August 19). It's guilt by association: With disgraced Donaghy ready to provide info about other refs to the Feds, Stern's NBA finds itself in PR nightmare. *Chicago Sun-Times*, p. A85.

54. Smallwood, John. (2007, August 21). If other refs gambled, that's a foul situation. Knight Ridder Tribune News Service. Retrieved August 22, 2007, from LexisNexis Academic database.

55. Smith, Sam. (2007, October 25). New rules for NBA referees: Can make some trips to casinos, officials disclosed. *Chicago Tribune* [online version]. Retrieved November 16, 2007, from LexisNexis Academic database.

56. Dilbeck. (2007).

CHAPTER 4

1. Adams doubles suit vs. Boggs. (1988, August 26). *Chicago Sun-Times*, p. 111.

2. Wade Boggs affair: Adams tells tales of infidelity, racism, superstition in Penthouse article on life with Red Sox slugger. (1989, February 23) *Austin American Statesman*, p. C3.

3. Howard, Johnette. (1993, June 7). Olson's battle has yet to be won. *Washington Post*, p. C3.

4. Ibid.

5. Dell'Apa, Frank. (1991, February 7). Kiam offers an apology: Joke about Olson causes furor. *Boston Globe*, p. 45.

6. Brown, Curt. (1993, May 31). Reporter still feels pain of harassment: Patriots locker room episode continues to haunt Lisa Olson. *Star Tribune*, p. 1C.

7. Ibid.

8. Shuster, Rachel. (1993, June 1). Locker room still a battleground for female journalists. *USA Today*, p. C3.

9. Lowenkron, H. (1992, July 10). Supporters of Mike Tyson say the former heavyweight champion is in prison for rape because justice is different for black men than white men. Associated Press. Retrieved June 21, 2007, from LexisNexis Academic database.

10. Ibid.

11. Ibid.

12. Ibid.

13. Ibid.

14. Ibid.

15. Jones, K. (1992, February 12). *The Independent* (London), p. 30.

16. Albert gets 12-month suspended sentence in hotel room attack. (1997, October 24). CNN. Retrieved June 29, 2007, http://edition.cnn.com/US/9710/24/albert/index.html.

17. Jones. (1992).

18. Bunn, Curtis. (2000, October 28). Falcons' fall can be traced to Robinson. *Atlanta Journal-Constitution*, p. 2C.

19. Freeman, Mike. (1999, February 2). Robinson's arrest looms larger after the Falcons' defeat. *New York Times*, p. D1.

20. Heath, Thomas. (1999, February 1). Falcons' Robinson opts to play despite arrest: Coach Reeves left decision to veteran safety. *Washington Post*, p. D7.

21. O' Brien, S. (2004, February 18). University of Colorado football sex scandal. CNN American Morning. Retrieved June 29, 2007, from http://transcripts.cnn.com/TRANSCRIPTS/0402/18/ltm.03.html.

22. Ibid.

23. Sixth rape allegation surfaces at CU. (2004, February 20). CNN.com. Retrieved June 29, 2007, from http://edition.cnn.com.2004/US/Central/02-19/colorado.football.

24. Jacobson, J. (2004, February 10). A scandal at the U. of Colorado at Boulder points to nationwide problems in recruiting. *Chronicle of Higher Education 50*(25), A33.

25. Chernus, I. (2004, February 21). Football and sex at Colorado: The real scandal. Common Dreams News Center. Retrieved April 2, 2007, from www.commondreams.org/cgi-bin/print.cgi?file=/views04/0221-05.htm.

26. Jacobson. (2004).

27. Complete text of Kobe Bryant's statement. (2004, September 1). CourtTV.com. Retrieved June 29, 2007, from www.courtv.com/trials/bryant/090104-statement.html.

28. Navarro, M. (2006, December 8). Easterling charged with sex crime. *Miami Herald.* Retrieved July 11, 2007, from LexisNexis Academic database.

29. Collings, B. (2006, December 8). Miami prep back arrested: Antwain Easterling's status for the Class 6A final against Lake Brantley is in doubt. *Orlando Sentinel.* Retrieved July 11, 2007, from LexisNexis Academic database.

30. Gordon, J. (2007, June 13). The Anti-fan: What's the "glory of football" worth? *Santa Fe New Mexican,* p. B1.

31. deLuzuriaga, T. (2007, July 10). Sex scandal could sink Northwestern football. *Miami Herald,* pp. 1, 5B.

32. Ibid., p. 5B.

33. Ibid.

34. Acquitted of rape, Neal returns to court. (2005, December 21). Associated Press. Retrieved June 12, 2007, from LexisNexis Academic database.

35. Smith, S. (2006, January 10). La Salle's bigwigs won't accept blame but deserve shame. *Philadelphia Inquirer.* Retrieved June 12, 2007, from LexisNexis Academic database.

36. La Salle faces sanctions for handling of alleged sex assaults. (2006, December 20). Associated Press. Retrieved June 12, 2007, from LexisNexis Academic database.

37. Leonard, J. (2007, July 9). Pressler finds a better life after Duke: Ex–Blue Devils coach survives the scandal that almost ruined his career. *Contra Costa Times.* Retrieved August 9, 2007, from LexisNexis Academic database.

38. Reitman, S. (2006, June 1). Sex and scandal at Duke. *Rolling Stone* [online edition]. Retrieved April 2, 2007, from www.rollingstone.com/news/story/10464110/sex_scandal_at_duke.

CHAPTER 5

1. Gregorian, V. (2004, August 1). Poor sports are as old as the games. *St. Louis-Dispatch,* p. A1.

2. Swezey, Christian. (2005, December 10). Dark days for the black knights in "Codebreakers," the cheating scandal that shook Army. *Washington Post,* p. C7.

3. Trouble at West Point. (1951, August 13). *Time* [online version]. Retrieved September 27, 2007, from www.time.com/time/printout/0,8816,889147,00.htm, para. 9.

4. Deford, Frank. (2000, November 13). Code breakers: Fifty years ago Red Blaik's football powerhouse at Army was decimated by the loss of players who violated the military academy's honor code—but who really acted dishonorably? *Sports Illustrated 93*(20).

5. Capozzi, Joe. (2001, October 1). Shattered shot fifty years later, fallout fractures friendship between Thomson, Branca. *Palm Beach* (Florida) *Post,* p. 1C.

6. Li, David. (2002, July 29). '51 Giants come clean—Admit to sign-stealing scheme. *New York Post*, p. 62.

7. Kelley, Steve. (2001, July 9). It was a cheap shot heard round the world. *Seattle Times*, p. D1.

8. Ibid.

9. Ibid.

10. Li. (2002), p. 62.

11. Neyer, Rob. (2001, September 27). It ain't cheatin' if you don't get caught. ESPN Classic [online version]. Retrieved August 18, 2007, from espn.go.com/classic/s/neyer_on%20_shot.html.

12. Neyer, Rob. (2001, September 27). It ain't cheatin' if you don't get caught. ESPN Classic [online version]. Retrieved August 18, 2007, from espn.go.com/classic/s/neyer_on%20_shot.html.

13. Heller, Dick. (2003, April 21). Ruiz ended up as big loser in '80 Boston Marathon ruse. *Washington Times*, p. C12.

14. Leavy, Jane. (1980, April 27). The saga of Rosie Ruiz: Saga of Rosie Ruiz unfolds with bitter confrontation. *Washington Post*, p. N1.

15. Ibid.

16. Amdur, Neil. (1981, April 2). Rosie Ruiz: It's been the longest year. *New York Times*, p. B13.

17. Nearman, Steve. (1998, April 26). Ready or not Boston, here comes Rosie Ruiz. *Washington Times*, p. C12.

18. Gareau gets to hear the cheers. (2005, April 19). *Boston Herald*, p. M17.

19. Ibid.

20. Heller, Dick. (2003, April 21). Ruiz ended up as big loser in '80 Boston Marathon ruse. *Washington Times*, p. C12.

21. Thompson, Rich. (2007, April 16). Officials ensure cheaters never win. *Boston Herald*, p. 70.

22. Amdur. (1981), p. B13.

23. Ibid.

24. Jenkins, Chris. (2000, April 18). Marathon organizers keeping the tabs on their runners: ChampionChip finds cheaters, posts results. *USA Today*, p. 16C.

25. Lota, Louinn. (1996, February 19). Computer timing chips to be used in first major U.S. marathon. Associated Press. Retrieved July 6, 2007, from LexisNexis Academic database.

26. Asher, Mark. (1987, February 26). NCAA cancels SMU's 1987 football. *Washington Post*, p. A1.

27. Ibid.

28. Ibid.

29. Wangrin, Mark. (2007, March 3). The last word: SMU's "death penalty" revisited. *San Antonio Express-News*, p. 14C.

30. Farrey, Tom. (2001, November 28). NCAA's once-rabid watchdog loses its bite. ESPN College Football [online version]. Retrieved August 24, 2007, from espn.go.com/ncf/s/2001/1126/1284940.html.

31. Heuser, John. (2003, May 9). NCAA blasts Michigan for violations: School plans to appeal additional postseason ban. *Grand Rapids Press*, p. B1.

32. Webber's community service includes reading to kids. (2004, August 6). *Grand Rapids Press*, p. D3.

33. Gone but not forgotten: Fab five brought glory and "shame" to Michigan. (2007, February 11). *Grand Rapids Press*, p. D8.

34. Heuser, John. (2003, May 9). NCAA blasts Michigan for violations: School plans to appeal additional postseason ban. *Grand Rapids Press*, p. B1.

35. Gone but not forgotten. (2007), p. D8.

36. Little league world series title voided. (1992, September 24). *Facts on File World News Digest*, p. 719.

37. Little league goes easy on the kids. (1992, November 15). *New York Times*, section 8, p. 10.

38. Ibid.

39. McCoy, Hal. (1994, July 23). Indians "batgate" a comedy of amateur skullduggery. *Dayton Daily News*, p. 3D.

40. Nightengale, Bob. (1995, October 19). Belle bat caper finally solved. *The Sporting News*, p. 4B.

41. McCoy. (1994).

42. Ibid.

43. One of Belle's biggest capers came in Chicago. (1996, November 19). Associated Press, Retrieved June 12, 2007, from LexisNexis Academic database.

44. Willon, Phil and Metz, Kevin. (1994, December 10). Law firm clears FSU officials: The NCAA plans to review the findings, which indicts Seminole players and booster. *Tampa Tribune*, Sports section, p. 1.

45. Ibid.

46. Johnston, Joey. (2005, November 25). Memorable quotes. *Tampa Tribune*, Sports section, p. 6.

47. Ibid.

48. Ibid.

49. Rubin, Adam. (2002, August 25). Bought and sold: Coaches pay price for peddling prep star Albert Means. *Daily News* (New York), p. 102.

50. Baird, Woody. (2005, February 1). Former Michigan State coach testifies he was told of recruiting payoff. Associated Press. Retrieved July 12, 2007, from LexisNexis Academic database.

51. Barnhart, Tony. (2005, January 30). College football on trial: Stakes, drama in booster case—outcome of trial could affect parties across spectrum of college athletics. *Atlanta-Journal Constitution*, p. 1D.

52. Seymour Jr., Add, and Billeaud, Jacques. (1999, September 28). UT under a cloud: School launches probe into alleged plagiarism. *News Sentinel*, p. A1.

53. ESPN alleges UT academic fraud, cover-up: Dickey says players are out until probe is complete. (1999, September 27). *News Sentinel*, p. A1.

54. Billeaud, Jacques, and Seymour Jr., Add. (2000, February 6). NCAA told UT athletic tutoring still out of control: English professor says problems unresolved. *News Sentinel*, p. A1.

55. Ibid.

56. Lundy, Gary. (2002, May 22). 2000 UT probe likely to fade. *Commercial Appeal* (Memphis), p. D4.

57. Minnesota dismisses academic counselor. (1999, June 19). *Pittsburgh Post-Gazette*, p. C10.

58. Becker, Bob. (2001, September 5). Level of deceit shocking: Too bad adults involved can't be more severely punished. *Grand Rapids Press*, p. C1.

59. Ibid., p. C1.

60. Cala, Andres. (2001, August 31). Answers expected today concerning Almonte's age. *South Bend Tribune*, p. B6.

61. After little league scandal, Almonte finds his place: Pitcher is emerging as a major league prospect. (2004, May 10). *Grand Rapids Press*, p. D4.

62. Armour, Nancy. (2003, October 10). Corked bat, homers part of Sosa's legacy. Retrieved August 14, 2007, from LexisNexis Academic database.

63. Unsplendid splinter: Cubs rally past Rays after Sosa's ignominious ejection. (2003, June 3). *Sports Illustrated* [online version]. Retrieved August 14, 2007, from sportsillustrated.cnn.com/baseball/news/2003/06/03/sosa_ejected_ap.

64. Newberry, Paul. (2003, March 6). Harrick's son fired by Georgia: Father's future in doubt. *Advocate*, p. 4C.

65. Schlabach, Mark. (2003, March 11). UGA finds "academic fraud," cancels season: Harrick suspended, Dogs pull out of tournaments. *Atlanta Journal-Constitution*, p. A1.

66. Ibid.

67. Bona, Van Breda Kolff settle out of court. (2005, April 20). *Buffalo News*, p. D3.

68. NCAA puts St. Bonaventure on probation. (2004, February 20). *Chicago Sun-Times*, p. 146.

69. Lieber, Jill. (2003, November 18). St. Bonaventure scandal leaves heavy human toll: Head of trustees' suicide, driven by passion for school, haunts widow. *USA Today*, p. C1.

70. Ibid.

71. Ibid.

72. Herbeck, Dan. (2005, December 5). Whistle-blower seeks judgment to clear his name: Former St. Bonaventure athletic director claims in suit he was a scapegoat. *Buffalo News*, p. A1.

73. Ibid.

74. Bowen, Fred. (2007, September 21). I spy ... a cheater. *Washington Post*, p. C12.

75. Mulligan, Mike. (2007, September 16). Call them the New England Stealers: Many around the league happy to see Belichick's reputation take a big hit. *Chicago Sun-Times*, p. A85.

76. Canepa, Nick. (2007, September 14). NFL fines Belichick, Patriots for spying: Goodell doesn't go far enough. *San Diego Union-Tribune*, p. D1.

CHAPTER 6

1. Asher, Mark. (1987, April 9). Dodgers fire Campanis: Racial comments spur dismissal of team executive. *Washington Post*, p. B1.

2. Ibid.

3. Ibid.

4. Ibid.

5. Controversial Campanis recalled with fondness. (1998, June 22). *Denver Post*, p. C5.

6. Wilbon, Michael. (1988, January 17). The Greek's apology is difficult to accept. *Washington Post*, p. D1.

7. Chad, Norman. (1988, January 18). CBS and Jimmy the Greek: A time to look inward. *Washington Post*, p. D9.

8. Wilbon. (1988), p. D1.

9. Ibid.

10. Nolan, J. (1992, November 26). Dateline: Cincinnati. Associated Press. Retrieved August 14, 2007, from LexisNexis Academic database.

11. Ibid.

12. Bodley, H. (1994, June 4). Schott won't change ways "for anything." *USA Today*, p. 1C.

13. Teaford, E. (2004, March 3). Despite troubles, Schott had plenty of admirers. *Charleston* (West Virginia) *Daily Mail*, p. 1B.

14. Maske, M. (1996, June 5). Schott may be removed: Baseball leaders considering action. *Washington Post*, p. B1.

15. Teaford. (2004).

16. Ibid.

17. Ibid.

18. Ibid.

19. Concannon, Joe. (1998, April 10). Zoeller still feeling heat. *Boston Globe*, p. E11.

20. Woods, Zoeller finally talk. (1997, May 21). *Charleston Gazette*, p. 1B.

21. Sheeley, Glenn. (1997, May 21). The Fuzzy-Tiger summit: Woods, "Now it's done"—both seek closure after discussing Zoeller's remark. *Atlanta Journal-Constitution*, p. 1B.

22. Woods, Zoeller finally talk. (1997), p. 1B.

23. Daniels, Earl. (1998, February 1). Zoeller lands new endorsement deals. *Florida Times-Union*, p. C11.

24. Ibid.

25. Sirak, Ron. (1998, April 5). Zoeller's comments won't stop echoing: Joke about Woods still haunts veteran golfer. *Milwaukee Journal Sentinel*, p. 7.

26. Ibid.

27. Ford, Bob. (2004, December 27). Complex legacy left by White: One of NFL's greatest linemen died yesterday. *National Post*, p. S6.

28. Stapleton, Arnie. (1998, April 3). Reggie White apologizes: "My intent was not to demean anyone.... If I did, I humbly ask for your forgiveness." *Madison* (Wisconsin) *Capital Times*, p. 1A.

29. Carlson, Michael. (2004, December 30). Obituary: Reggie White: Green Bay Packers football player known as the minister of defense—and offence. *Guardian*, p. 20.

30. Youngblood, Kent. (1998, August 7). White is tight-lipped after Smith's blasts: Viking running back Robert Smith calls Reggie White's comments on homosexuals "ignorant" and says religion can be a divisive issue in NFL locker rooms. *Wisconsin State Journal*, p. 1B.

31. Ibid.

32. Hershey, Steve. (1998, July 17). White criticized for wearing uniform in ad. *USA Today*, p. 7C.

33. Chandler, Charles, and Garfield, Ken. (2000, August 1). White won't back down from remarks: He says he still believes homosexuality is a sin, although he has nothing personal against gays. *Wisconsin State Journal*, p. 4C.

34. Pearlman, Jeff. (1999, December 23). Shooting outrageously from the lip, Braves closer John Rocker bangs away at his favorite targets: The Mets, their fans, their city, and just about everyone in it. *Sports Illustrated* [online version]. Retrieved August 8, 2007, from sportsillustrated.cnn.com/features/cover/news/1999/12/22/rocker.

35. Ibid.

36. Ibid.

37. Newberry, Paul. (2000, February 8). Arbitrator being asked to overturn Rocker suspension. Associated Press. Retrieved July 11, 2007, from LexisNexis Academic database.

38. Anatomy of a controversy. (2000, June 29). *USA Today*, p. 2C.

39. Rogers, Carroll. (2000, March 3). A day of healing for Rocker: Meeting, apologies clear air on return. *Atlanta Journal-Constitution*, p. 1C.

40. Ibid.

41. Report: A matured Rocker wants to put disparaging comments behind him. (2005, April 14). Associated Press. Retrieved July 11, 2007, from LexisNexis Academic database.

42. Vacchiano, Ralph. (2004, January 18). In no rush to forget: McNabb's dad still irate over Limbaugh's attack. *Daily News* (New York), p. 56.

43. O'Connor, Ian. (2004, January 14). McNabb's amazing career built on proving doubters wrong. *USA Today*, p. 2C.

44. Ibid.

45. Kay, Joe. (2004, January 29). Black QBs lament Limbaugh's comments. Associated Press. Retrieved June 13, 2007, from LexisNexis Academic database.

46. Olson, L. (2007, April 10). Two weeks? He needs at least a summer vacation. *Daily News* (New York), p. 58.

47. Ibid.

48. Bondy, F. (2007, April 11). Imus the ignoramus: Host knows nothing of players he has hurt. *Daily News* (New York), p. 63.

49. Coffey, W. (2007, April 15). Sex games. Imus's bile places spotlight on women's sports. *Daily News* (New York), p. 82.

CHAPTER 7

1. The life and times of Muhammad Ali. (n.d.). Retrieved September 8, 2007, from www.africanamericans.com/MuhammadAli.htm.

2. Heller, D. (2005, June 27). Ali had Supreme Court in his corner in 1971. *Washington Times*, p. C4. Retrieved September 10, 2007, from ProQuest database.

3. Ibid.

4. Todd, J. (2000, May 20). The fights of their lives. *Gazette* (Montreal), p. J1. Retrieved September 10, 2007, from ProQuest database.

5. The life and times. (n.d.).

6. Zirin, D. (2007). *Welcome to the terrordome*. Chicago: Haymarket Press, p. 180.

7. Heller. (2005).

8. Todd. (2000).

9. On this day. (2006). BBC News [online version]. Retrieved September 8, 2007, from http://news.bbc.co.uk/onthisday/hi/dates/stories/october/17/newsid_3535000/3535348.stm.

10. The black boycott. (1968, February 23). *Time* [online version]. Retrieved September 8, 2007, from www.time.com.

11. Fitzpatrick, F. (2007, March 27). As decades go by, Tommie Smith remains complex figure. Knight Ridder Tribune News Service. Retrieved September 10, 2007, from ProQuest database.

12. On this day. (2006).

13. Ibid.

14. Zirin, D. (2005). *What's my name, fool?* Chicago: Haymarket Press, p. 76.

15. Fitzpatrick. (2007).

16. Harasta, C. (2005, May 27). History won't forget Tommie Smith, who will get an honorary degree. Knight Ridder Tribune News Service. Retrieved September 10, 2007, from ProQuest database.

17. Zirin. (2005), p. 86.

18. Zirin. (2007), p. 146.

19. Saraceno, Frank. (2004, August 6). Classic 1972 USA vs. USSR basketball game. ESPN Classic [online version]. Retrieved September 10, 2007, from sports.espn.go.com/classic/s/classic_1972_usa_ussr_gold_medal_hoop.htm, para. 20.

20. Ibid., para. 24.

21. Ibid., para. 29.

22. Ibid., para. 28.

23. Free agents' big win: Baseball owners found guilty of collusion. (1987, September 22). *San Francisco Chronicle*, p. D1.

24. Ibid.

25. Hoynes, Paul. (1990, December 26). Collusion may be worst scandal, Miller says. *Plain Dealer* [online version]. Retrieved August 25, 2007, from ProQuest database.

26. Denlinger, Ken. (1988, October 3). Rawest ring decision: Some saw it coming. *Washington Post*, p. B1.

27. Anderson, Dave. (1989, March 22). Roy Jones Jr. still fighting for the gold. *New York Times*, p. B9.

28. Ibid.

29. Denlinger. (1988), p. B1.

30. Ibid.

31. Woodward, Steve. (1989, March 8). Boxer still has hopes of getting gold medal. *USA Today*, p. 5C.

32. Anderson. (1989), p. B9.

33. Chass, Murray. (1990, July 31). Steinbrenner's control of Yanks severed. *New York Times*, p. A1.

34. Heller, M. F. (1990, August 1). Sending a message: Vincent's action shows that he won't abide by questionable conduct. *Washington Times*, p. D1.

35. Ibid.

36. Ibid.

37. Curry, Jack. (1992, March 23). Steinbrenner back, but not really. *New York Times*, p. C5.

38. Ibid.

39. Rhoden, William C. (1992, September 28). Jackie Sherrill teaches us about priorities: Is castrating a bull the type of education NCAA strives for? *The Sporting News*, p. 6.

40. Litke, Jim. (1992, September 16). Associated Press. Retrieved July 5, 2007, from LexisNexis Academic database.

41. Ibid.

42. Fitzgerald, Tom. (1992, September 21). Top of the sixth. *San Francisco Chronicle*, p. C8.

43. D'Angelo, Tom. (1996, November 23). Abdul-Rauf learns art of compromise. *Palm Beach* (Florida) *Post*, p. 1C.

44. Ibid.

45. Ibid.

46. Golfer apologizes for anthem remark. (1996, March 23). *News and Record* (Greensboro, NC), p. C4.

47. Michaelis, Vicki. (1996, December 18). Interest in Abdul-Rauf hasn't flagged yet. *Denver Post*, p. C1.

48. Fitzgerald, Joe. (2006, August 19). Guilty even of proven innocent. *Boston Herald*, p. 4.

49. Wood, Lin L. (1999, April 15). When private lives become the story: The rush to hang Richard Jewell—security guard's attorney takes the press to task. *San Francisco Chronicle*, p. A25.

50. Ibid.

51. Fitzgerald. (2006), p. 4.

52. Goodman, Brenda. (2006, May 27). Falsely accused suspect pursues libel case. *New York Times*, p. A11.

53. Johnson, Kevin. (1999, November 26). Richard Jewell's libel lawsuit: Big case, big issues. *USA Today*, p. 15A.

54. Wilkie, Curtis. (1997, February 15). Jewell is still waiting for a "thank you": Ex-Olympic bomb suspect ponders absence of accolades. *Boston Globe*, p. A1.

55. Ibid.

56. Fitzgerald. (2006), p. 4.

57. Scott, Jeffrey and Morris, Mike. (2007, August 30). Richard Jewell found dead at 44. *Atlanta Journal-Constitution*, p. B1.

58. Struby, Tim. (2001, February 18). On the rebound a year after hazing scandal ended Vermont's hockey season, Cats are keeping the faith. *Chicago Sun-Times*, p. 132.

59. Denlinger, Ken. (2000, February 6). Hazing incident ends season for Vermont hockey. *Seattle Times*, p. C9.

60. Dupont, Kevin Paul. (2000, October 15). Haze clears at UVM: Hockey reappears. *Boston Globe*, p. D1.

61. Struby. (2001), p. 132.

62. Coffey, Wayne. (2003, October 26). O'Leary rewrites resume: Emerges from ND scandal to fix Vikings defense. *Daily News* (New York), p. 114.

63. Wilson, Stephen. (1998, December 14). Hodler says Salt Lake was blackmailed. Associated Press. Retrieved July 11, 2007, from LexisNexis Academic database, para. 12.

64. Strickland, Carter. (2003, November 8). Price regrets having trusted school officials: Wanted to tell his story, but was advised to remain quiet ... then he was fired. *Spokesman Review*, C6.

65. Ibid.

66. UTEP hires former 'Bama coach. (2003, December 22). *Charleston* (West Virginia) *Daily Mail*, p. 3B.

67. Ibid.

68. Berkow, Ira. (2004, September 10). The most infamous seat in the house. *New York Times*, p. D1.

69. Spielman, Fran. (2003, October 17). Mayor unloads on media for naming Cubs fan: "You'd better be careful how you present him." *Chicago Sun-Times*, p. 10.

70. Isaacson, Melissa. (2004, February 26). Infamous foul ball is blown to smithereens. Knight Ridder Tribune News Service. Retrieved August 25, 2007, from ProQuest database.

71. Berkow. (2004), p. D1.

72. Dvorak, Todd. (2003, May 6). Eustachy, Iowa State part ways. *Advocate* (Baton Rouge), p. 1C.

73. Ibid.

74. Merrill, Elizabeth. (2004, March 19). Friends say there's life after ISU for fired coach. *Omaha World-Herald*, p. 1A.

75. Schmitz, Brian. (2006, December 22). Win for Bob Knight means dark days for college basketball. Knight Ridder Tribune News Service. Retrieved August 25, 2007, from ProQuest database.

76. Imrem, Mike. (2006, November 15). Knight's conduct? Defenseless. *Daily Herald* (Arlington Heights, IL), p. 1.

77. Outside the lines: Bob Knight and anger management. (2000, May 21). Retrieved August 25, 2007, from sports.espn.go.com/page2/tvlistings/show8transcript.html.

78. Ibid.

79. Knight is all-time wins leader in Division I after Texas Tech tops New Mexico. (2007, January 2). *USA Today* [online version]. Retrieved August 27, 2007, from usatoday. com/sports/college/mensbasketball/games/2007-01-01-texastech-newmexico_x.htm.

80. Schmitz. (2006), para. 16.

81. Knight is all-time. (2007), para. 3.

82. Ibid., para. 17.

83. Ibid., para. 5.

BIBLIOGRAPHY

Acquitted of rape, Neal returns to court. (2005, December 21). Associated Press. Retrieved June 12, 2007, from LexisNexis Academic database.

Adams doubles suit vs. Boggs. (1988, August 26). *Chicago Sun-Times*, p. 111.

After little league scandal, Almonte finds his place: Pitcher is emerging as a major league prospect. (2004, May 10). *Grand Rapids Press*, p. D4.

Albert gets 12-month suspended sentence in hotel room attack. (1997, October 24). CNN. Retrieved June 29, 2007, from http://edition.cnn.com/US/9710/24/albert/index.html.

Allen, K. (2000, March 8). McSorley faces charge of assault. Incident opens new debate over sports leagues "policing own." *USA Today*, 1C.

Amdur, N. (1981, April 2). Rosie Ruiz: It's been the longest year. *New York Times*, p. B13.

Anatomy of a controversy. (2000, June 29). *USA Today*, p. 2C.

Anderson, D. (1989, March 22). Roy Jones Jr. still fighting for the gold. *New York Times*, p. B9.

Anderson, R. (2003, December 10). Neuheisel returns the kick. *Seattle Weekly*. Retrieved August 11, 2007, from seattleweekly.com/2003-12-10/news/neuheisel-returns-the-kick.php.

Armour, N. (2003, October 10). Corked bat, homers part of Sosa's legacy. Retrieved August 14, 2007, from LexisNexis Academic database.

Asher, M. (1987, February 26). NCAA cancels SMU's 1987 football. *Washington Post*, p. A1.

Asher, M. (1987, April 9). Dodgers fire Campanis: Racial comments spur dismissal of team executive. *Washington Post*, p. B1.

Attner, P. (1993, October 18). Retired or just tired? In retirement, Michael Jordan may find the challenge he needs: To reclaim his position as the best ever. *The Sporting News*, p. 29.

Baird, W. (2005, February 1). Former Michigan State coach testifies he was told of recruiting payoff. Associated Press. Retrieved July 12, 2007, from LexisNexis Academic database.

Barnhart, T. (2005, January 30). College football on trial: Stakes, drama in booster case—outcome of trial could affect parties across spectrum of college athletics. *Atlanta-Journal Constitution*, p. 1D.

Becker, B. (2001, September 5). Level of deceit shocking: Too bad adults involved can't be more severely punished. *Grand Rapids Press*, p. C1.

Berkow, I. (2004, September 10). The most infamous seat in the house. *New York Times*, p. D1.

Berlinicke, J. (2000, November 5). McSore sports: Clean up the game—the NHL. *Lakeland* (Florida) *Ledger*, p. C11.

Bertuzzi back on the ice after long suspension. (2005, August 16). Associated Press. Retrieved July 16, 2007, from LexisNexis Academic database.

Bias grand jury blasts Maryland's athletic department. (1987, February 27). United Press International. Retrieved July 12 from LexisNexis Academic database.

Bias reportedly suffered three seizures before help called. (1986, October 17). United Press International. Retrieved July 11, 2007, from LexisNexis Academic database.

Bias's death shook Maryland. (1987, June 5). United Press International. Retrieved July 11, 2007, from LexisNexis Academic database.

Biggane, B. (2004, March 12). *Palm Beach* (Florida) *Post*, p. 1C.

Billeaud, J., and Seymour, A., Jr. (2000, February 6). NCAA told UT athletic tutoring still out of control: English professor says problems unresolved. *News Sentinel*, p. A1.

Bisher, F. (1993, October 15). Maybe Jordan's decision wasn't totally his own. *Atlanta Journal-Constitution*, p. C1.

The black boycott. (1968, February 23). *Time* [online version]. Retrieved September 8, 2007, from www.time.com.

Bodenrader, T. (1997, June 30). Bite of the century: Chomp at the bit—glove cutter gets himself an earful. *Boston Herald*, p. 102.

Bodley, H. (1994, June 4). Schott won't change ways "for anything." *USA Today*, p. 1C.

Bodley, H. (2004, March 4). Ueberroth took action in 1986 cocaine scandal. *USA Today*. Retrieved August 30, 2007, from usatoday.com/sports/baseball/columnist/bodley/2004-03-04-bodley_x.htm.

Bona, Van Breda Kolff settle out of court. (2005, April 20). *Buffalo News*, p. D3.

Bonds gets call from Bush, ripped by tabloids. (2007, August 9). Associated Press. Retrieved August 11, 2007, from LexisNexis Academic database.

Bondy, F. (2007, April 11). Imus the ignoramus. Host knows nothing of players he has hurt. *Daily News* (New York), p. 63.

Bowen, F. (2007, September 21). I spy … a cheater. *Washington Post*, p. C12.

Brennan, J. (2007, July 17). Part of 911 call tossed: Judge issues rulings for Jayson Williams retrial. *The Record* (Bergen County, NJ), p. A3.

Brioso, C., and Barzalai, P. (n.d.). The Rose Scandal. *USA Today* [online version]. Retrieved September 21, 2007, from usatoday.com.

Brown, C. (1993, May 31). Reporter still feels pain of harassment: Patriots locker room episode continues to haunt Lisa Olson. *Star Tribune*, p. 1C.

Brubaker, B. (1986, August 17). Drug use by players may lead to more surveillance by NBA. *Washington Post*, B1.

Brubaker, B. (1993, October 9). Jordan is cleared in probe: No betting violations uncovered by NBA. *Washington Post*, p. G1.

Brunt, S. (1997, June 30). Holyfield more than a mouthful for Tyson. *Globe and Mail* (Toronto), p. C12.

Bunn, C. (2000, October 28). Falcons' fall can be traced to Robinson. *Atlanta Journal-Constitution*, p. 2C.

Cala, A. (2001, August 31). Answers expected today concerning Almonte's age. *South Bend Tribune*, p. B6.

Canepa, N. (2007, September 14). NFL fines Belichick, Patriots for spying: Goodell doesn't go far enough. *San Diego Union-Tribune*, p. D1.

Canucks' Bertuzzi charged with assault. (2004, June 24). The Sports Network. Retrieved July 16, 2007, from LexisNexis Academic database.

Capozzi, J. (2001, October 1). Shattered shot fifty years later, fallout fractures friendship between Thomson, Branca. *Palm Beach* (Florida) *Post*, p. 1C.

Carlson, M. (2004, December 30). Obituary: Reggie White: Green Bay Packers football player known as the minister of defense—and offence. *Guardian*, p. 20.

Carter, R. (1979, August 11). Tomjanovich: It felt like "Scoreboard fell on me." *Washington Post*, p. C5.

Chad, N. (1988, January 18). CBS and Jimmy the Greek: A time to look inward. *Washington Post*, p. D9.

Chandler, C., and Garfield, K. (2000, August 1). White won't back down from remarks: He says he still believes homosexuality is a sin, although he has nothing personal against gays. *Wisconsin State Journal*, p. 4C.

Chass, M. (1990, July 31). Steinbrenner's control of Yanks severed. *New York Times*, p. A1.

Chernus, I. (2004, February 21). Football and sex at Colorado: The real scandal. Common Dreams News Center. Retrieved April 2, 2007, from www.commondreams.org/cgi-bin/print.cgi?file=/views04/0221-05.htm.

Coffey, W. (2003, October 26). O'Leary rewrites resume: Emerges from ND scandal to fix Vikings defense. *Daily News* (New York), p. 114.

Coffey, W. (2007, April 15). Sex games. Imus's bile places spotlight on women's sports. *Daily News* (New York), p. 82.

Collier, G. (2007, August 9). It's history: The chase is over—Bonds hit no. 756. While many points are moot, the debate over the San Francisco slugger's status has only just begun. *Pittsburgh Post-Gazette*, p. D1.

Collings, B. (2006, December 8). Miami prep back arrested: Antwain Easterling's status for the Class 6A final against Lake Brantley is in doubt. *Orlando Sentinel*. Retrieved July 11, 2007, from LexisNexis Academic database.

Complete text of Kobe Bryant's statement. (2004, September 1). CourtTV.com. Retrieved June 29, 2007, from www.courtv.com/trials/bryant/090104-statement.html.

Concannon, J. (1998, April 10). Zoeller still feeling heat. *Boston Globe*, E11.

Connolly, D. (2007, August 9). Is Bonds fit for crown? With no. 756, Barry Bonds stands alone atop the home run list. But he begins his reign facing some king-sized doubts. *Baltimore Sun* [online version]. Retrieved August 8, 2007, from LexisNexis Academic database.

Controversial Campanis recalled with fondness. (1998, June 22). *Denver Post*, p. C5.

Convicted NFL player says he didn't know victim well. (2001, February 14). Associated Press. Retrieved July 12, 2007, from LexisNexis Academic database.

Cook, W. A. (2005). *The Louisville Grays scandal of 1877: The taint of gambling at the dawn of the National League*. Jefferson, NC: McFarland & Co.

Corbett, S. (2007, August 19). The outcast. *New York Times*, p. 60.

Curry, J. (1992, March 23). Steinbrenner back, but not really. *New York Times*, p. C5.

Dabe, C. (2007, August 9). Is Barry Bonds a home run king? A cheater? It's all about … perceptions. *Beaumont* (Texas) *Enterprise*. Retrieved August 11, 2007, from LexisNexis Academic database.

Daly, D. (2007, July 24). Not exactly a novel concept: Donaghy scandal like NFL in '46. *Washington Times*, p. C1.

D'Angelo, T. (1996, November 23). Abdul-Rauf learns art of compromise. *Palm Beach* (Florida) *Post*, p. 1C.

Daniels, E. (1998, February 1). Zoeller lands new endorsement deals. *Florida Times-Union*, p. C11.

Dedman, B. (1998, December 4). College football: 4 are indicted in Northwestern football scandal. *New York Times*, p. D1.

Deford, F. (2000, November 13). "Code breakers: Fifty years ago Red Blaik's football powerhouse at Army was decimated by the loss of players who violated the military academy's honor code. But who really acted dishonorably?" *Sports Illustrated* 93(20).

Dell'Apa, F. (1991, February 7). Kiam offers an apology: Joke about Olson causes furor. *Boston Globe*, p. 45.

deLuzuriaga, T. (2007, July 10). Sex scandal could sink Northwestern football. *Miami Herald*, p. 1, 5B.

Denlinger, K. (1988, October 3). Rawest ring decision: Some saw it coming. *Washington Post*, p. B1.

Denlinger, K. (2000, February 6). Hazing incident ends season for Vermont hockey. *Seattle Times*, p. C9.

Dilbeck, S. (2007, August 17). Whole truth shall set NBA free. *Daily News* (New York), p. S1.

Drew, J. (2007, September 21). CEO: Landis ruling a relief. *Salt Lake Tribune* [online version]. Retrieved September 21, 2007, from ProQuest database.

Dunham, W. (1987, June 10). Driesell: Cocaine comment misinterpreted. United Press International. Retrieved July 11, 2007, from LexisNexis Academic database.

Dunn, S. (2007, August 7). Punter's interview with police highlights day 6 of attempted murder case. *Greeley* (Colorado) *Tribune* [online version]. Retrieved August 12, 2007, from LexisNexis Academic database.

Dupont, K. P. (2000, October 15). Haze clears at UVM: Hockey reappears. *Boston Globe*, p. D1.

Dvorak, T. (2003, May 6). Eustachy, Iowa State part ways. *Advocate* (Baton Rouge), p. 1C.

Eng, R. (2003, March 28). Pick six tales add to racing's rich lore. *Las Vegas Review-Journal*, p. 9C.

ESPN alleges UT academic fraud, cover-up: Dickey says players are out until probe is complete. (1999, September 27). *News Sentinel*, p. A1.

Ex-Arizona State player writes about point-shaving. (1998, November 5). Associated Press. Retrieved June 13, 2007, from LexisNexis Academic database.

Fainaru-Wada, M., and Williams, L. (2006, December 24). From children to pros, the heat is on to stop use of performance enhancers. *San Francisco Chronicle*, p. A1.

Farrey, T. (2001, November 28). NCAA's once-rabid watchdog loses its bite. ESPN College Football [online version]. Retrieved August 24, 2007, from espn.gp.com/ncf/s/2001/1126/1284940.html.

Fignone, A. J. (1989). Gambling and college basketball: The scandal of 1951. *Journal of Sport History 16*(1), pp. 44–61.

Finley, B. (2003, October 29). Winner of the pick six may now go to a track. *New York Times*, p. D2.

Fitzgerald, J. (2003, March 21). Pick six defendants sentenced. *Times Union*, p. C3.

Fitzgerald, J. (2006, August 19). Guilty even of proven innocent. *Boston Herald*, p. 4.

Fitzgerald, T. (1992, September 21). Top of the sixth. *San Francisco Chronicle*, p. C8.

Fitzpatrick, F. (2007, March 27). As decades go by, Tommie Smith remains complex figure. Knight Ridder Tribune News Service, p. 1. Retrieved September 10, 2007, from ProQuest database.

Ford, B. (2004, December 27). Complex legacy left by White: One of NFL's greatest linemen died yesterday. *National Post*, p. S6.

Free agents' big win: Baseball owners found guilty of collusion. (1987, September 22). *San Francisco Chronicle*, p. D1.

Freeman, M. (1999, February 2). Robinson's arrest looms larger after the Falcons' defeat. *New York Times*, p. D1.

Fryer, J. (2001, April 6). Triggerman in Carruth shooting sentenced to 40 years behind bars. Associated Press. Retrieved July 12, 2007, from LexisNexis Academic database.

Gareau gets to hear the cheers. (2005, April 19). *Boston Herald*, p. M17.

Gearan, J. (1997, December 5). Is league's penalty excessive? *Telegram and Gazette* (Massachusetts), p. D1.

Gerstner, J. C. (1998, December 14). Northwestern cases: It "can happen anywhere": Time, academic focus temper "embarrassment." *USA Today*, p. 10C.

Goldstein, J. (2003, November 19). Explosion: 1951 scandals threaten college hoops. ESPN Classic [online version]. Retrieved August 30, 2007, from espn.go.com/classic/s/basketball_scandals_explosion.html.

Golfer apologizes for anthem remark. (1996, March 23). *News and Record* (Greensboro, NC), p. C4.

Gone but not forgotten: Fab five brought glory and "shame" to Michigan. (2007, February 11). *Grand Rapids Press*, p. D8.

Goodman, B. (2006, May 27). Falsely accused suspect pursues libel case. *New York Times*, p. A11.

Gregorian, V. (2004, August 1). Poor sports are as old as the games. *St. Louis-Dispatch*, p. A1.

Hamilton, W. (1994, January 15). Three held in assault on Kerrigan. *Washington Post*, p. A1.

Hanna, B., and Caplan, J. (2004, May 12). Baylor, basketball player's mother settle lawsuit. Knight Ridder Tribune News Service. Retrieved August 28, 2007, from ProQuest database.

Harasta, C. (2005, May 27). History won't forget Tommie Smith, who will get an honorary degree. Knight Ridder Tribune News Service. Retrieved September 10, 2007, from ProQuest database.

Heath, T. (1999, February 1). Falcons' Robinson opts to play despite arrest: Coach Reeves left decision to veteran safety. *Washington Post*, p. D7.

Heath, T. (2001, January 23). Carruth sentenced to almost 19 years: Appeal is likely in shooting death. *Washington Post*, p. D1.

Heller, D. (2003, April 21). Ruiz ended up as big loser in '80 Boston Marathon ruse. *Washington Times*, p. C12.

Heller, D. (2005, June 27). Ali had Supreme Court in his corner in 1971. *Washington Times*, p. C4. Retrieved September 10, 2007, from ProQuest database.

Heller, M. F. (1990, August 1). Sending a message: Vincent's action shows that he won't abide by questionable conduct. *Washington Times*, p. D1.

Herbeck, D. (2005, December 5). Whistle-blower seeks judgment to clear his name: Former St. Bonaventure athletic director claims in suit he was a scapegoat. *Buffalo News*, p. A1.

Hershey, S. (1998, July 17). White criticized for wearing uniform in ad. *USA Today*, p. 7C.

Heuser, J. (2003, May 9). NCAA blasts Michigan for violations: School plans to appeal additional postseason ban. *Grand Rapids Press*, p. B1.

Howard, J. (1993, June 7). Olson's battle has yet to be won. *Washington Post*, p. C3.

Howard, J. (1994, January 28). Harding admits knowledge of plot after the attack. *Washington Post*, A1.

Hoynes, P. (1990, December 26). Collusion may be worst scandal, Miller says. *Plain Dealer* [online version]. Retrieved August 25, 2007, from ProQuest database.

Huff, D. (1979, August 7). Jury selected to hear Kermit Washington case. *Washington Post*, p. D5.

Imrem, M. (2006, November 15). Knight's conduct? Defenseless. *Daily Herald* (Arlington Heights, IL), p. 1.

Isaacs, N. D. (2001). *You bet your life: The burdens of gambling.* Lexington: University Press of Kentucky.

Isaacson, M. (2004, February 26). Infamous foul ball is blown to smithereens. Knight Ridder Tribune News Service. Retrieved August 25, 2007, from ProQuest database.

Isola, F. (2004, November 4). Spree backpedals: Says media distorts position. *Daily News* (New York), p. 76.

Italie, H. (1989, September 3). Black Sox gambling scandal was part of times. *Houston Chronicle*, p. 7.

Jacobson, J. (2004). A scandal at the U. of Colorado at Boulder points to nationwide problems in recruiting. *Chronicle of Higher Education 50*(25), A33.

Jasner, P. (2007, August 21). Reffing degrading: Two former striped shirts say officiating needs overhaul. *Philadelphia Daily News*, p. 70.

Jenkins, C. (2000, April 18). Marathon organizers keeping the tabs on their runners: ChampionChip finds cheaters, posts results. *USA Today*, p. 16C.

Jenkins, S. (1987, June 5). Driesell: Acquittal helps Bias's reputation. *Washington Post*, G3.

Johnson, K. (1999, November 26). Richard Jewell's libel lawsuit: Big case, big issues. *USA Today*, p. 15A.

Johnston, J. (2005, November 25). Memorable quotes. *Tampa Tribune*, Sports section, p. 6.

Johnstone, D. (1997, December 28). The "ear that was": Bizarre biting runaway best story winner. *Sunday Star Times* (Wellington, New Zealand), p. B2.

Jones, K. (1992, February 12). *The Independent* (London), p. 30.

Jordan tells *60 Minutes* he was "stupid" about gambling. (2005, October 19). Associated Press. Retrieved August 16, 2007, from LexisNexis Academic database.

Kay, J. (2004, January 29). Black QBs lament Limbaugh's comments. Associated Press. Retrieved June 13, 2007, from LexisNexis Academic database.

Kelley, S. (2001, July 9). It was a cheap shot heard round the world. *Seattle Times*, p. D1.

Killion, A. (2007, August 20). Michael Vick experience was a horror show. Knight Ridder Tribune News Service. Retrieved August 22, 2003, from ProQuest database.

Klapisch, B. (2007, August 9). Hank strikes out: Aaron's video tribute doesn't mask his insincerity toward baseball's all-time lie king. *The Record* (Bergen County, NJ), p. S1.

Knight is all-time wins leader in Division I after Texas Tech tops New Mexico. (2007, January 2). *USA Today* [online version]. Retrieved August 27, 2007, from usatoday.com/sports/college/mensbasketball/games/2007,-01-01-texastech-newmexico_x.htm.

Korte, T. (2005, February 8). Neuheisel lawyer explores UW's different accounts of why coach was fired. Associated Press. Retrieved July 11, 2007, from LexisNexis Academic database.

Lacayo, R. (1985, September 23). The cocaine agonies. *Time.* Retrieved September 18, 2007, from time.com/time/printout/0,8816,959943,00.html.

Landis has more to say on Web site. (2007, September 26). *Washington Post*, p. E2.

Lane, W. E. (1995, December 18). "I'm Back"—Jordan returns and rules again. Retrieved August 16, 2007, from LexisNexis Academic database.

La Salle faces sanctions for handling of alleged sex assaults. (2006, December 20). Associated Press. Retrieved June 12, 2007, from LexisNexis Academic database.

Leavy, J. (1980, April 27). The saga of Rosie Ruiz: Saga of Rosie Ruiz unfolds with bitter confrontation. *Washington Post*, p. N1.

Leibovich, L. (1998). The mystery of O.J. Simpson. Salon. Retrieved July 12, 2007, from www.salon.com/media.

Leonard, J. (2007, July 9). Pressler finds a better life after Duke: Ex-Blue Devils coach survives the scandal that almost ruined his career. *Contra Costa Times.* Retrieved August 9, 2007, from LexisNexis Academic database.

Lewis avoids civil trial. (2004, May 3). *Milwaukee Journal Sentinel*, p. 3C.

Lewis murder charges dropped: Ravens star accepts misdemeanor charge, will testify. (2000, June 5). CNN/Sports Illustrated. Retrieved September 11, 2007, from sportsillustrated. cnn.com/football/nfl/news/19/06/04/lewis_agreement.

Li, D. (2002, July 29). '51 Giants come clean—Admit to sign-stealing scheme. *New York Post*, p. 62.

Lidz, F. (1985, June 10). Embarrassing evidence. *Sports Illustrated*, p. 15.

Lieber, J. (2003, November 18). St. Bonaventure scandal leaves heavy human toll: Head of trustees' suicide, driven by passion for school, haunts widow. *USA Today*, p. C1.

Lieber, J., and Neff, C. (1989, July 3). The case against Pete Rose. *Sports Illustrated*, p. 20.

The life and times of Muhammad Ali. (n.d.). Retrieved September 8, 2007, from www. africanamericans.com/MuhammadAli.htm.

Linder, D. (2001). The Black Sox trial: An account. Retrieved August 30, 2007, from www.law.umkc.edu/faculty/projects/ftrials/blacksox/blacksoxaccount.html.

Litke, J. (1992, September 16). Associated Press. Retrieved July 5, 2007, from LexisNexis Academic database.

Litke, J. (2001, January 24). Lewis unrepentant over Atlanta stabbings. *Post-Tribune* (Gary, IN), p. C4.

Little league goes easy on the kids. (1992, November 15). *New York Times*, section 8, p. 10.

Little league world series title voided. (1992, September 24). *Facts on File World News Digest*, p. 719.

Lomax, M. E. (2002). "Detrimental to the league." Gambling and the governance of pro-fessional football, 1946–1963. *Journal of Sport History 29*(2), p. 303.

Lopresti, M. (1997, December 4). NBA could soon choke on its troubles. *USA Today*, p. 3C.

Lota, L. (1996, February 19). Computer timing chips to be used in first major U.S. mara-thon. Associated Press. Retrieved July 6, 2007, from LexisNexis Academic database.

Lovinger, J. (2002). *The gospel according to ESPN*. New York: Hyperion.

Lowenkron, H. (1992, July 10). Supporters of Mike Tyson say the former heavyweight champion is in prison for rape because justice is different for black men than white men. *Associated Press*. Retrieved June 21, 2007, from LexisNexis Academic database.

Lundy, G. (2002, May 22). 2000 UT probe likely to fade. *Commercial Appeal* (Memphis), p. D4.

Maher, J. (2005, June 24). NCAA spares death penalty for Baylor: Beleaguered program to lose nonconference schedule for a year. *Austin American Statesman*, p. D2.

Maske, M. (1996, June 5). Schott may be removed: Baseball leaders considering action. *Washington Post*, p. B1.

McCoy, H. (1994, July 23). Indians "batgate" a comedy of amateur skullduggery. *Dayton Daily News*, p. 3D.

Merrill, E. (2004, March 19). Friends say there's life after ISU for fired coach. *Omaha World-Herald*, p. 1A.

Met testifies of "romance" between players and drugs. (1985, September 6). *Seattle Times*, p. D2.

Michaelis, V. (1996, December 18). Interest in Abdul-Rauf hasn't flagged yet. *Denver Post*, p. C1.

Michael Vick timeline. (2007, August 21). *Times-Picayune* (New Orleans), p. 7.

Miller, E., and Wagner, D. (1997, December 7). ASU's player gambling debt tied to point-shaving scandal. *Pittsburgh Post-Gazette*, p. D15.

Minnesota dismisses academic counselor. (1999, June 19). *Pittsburgh Post-Gazette*, p. C10.

Moore, D. L. (2003, April, 18). Stunned family, friends of Dennehy rip Bliss: Secretly recorded tapes reveal plot to say Dennehy dealt drugs. *USA Today*, p. C3.

Moore surprised Bertuzzi cleared to play. (2005, August 11). Associated Press. Retrieved July 16, 2007, from LexisNexis Academic database.

Mueller, M., Crittenden, J., and Ford, B. (1996, November 14). Suspended BC player says betting more widespread. *Boston Herald*, p. 34.

Mulligan, M. (2007, September 16). Call them the New England Stealers: Many around the league happy to see Belichick's reputation take a big hit. *Chicago Sun-Times*, p. A85.

Navarro, M. (2006, December 8). Easterling charged with sex crime. *Miami Herald*. Retrieved July 11, 2007, from LexisNexis Academic database.

NCAA puts St. Bonaventure on probation. (2004, February 20). *Chicago Sun-Times*, p. 146.

Nearman, S. (1998, April 26). Ready or not Boston, here comes Rosie Ruiz. *Washington Times*, p. C12.

Neff, C., and Lieber, J. (1989, April 3). Rose's grim vigil: As gambling charges—and the media—engulf him, Pete Rose awaited his fate. *Sports Illustrated*, p. 52.

Newberry, P. (2000, February 8). Arbitrator being asked to overturn Rocker suspension. Associated Press. Retrieved July 11, 2007, from LexisNexis Academic database.

Newberry, P. (2003, March 6). Harrick's son fired by Georgia: father's future in doubt. *Advocate*, p. 4C.

Neyer, R. (2001, September 27). It ain't cheatin' if you don't get caught. ESPN Classic [online version]. Retrieved August 18, 2007, from espn.go.com/classic/s/neyer_on%20_shot.html.

Nightengale, B. (1995, October 19). Belle bat caper finally solved. *The Sporting News*, p. 4B.

Nolan, J. (1992, November 26). Dateline: Cincinnati. Associated Press. Retrieved August 14, 2007, from LexisNexis Academic database.

O'Brien, S. (2004, February 18). University of Colorado football sex scandal. CNN American Morning. Retrieved June 29, 2007, from http://transcripts.cnn.com/TRANSCRIPTS/0402/18/ltm.03.html.

O'Connor, I. (2004, January 14). McNabb's amazing career built on proving doubters wrong. *USA Today*, p. 2C.

O'Keeffe, M. (2000, May 22). Seeking another shot: Isaac Burton, NBA hopeful. *Daily News* (New York), p. 67.

Okimoto, J. (1999, June 22). Five men sentenced in college basketball point-shaving scandal. Associated Press. Retrieved June 13, 2007, from LexisNexis Academic database.

Olson, L. (2007, April 10). Two weeks? He needs at least a summer vacation. *Daily News* (New York), p. 58.

O'Neill, D. (2007, September 18). Fashion maven seeks input on future of 756th home run ball. *St. Louis Post-Dispatch*, p. D2.

One of Belle's biggest capers came in Chicago. (1996, November 19). Associated Press, Retrieved June 12, 2007, from LexisNexis Academic database.

On this day. (2006). BBC News [online version]. Retrieved September 8, 2007, from http://news.bbc.co.uk/onthisday/hi/dates/stories/october/17/newsid_3535000/3535348.stm.

Outside the lines: Bob Knight and anger management. (2000, May 21). Retrieved August 25, 2007, from sports.espn.go.com/page2/tvlistings/show8transcript.html.

Paul, K. (2000, November 8). McSorley's verdict: One year. *Boston Globe*, p. E4.

Pearlman, J. (1999, December 23). Shooting outrageously from the lip, Braves closer John Rocker bangs away at his favorite targets: The Mets, their fans, their city, and just about everyone in it. *Sports Illustrated* [online version]. Retrieved August 8, 2007, from sportsillustrated.cnn.com/features/cover/news/1999/12/22/rocker.

Pells, E. (2007, September 21). Landis's bid to retain Tour title fails: Arbitration panel upholds DQ. *Chicago Sun-Times*, p. 83.

Perkins, D. (2007, August 21). If NBA ref sings, Stern will hang. *Toronto Star*, p. S1.

Pistons ban Green for life. (2006, November 17), *Seattle Times*, p. D4.

Podell, I. (2000, February 23). McSorley suspended after attack on Brashear. Associated Press. Retrieved July 16, 2007, from LexisNexis Academic database.

Red, C. (2007, August 21). With Vick plea, dog bites man: Reverses field, agrees to accept Fed deal. *Daily News* (New York), p. 48.

Reitman, S. (2006, June 1). Sex and scandal at Duke. *Rolling Stone* [online edition]. Retrieved April 2, 2007, from www.rollingstone.com/news/story/10464110/sex_scandal_at_duke.

Report: A matured Rocker wants to put disparaging comments behind him. (2005, April 14). Associated Press. Retrieved July 11, 2007, from LexisNexis Academic database.

Reusse, P. (1997, December 14). Iron Mike unmasked: The world was shocked when Mike Tyson bit a piece of Evander Holyfield's ear. But trainer Teddy Atlas was not surprised. He knew Tyson would opt for easy way out. *Star Tribune*, p. C4.

Rhoden, W. C. (1992, September 28). Jackie Sherrill teaches us about priorities: Is castrating a bull the type of education NCAA strives for? *The Sporting News*, p. 6.

Rogers, C. (2000, March 3). A day of healing for Rocker: Meeting, apologies clear air on return. *Atlanta Journal-Constitution*, p. 1C.

Roughness: Lewis pitching slam bam video doesn't do much for his image, or the NFL's either. (2002, November 24). *Post Tribune* (Gary, IN), p. C2.

Rubin, A. (2002, August 25). Bought and sold: Coaches pay price for peddling prep star Albert Means. *Daily News* (New York), p. 102.

Rushlo, M. (1999, November 16). Former ASU player sentenced to one year for point shaving. Associated Press. Retrieved June 13, 2007, from LexisNexis Academic database.

Ryan, B. (1996, November 7). BC will pay the price for inexcusable acts. *Boston Globe*, p. E1.

Ryan, B. (2000, June 8). His name linked to "contact," but Washington should be known for project, not punch. *Boston Globe*, p. D1.

Saraceno, F. (2004, August 6). Classic 1972 USA vs. USSR basketball game. ESPN Classic [online version]. Retrieved September 10, 2007, from sports.espn.go.com/classic/s/classic_1972_usa_ussr_gold_medal_hoop.htm.

Schlabach, M. (2003, March 11). UGA finds "academic fraud," cancels season: Harrick suspended, Dogs pull out of tournaments. *Atlanta Journal-Constitution*, p. A1.

Schmitz, B. (2006, December 22). Win for Bob Knight means dark days for college basketball. Knight Ridder Tribune News Service. Retrieved August 25, 2007, from ProQuest database.

Scott, J. and Morris, M. (2007, August 30). Richard Jewell found dead at 44. *Atlanta Journal-Constitution*, p. B1.

Seymour, A., Jr., and Billeaud, J. (1999, September 28). UT under a cloud: School launches probe into alleged plagiarism. *News Sentinel*, p. A1.

Sheeley, G. (1997, May 21). The Fuzzy-Tiger summit: Woods, "Now it's done"—both seek closure after discussing Zoeller's remark. *Atlanta Journal-Constitution*, p. 1B.

Shuster, R. (1993, June 1). Locker room still a battleground for female journalists. *USA Today*, p. C3.

Sirak, R. (1998, April 5). Zoeller's comments won't stop echoing: Joke about Woods still haunts veteran golfer. *Milwaukee Journal Sentinel*, p. 7.

Sixth rape allegation surfaces at CU. (2004, February 20). CNN.com. Retrieved June 29, 2007, from http://edition.cnn.com.2004/US/Central/02-19/colorado.football.

Smallwood, J. (2007, August 21). If other refs gambled, that's a foul situation. Knight Ridder Tribune News Service. Retrieved August 22, 2007, from LexisNexis Academic database.

Smith, S. (2006, January 10). La Salle's bigwigs won't accept blame but deserve shame. *Philadelphia Inquirer.* Retrieved June 12, 2007, from LexisNexis Academic database.

Smith, S. (2007, October 25). New rules for NBA referees: Can make some trips to casinos, officials disclosed. *Chicago Tribune* [online version]. Retrieved November 16, 2007, from LexisNexis Academic database.

Smizik, B. (1985, September 15). Baseball and Pirates on trial, and they're losing. *Seattle Times*, p. C3.

Soshnick, S. (2005, January 13). Williams joins minors while awaiting retrial. *National Post*, p. S5.

Spielman, F. (2003, October 17). Mayor unloads on media for naming Cubs fan: "You'd better be careful how you present him." *Chicago Sun-Times*, p. 10.

Springer, S. (2007, August 8). Bonds slugs home run no. 756 to pass Aaron. *Los Angeles Times*, p. A1.

Stapleton, A. (1998, April 3). Reggie White apologizes: "My intent was not to demean anyone.... If I did, I humbly ask for your forgiveness." *Madison* (Wisconsin) *Capital Times*, p. 1A.

Steinmetz, M. (1997, December 2). Sprewell suspended for Carlesimo attack—Warriors chokes, punches his coach. *Seattle Times*, p. C1.

Strickland, C. (2003, November 8). Price regrets having trusted school officials: Wanted to tell his story, but was advised to remain quiet ... then he was fired. *Spokesman Review*, C6.

Struby, T. (2001, February 18). On the rebound a year after hazing scandal ended Vermont's hockey season, Cats are keeping the faith. *Chicago Sun-Times*, p. 132.

Sullivan, R. (1985, May 20). In Pittsburgh, the party may soon be over. *Sports Illustrated*, p. 34.

Swezey, C. (2005, December 10). Dark days for the black knights in "Codebreakers," the cheating scandal that shook Army. *Washington Post*, p. C7.

Teaford, E. (2004, March 3). Despite troubles, Schott had plenty of admirers. *Charleston* (West Virginia) *Daily Mail*, p. 1B.

Telander, R. (2007, August 19). It's guilt by association: With disgraced Donaghy ready to provide info about other refs to the Feds, Stern's NBA finds itself in PR nightmare. *Chicago Sun-Times*, p. A85.

Thompson, R. (2007, April 16). Officials ensure cheaters never win. *Boston Herald*, p. 70.

Todd, J. (2000, May 20). The fights of their lives. *Gazette* (Montreal), p. J1. Retrieved September 10, 2007, from Proquest database.

Trouble at West Point. (1951, August 13). *Time* [online version]. Retrieved September 27, 2007, from www.time.com/time/printout/0,8816,889147,00.htm.

Tulane scandal: 8 indicted, coaches quit. (1985, April 5). *San Francisco Chronicle*, p. 69.

Tulane star confesses he was paid by coaches. (1985, April 5). *Seattle Times*, p. E1.

Unsplendid splinter: Cubs rally past Rays after Sosa's ignominious ejection. (2003, June 3). *Sports Illustrated* [online version]. Retrieved August 14, 2007, from sportsillustrated. cnn.com/baseball/news/2003/06/03/sosa_ejected_ap.

UTEP hires former 'Bama coach. (2003, December 22). *Charleston* (West Virginia) *Daily Mail*, p. 3B.

Vacchiano, R. (2004, January 18). In no rush to forget: McNabb's dad still irate over Limbaugh's attack. *Daily News* (New York), p. 56.

Vample, R. (2006, August 16). Artest does community service in Detroit, part of brawl sentence. Associated Press. Retrieved August 9, 2007, from LexisNexis Academic database.

Views on a champ, a chomp, a chump. (1997, June 30). *Austin American Statesman*, p. D8.

Vivlamore, C. (2007, September 27). Vick's woes multiple with failed drug test: Confined to home, QB facing sentence in dogfighting case sends bad signal to judge, NFL. *Atlanta Journal Constitution*, p. A1.

Voisin, A. (1993, June 5). Mike's mess: Jordan says book's claims "preposterous"—Bull breaks his silence, denies gambling losses. *Atlanta Journal-Constitution*, p. D1.

Wade Boggs affair: Adams tells tales of infidelity, racism, superstition in *Penthouse* article on life with Red Sox slugger. (1989, February 23). *Austin American Statesman*, p. C3.

Wangrin, M. (2007, March 3). The last word: SMU's "death penalty" revisited. *San Antonio Express-News*, p. 14C.

Webber's community service includes reading to kids. (2004, August 6). *Grand Rapids Press*, p. D3.

Wesch, H. (2002, November 2). Pick six betting scandal is cup of worms: Racing officials from N.Y. to Arcadia aim to restore confidence. *San Diego Union-Tribune*, p. D1.

Whicker, M. (1997, June 30). Call him ear-responsible: Tyson delivers punchline to the joke that is boxing. *Orange County Register*, p. S7.

Whisler, J. (1997, November 9). Post-bite therapy hasn't helped Tyson. *San Antonio Express-News*, p. 5C.

Wilbon, M. (1988, January 17). The Greek's apology is difficult to accept. *Washington Post*, p. D1.

Wilkie, C. (1997, February 15). Jewell is still waiting for a "thank you": Ex-Olympic bomb suspect ponders absence of accolades. *Boston Globe*, p. A1.

Williams, L., and Fainaru-Wada, M. (2005, October 19). Short prison terms for BALCO defendants: Judge blasts steroid dealer for continuing to protect his superstar drug clients. *San Francisco Chronicle*, p. A1.

Williams guilty of four charges: Ex-player acquitted of manslaughter. (2004, May 1). *Charleston* (West Virginia) *Gazette*, p. 3B.

Willon, P. and Metz, K. (1994, December 10). Law firm clears FSU officials: The NCAA plans to review the findings, which indicts Seminole players and booster. *Tampa Tribune*, Sports section, p. 1.

Wilson, S. (1998, December 14). Hodler says Salt Lake was blackmailed. Associated Press. Retrieved July 11, 2007, from LexisNexis Academic database.

Wise, M. (1997, December 7). Pro basketball: A suspended player, a shaken league. *New York Times*, Section 8, p. 1.

Withers, B. (2005, January 11). Lawsuit vs. UW headed to trial: Neuheisel suing for wrongful termination—attempt to have case dismissed fails. *Seattle Times*, p. D1.

Wood, L. L. (1999, April 15). When private lives become the story: The rush to hang Richard Jewell—security guard's attorney takes the press to task. *San Francisco Chronicle*, p. A25.

Woods, Zoeller finally talk. (1997, May 21). *Charleston* (West Virginia) *Gazette*, p. 1B.

Woodward, S. (1989, March 8). Boxer still has hopes of getting gold medal. *USA Today*, p. 5C.

Youngblood, K. (1998, August 7). White is tight-lipped after Smith's blasts: Viking running back Robert Smith calls Reggie White's comments on homosexuals "ignorant" and says religion can be a divisive issue in NFL locker rooms. *Wisconsin State Journal*, p. 1B.

Zirin, D. (2005). *What's my name, fool?* Chicago: Haymarket Press.

Zirin, D. (2007). *Welcome to the terrordome.* Chicago: Haymarket Press.

INDEX

About the Authors

PETER FINLEY is an assistant professor of sport and recreation management in the H. Wayne Huizenga School of Business and Entrepreneurship at Nova Southeastern University, where he specializes in sociology of sport and sport ethics. He is the author of several publications about sport-related issues, including use of the Web for recruiting, privacy rights, and a variety of other sociology of sport topics. He and Laura Finley are co-authors of *The Sports Industry's War on Athletes* (Praeger, 2006).

LAURA FINLEY is an adjunct faculty member in the Women's Studies program and director of the Center for Living and Teaching Peace, which provides training and consultation on topics relevant to creating and sustaining a more peaceful world. She holds a Ph.D. in sociology from Western Michigan University, as well as two degrees in education. She has presented at numerous national and international conferences and is the author or co-author of five books and many journal articles and book chapters.

JEFFREY FOUNTAIN is an assistant professor of sport and recreation management in the H. Wayne Huizenga School of Business and Entrepreneurship at Nova Southeastern University, where he specializes in sport marketing, sport finance, and organization and administration of sport. He recently created a course on sport in popular culture that examines the issues and roles of sport in the movies, on television, and in the print media. His current research focuses on purchasing power and how increasing costs of sporting events is affecting sports fans.